Creation in the Bible series*
Ekkehardt Mueller, DMin, ThD, general editor

He Spoke and It Was: Divine Creation in the Old Testament
Gerald A. Klingbeil, DLitt, volume editor

Gary Swanson, MA, editor for general readership

The following entities collaborated in the preparation of this volume.

Biblical Research Institute
A doctrinal and theological resource center that serves the General Conference of Seventh-day Adventists through research, publication, and presentations. https://adventistbiblicalresearch.org/

Geoscience Research Institute
The institute assists the General Conference of Seventh-day Adventists through the scientific study of the natural world in the area of origins and other related matters. Findings are made available through publications and presentations. http://grisda.org/

Faith and Science Council
A body of the General Conference of Seventh-day Adventists created to study the interrelationships of science and Scripture with particular attention to Creation. It provides for the two institutes above to interact and collaborate on projects. http://fscsda.org/

*The next volume in this series will address Creation in the New Testament.

CREATION SERIES
VOLUME ONE

DIVINE CREATION IN THE OLD TESTAMENT

GERALD A. KLINGBEIL, EDITOR

 Pacific Press®
Publishing Association
Nampa, Idaho | Oshawa, Ontario, Canada
www.pacificpress.com

Cover design by Gerald Lee Monks
Cover resources from Dreamstime.com
Inside design by Aaron Troia

You can obtain additional copies of this book by calling toll-free 1-800-765-6955 or by visiting http://www.adventistbookcenter.com.

ISBN 13: 978-0-8163-5833-5
ISBN 10: 0-8163-5833-8

April 2015

Contents

Introduction

Gerald A. Klingbeil

Creation is a topic eliciting a plethora of responses. Biblical scholars love to discuss the minutiae and nuances of the Hebrew (or Greek) text, ponder the significance of the linguistic data as well as the theological reflection, and debate the interconnection of all these elements. Scholars engaged in the natural sciences, on the other hand, often wonder about the relevance of the biblical statements and the import of the careful linguistic work as they consider the data of scientific research.

The present volume provides a penetrating review of the relevant data regarding creation in the Old Testament or, as some prefer to call it, the Hebrew Bible. It is the first volume in a series featuring careful scholarly engagement with the biblical text itself that is aimed at helping scientists and interested nonspecialists grasp the significance of biblical Creation terminology and theology. A second volume, currently in the process of preparation, will focus upon the relevant New Testament data. The biblical focus of these two volumes should not, however, be interpreted as a retreat from the larger debate related to Creation and evolution. All studies included in this volume have been read by a standing committee of Adventist biblical scholars and scientists who are engaged in careful dialogue and thoughtful interaction. The work of the Faith and Science Council underlines the commitment of administrators, Bible scholars, and scientists within the Seventh-day Adventist Church to listen to one another and engage contemporary science and scholarship constructively on this important issue. This engagement has its foundation in the abiding biblical statement of faith, describing the beginning of life through the word of an all-powerful Creator, who simply spoke life into existence. "In the beginning God created the heavens and the earth" (Gen. 1:1, NIV) functions as the foundational credo of biblical theology, because life begins with God. It also represents the underlying philosophical and theological framework of this volume's contributors.

When the diverse group of scholars who were invited to contribute to this volume received their assignment, they were asked to interact particularly with one key question: What is the relationship of Genesis 1; 2 and its inherent creation theology to other texts and textual genres in the Hebrew Bible? Would a prophet referring directly or indirectly to Genesis 1; 2 share the original author's concept of Creation? Would the use of Creation terminology and theology in later texts evidence a changed perspective from the one visible in Genesis, or would they reflect an underlying Creation framework, similar to the one informing the first chapters of Scripture?

Considering the main question involving the relationship between Genesis 1, 2, and later Creation theology, begins with chapter 1, "The Unique Cosmology of Genesis 1," by Gerhard F. Hasel and Michael G. Hasel, which represents a revised edition of a landmark study, originally published by the late Gerhard and significantly updated by his son Michael, that focuses upon the unique elements of biblical cosmology. Chapter 2, "The Myth of the Solid Heavenly Dome," by Andrews University professors Randall W. Younker and Richard M. Davidson, critically reviews the research history involving the interpretation of the *rāqîaʿ*, described in Genesis 1:6–8, and questions the often uncritical consensus that "primitive" biblical authors (and later commentators) considered the heavenly dome to be a flat, solid expansion.

Davidson's ("The Genesis Account of Origins") comprehensive discussion of the when, who, how, and what of Creation in Genesis 1; 2 leaves no stone unturned and no reference unmentioned. It not only represents a veritable tour de force of opinions and positions, but it also engages the Hebrew text meticulously and thoroughly. Paul Gregor, "Creation Echoes of Genesis 1 and 2 in the Pentateuch," picks up the baton and discusses Creation terminology and theology in the remainder of the Pentateuch, outside Genesis 1; 2. Following the canonical sequence, Davidson's "Creation in the Psalms: Psalm 104" focuses exclusively upon Psalm 104—the key text involving Creation theology in the Psalter. "The Creation Theme in the Book of Psalms," by Alexej Muráň, continues

Davidson's discussion of Creation imagery and theology in the psalms, covering the remainder of the Psalter. Muráň's use of intertextuality and attention to significant clusters of Creation terminology provide a helpful methodological frame for further studies on Creation in other biblical genres.

Practical counsel characterizes biblical wisdom literature. Ángel M. Rodríguez, "Genesis and Creation in the Wisdom Literature," reviews the relevant data and comes to the conclusion that Creation theology and terminology in Job, Proverbs, and Ecclesiastes is deeply rooted in Genesis 1; 2. Pain and death, the result of the undoing of creation in Genesis 3, is recognized as foreign to the original creation and due to human sin. Particularly, the personification of wisdom and its link to creation in Proverbs contributes to the theology of Genesis and its focus upon the Divine Word.

Martin G. Klingbeil's "Creation in the Prophetic Literature of the Old Testament" focuses upon the prophetic literature of the Old Testament and includes a handy introduction to intertextuality per se and Creation markers, not only focusing upon particular key words but also involving the helpful notion of semantic domains, literary markers (involving metaphors and poetry), and conceptual Creation markers (involving motifs and typologies). Klingbeil concludes that "creation in the prophetic literature of the Old Testament is employed as a constant literary and theological reference that connects to a historical past, motivates the interpretation of the present, and moves toward a perspective for the future by means of a continuous contextualization of the topic via the triad: creation, de-creation, and re-creation."

Rodríguez's unique study ("Biblical Creationism and Ancient Near-Eastern Evolutionary Ideas") is interested in discovering the concept of natural evolution in ancient Near-Eastern creation accounts, focusing particularly upon Egyptian texts. Rodríguez concludes that ancient Near-Eastern texts contained latent evolutionary thoughts (e.g., as related to development from simple elements like water, matter, and time), even though they are not referring, technically, to the concept of natural evolution as used in modern science. In view of this surprising recognition, the stark difference between the biblical cosmogony and anthropogony to its ancient Near-Eastern contemporaries, highlights a very different perspective and invites the modern reader to use the biblical text "as a hermeneutical tool to evaluate and deconstruct contemporary scientific evolutionary theories."

Jacques B. Doukhan's " 'When Death Was Not Yet' " wonders about the entrance of death into a post-Creation world, considering its particular role in evolutionary theories. Doukhan's close reading of the biblical text highlights the reversal motif in Genesis and emphasizes that death stands in stark contrast to God's creation, which was considered *ṭôb měʾōd,* or "very good" (Gen. 1:31).

The current volume does not pretend to claim that all questions and issues related to the concept of Creation in the biblical text are easily answered or have been resolved. That would be presumptuous. However, the weight of the textual data of the Old Testament clearly argues for an overarching understanding and theology of Creation that permeates every biblical genre and book. Creation by fiat, in seven literal twenty-four-hour days, and through God's Divine Word was a given in biblical times and represented the framework for a biblical anthropology, cosmology, and—ultimately—soteriology. Following the Fall, described in Genesis 3, it is God who takes the initiative and begins His search for humanity. His question—"Adam, where are you?"—is still echoing through the ages and speaks to human hearts in need of hope, healing, and restoration. The earth-made-new reflects God's original creation and represents a key moment in the cosmic battle between good and evil. When John sees a new earth and a new heaven in Revelation, he stands solidly on the foundation laid in Genesis 1; 2. The God of creation is also the God of salvation, whose might and power ultimately will re-create an earth that has been corrupted by thousands of years of sin. At its core, Creation theology is all about *who* we are, *what* our destiny is, and *how* God chooses to save a world that is in direct rebellion to its Creator. It contains an echo of hope that rings through the centuries—and keeps tugging at our hearts.

The Unique Cosmology of Genesis 1

Gerhard F. Hasel
Michael G. Hasel

The opening chapters of the Bible (Gen. 1–11) contain the history of beginnings, focusing on natural and historical beginnings and the ensuing history of the world and humankind.[1] Nowhere else in Scripture is found such a comprehensive and detailed narration of the origin of the earth and humanity.

While this is important in itself, it receives greater significance when one recognizes that the Genesis account for the origin of the universe (cosmology) in the Creation account is without rival. Nowhere in the ancient Near East or Egypt has anything similar been recorded. The unique words about Creator, creation, and creature—of God, world, and humanity in Genesis 1; 2—set the entire tone for the wonderful and unique saving message of the Bible. It can be said without hesitation that the world and humankind were in the beginning and remain now in the hands of the Creator. Scripture is able to speak about an end of the world and humanity only because God is the Creator of that world and humanity.

The Genesis Cosmogony of Totality

This awe-inspiring Creation account in Genesis contains the first conception of the world and humankind as totalities from their beginning. No one experiences and "knows" humanity in its totality. But in the biblical Creation, these realities are expressed in their totalities as originating from the Creator. The totalities of God's created world and what is in it depicts how the origin and continuing existence of the world and life is expressed in time and space.

Today, there are many who believe that it is unnecessary to engage in a dialogue between the biblical presentation of Creation and the scientific quest for understanding the world and humanity. But such dialogue and interaction are not only desirable, they are essential. The sciences can deal only with partial spheres of knowledge but not with totalities.

This totality is already revealed in the first verse of the Bible: "In the beginning God created the heaven and the earth" (Gen. 1:1).[2] This simple sentence makes four basic affirmations that are completely new and profound in the human quest for an understanding of the world's origin and themselves.[3]

The first affirmation claims that God made the heaven and the earth "in the beginning." There was, then, a time when this globe and its surrounding atmospheric heavens did not exist. In ancient Near-Eastern mythologies, the earth had no beginning, and in Greek philosophical thought, the world existed from eternity. By the use of the words "in the beginning," however, the Genesis cosmology fixes an absolute beginning for Creation. The pregnant expression "in the beginning" separates the conception of the world once and for all from the cyclical rhythm of pagan mythology and the speculation of ancient metaphysics. This world, its life and history, is not dependent upon nature's cyclical rhythm but is brought into existence as the act of Creation by a transcendent God.

The second affirmation is that God is the Creator. As God, He is completely separate from and independent of nature. Indeed, God continues to act upon nature, but God and nature are separate and can never be equated in some form of emanationism or pantheism. This is in contrast to the Egyptian concepts in which creator-god Atum himself is the primordial mound from which arose all life in the Heliopolis cosmology, or where, in another tradition, Ptah is combined with "the land that rises" in the Memphis theology. In Egyptian cosmologies, "everything is contained within the inert monad, even the creator God."[4] There is no separation in Egypt between god and nature.

The third affirmation is that God has acted in fiat creation. The special verb for "create," *bara'*, has only God as its subject throughout the Bible. That is in the Hebrew language—no one can *bara'*, or "create," but God. God alone is Creator, and no one else may share in this special activity. The verb *bara'* is never employed with matter or stuff from which God creates; it contains— along with the emphasis of the phrase "in the beginning"—the idea of creation out of nothing (*creatio ex nihilo*). Since the earth is described in verse 2 as being in a rude state

of desolation and waste, the word *create* in the first verse of Genesis must signify the calling into existence of original matter in the formulation of the world.

The fourth affirmation deals with the object of Creation, the material that is brought forth by divine creation, namely "the heaven and the earth." These words, "the heaven and the earth," are in the Hebrew language a synonym for our term *cosmos*. A close study of the forty-one usages of the phrase "heaven and the earth" reveals that they do not mean that God created the entire universe with its thousands of galaxies at the time He created the world. The focus remains on the planet Earth and its more or less immediate surroundings. The elevated ideas expressed in this first verse of the Bible set the tone for the entire Genesis cosmology.

Modern Interpretations of Biblical Cosmology

It is widely believed that the biblical cosmology is a myth describing a three-storied universe with a heaven above, a flat earth, and the netherworld underneath. If this understanding is coupled with the assumption that the Bible supports a geocentric, or "earth-centered," universe, then it seems hopelessly dated. Thus, many modern scholars have become convinced that the biblical cosmology is historically and culturally conditioned, reflecting a primitive and outdated cosmology of the ancient world. They argue that the biblical cosmology should be abandoned and replaced by a modern, scientific one.

New Testament scholar Rudolf Bultmann wrote some decades ago that, in the

New Testament, "the world is viewed as a three-storied structure, with the earth in the centre, the heaven above, and the underworld beneath"[5] made up of hell, the place of torment. Other modern scholars believe that the cosmology of the Old Testament literally depicts such a picture of a three-storied universe, with storehouses of water, chambers of snow and wind, and windows of heaven. This is depicted in a vaulted canopy of the heavens above a flat earth, at the center of which is a navel, with waters under the earth including rivers of the netherworld. Such a mythological cosmology is now out of date, wrote Bultmann. Modern people cannot believe in such a mythological cosmology while simultaneously flying in jets, browsing the Internet, and using smartphones.

In modernist thinking, this leaves open only two alternatives: (1) accept the assumed mythological picture of the world at the price of intellectual sacrifice, or (2) abandon the biblical cosmology and adopt whatever happens to be the latest scientific theory.

But these two alternatives are false. Do we find, after careful investigation, any evidence in the Bible for a three-storied universe? Does the Bible support the notion of a geocentric universe? If anything, the Bible is human-centered, or more accurately, it is centered on the interrelationship between God and humans. In the Old Testament, God is the center of everything but not the physical center. The Bible does not provide information for a physical center. According to it, the solar system could be geocentric, heliocentric, or something else.

Where has the interpretation come from that the Bible presents a geocentric picture? This idea arose in post—New Testament times, when leading theologians adopted the Greek Ptolemaic cosmology of second century A.D. and interpreted the Bible on the basis of this nonbiblical concept. The famous trial of Galileo in the seventeenth century could have been avoided had theologians of the church recognized that their interpretation of certain Bible texts was based on the cosmology of the pagan mathematician-geographer Ptolemy.

Although we are freed today from the Ptolemaic cosmology, a vast number of biblical scholars still read the cosmology of the Bible through the glasses of what they believe to be the pagan cosmologies of the ancient Near East and Egypt. In the final analysis, these ideas are based on a faulty interpretation of certain biblical passages. It is important to recognize this claim, stating that the cosmology of the Bible is mythological, is of fairly recent origin. But the Bible, properly and honestly interpreted on its own terms, is, in fact, acceptable to the modern mind and does not present the kind of cosmology so widely attributed to it.

The Biblical Concept of Cosmology

The widespread notion that the biblical cosmology reflects a pagan picture of the three-storied universe has cast its shadow broadly. But there is a question whether ancient mythological cosmologies truly had a clearly defined three-storied universe.

The ancient Egyptian view in the Memphite theology was that the permanent place of the dead was in the West. In the

Amduat of the New Kingdom, the deceased are swallowed with the sun by Nut in the West, travel through the twelve hours of the night, and emerge with the sun in paradise, experiencing daily regeneration and re-creation. In Canaanite mythology, the supreme deity El had his throne near the "sources of the Two Rivers, in the midst of the Double-Deep,"[6] which means that the gods did not always dwell in the heavens or the upper story of a supposed three-storied universe. The Canaanite god Baal, who, unfortunately, was also worshiped at times by the Israelites, had his place of abode on the mountain of Zaphon in northern Syria, at the mouth of the Orontes River.

Such examples make it clear that there was no uniform ancient mythical picture of a three-storied universe. The dead could dwell in the West, and the gods could dwell in various parts of the earth rather than in a heavenly world. The most comprehensive study on Mesopotamian cosmic geography concludes that there was no belief in a three-storied universe with a solid metal vault, but rather, it concludes that the Mesopotamians believed in six flat heavens, suspended one above the other by cables.[7] This concept is altogether absent in the biblical cosmology.

The original word for "deep" in Genesis 1:2 figures prominently in the argument of those scholars supporting the view that the Genesis cosmology is three storied. There is heaven above and earth below (v. 1), and underneath is "the deep," interpreted as the "primeval ocean." It has been claimed that the original word for "deep," or *těhôm*, is directly derived from the name *Tiamat*, the mythical Babylonian monster

and goddess of the primeval world ocean in the national epic *Enuma Elish*. *Těhôm* is said to contain an "echo of the old cosmogonic myth,"[8] in which the creator-god Marduk engages Tiamat in battle and slays her. The interpretation that the biblical term "deep" is linguistically dependent on Tiamat is known to be incorrect today on the basis of an advanced understanding of comparative Semitic languages. In fact, "it is phonologically impossible to conclude that [the original word translated as "deep"] was borrowed from *Tiamat*."[9] The thirty-five usages of this word and its derivative forms in the Old Testament reveal that it is generally "a poetic term for a large body of water,"[10] which is completely "nonmythical."[11] To suggest that verse 2 contains the remnant of a conflict from the pagan battle myth is to read ancient mythology into Genesis—something the text actually combats. The description of the passive, powerless, and unorganized state of the "deep" in verse 2 reveals that this term is nonmythical in content and antimythical in purpose.

More recently, a Canaanite background has been suggested for this chaos-battle myth embedded in Genesis, marking a shift of origin from Babylon to the West. But there is little evidence for this. The term translated as "seas" does not appear until verse 10, when one would expect it in the initial few verses of the account. Any connection with the Canaanite deity Yam is, therefore, not present, making it "difficult to assume that an earlier Canaanite dragon myth existed in the background of Gen 1:2."[12] In fact, several scholars reject that there even was a creation myth in Ugarit where these texts were found, and others question whether Baal ever functioned as a creator-god.

What can be said of "the fountains of the great deep" mentioned twice in the Genesis Flood account (7:11; 8:2)?[13] The "great deep" refers undoubtedly to subterranean water. But there is no suggestion in these texts that this underground water is connected with the mythology of an underworld sea on which the earth floats. During the Flood, the springs of the subterranean waters, that had fed the springs and rivers, split open with such might and force that, together with the torrential downpour of waters stored in the atmospheric heavens, the worldwide Flood came about.

The subterranean features, such as "the waters beneath the earth" (Exod. 20:4; Deut. 4:18; 5:8; Job 26:5; Ps. 136:6), fail, on close investigation, to uphold the supposed three-storied or triple-decked view of the world. And what about the underworld? *Šĕʾôl* is invariably the place where dead people go.[14] It is a figurative expression of the grave and may be equated with the regular Hebrew term for "grave." In the Bible, *šĕʾôl* never refers to an underworld of gloomy darkness or waters as the abode of the dead, as was conceived in pagan mythology among Babylonians and Greeks. As a designation of the grave, *šĕʾôl*, of course, is subterranean, because it is in the ground. The three usages of the phrase "the waters beneath the earth" (Exod. 20:4; Deut. 4:18; 5:8) easily refer to waters below the shoreline, because, in one of the texts (Deut. 4:18), it is indeed the place where fish dwell.

Some poetic passages describe the "foundations" of the earth as resting on "pillars" (1 Sam. 2:8; Job 9:6; Ps. 75:43). These words, however, are used only in poetry and are best understood as metaphors. They cannot be construed to refer to literal pillars. Even today, we speak metaphorically of "pillars of the church," referring to staunch supporters of the community of believers. So the pillars of the earth are metaphors describing that God can support or move the inner foundations that hold the earth in place and together, because He is Creator.

Moving from what is "below" the earth to what is "above," the act of fiat creation on the second day calls into existence the firmament (Gen. 1:7). The firmament is frequently associated with firmness and solidity, ideas derived from the Vulgate *firmamentum* and the Septuagint *stereōma* but not from the original term in the Hebrew. Following the Vulgate, many have suggested that this was a "vaulted solid body."[15] But this is a very recent interpretation, first suggested in the eighteenth century, by the French philosopher Voltaire. The Hebrew term *rāqîaʿ*, traditionally translated "firmament," is better rendered with "expanse." Some have tried to document on the basis of nonbiblical texts that the original word designated something solid, perhaps a strip of metal. But these attempts at explaining the Hebrew word fail to convince. Such interpretations are based on unsupported philological guesses and extrabiblical mythical notions but not on what the biblical texts actually demand.

In passages like Genesis 1:7; Psalm 19:1; Daniel 12:3, *firmament* has the meaning of the curved expanse of the heavens, which to an observer on the ground appears like a vast inverted vault. In Ezekiel (1:22, 23, 25, 26; 10:1), it has the sense of an extended platform or level surface. No text of Scripture teaches that the firmament, or expanse, of heaven is firm and solid and holds anything up.[16]

Rain does not come through "windows of heaven" in a solid firmament. Of the five texts in the Bible that refer to the "windows of heaven," only the Flood story (Gen. 7:11; 8:2) relates them to water, and here, the waters do not come from the firmament but from heaven. The remaining three texts clearly indicate that the expression "windows of heaven" is to be understood in a nonliteral sense; it is figurative language in the same way as we can speak today of the "windows of the mind" or the "vault of heaven" without implying that the mind has windows with sashes and glass or that heaven is a literal vault of solid bricks or concrete.

In 2 Kings 7:2, barley comes through the "windows in heaven." In Isaiah 24:18, it seems to be trouble and anguish that use this entrance, while in Malachi 3:10, blessings come through "the windows of heaven." Such figurative language does not lend itself to the reconstruction of biblical cosmology. This is underlined by the fact that the Bible makes abundantly clear that rain comes from clouds (Judg. 5:4; 1 Kings 18:45), which are under and not above the firmament of heaven (Job 22:13, 14). In Psalm 78:23, this association of clouds with the "doors of heaven" is explained in poetry, where the first line and second line repeat the same concept: "Yet He commanded the clouds above, and opened the doors of heaven" (NASB). In the Old Testament, whenever it rains heavily, this is expressed figuratively by the expression that the windows or doors of heaven are opened.

The recognition of the nonliteral, metaphorical use of words—pictorial language—in the Bible is important. If the Bible is read and interpreted on its own terms, it is usually not difficult to recognize such language. We still refer to "the sun setting in the horizon" today, when we, in fact, know that the earth is rotating on its axis away from the sun. Such language was used in ancient times in the same way as metaphor or poetic language.

On the basis of this evidence, the widespread view that the biblical cosmology describes a three-storied universe cannot be maintained. The so-called primitive or primeval view turns out to be an "assigned interpretation and not one which was derived from the texts themselves."[17] Even when certain narratives of the Bible date to the time of some of these pagan myths, this does not necessarily imply that every ancient writer used the same ideas, whether inspired or not.

Other Aspects of Contrast

The reality is that the Genesis account strongly contrasts with ancient Near-Eastern and Egyptian accounts so that there is an intended polemic or argument against these myths.

Sea Monster or Sea Creatures? On the fifth day of Creation (Gen. 1:20–23), God created the "great whales" (v. 21) or "great sea monsters," as more recent translations (RSV, NEB, NAB) render the Hebrew term.

In Ugaritic texts, a related term appears as a personified monster, a dragon, who was overcome by the goddess Anath, the creator-god. Is it justified to link the biblical term to mythology in this context? The word in verse 21 appears in a clearly "nonmythological context."[18] On the basis of other Creation passages in the Bible, it appears to be a generic name for large water creatures in contrast to the small water creatures created next (Gen. 1:21; Ps. 104:25, 26). God's totally effortless creation of these large aquatic creatures, as expressed through the verb "create," which always stresses effortless creation, exhibits a deliberate argument against the mythical idea of creation by battle and combat.

The Lack of Combat, Force, or Struggle. The red thread of opposition to pagan myth is also visible in the fiat creation of raising the "firmament," or "expanse" (Gen. 1:6, 7), without any struggle whatsoever. Ancient Near-Eastern and Egyptian mythologies link this act of separation to combat and struggle. The ancient cosmologies are not absorbed or reflected in Genesis but are overcome.

Creation by Word of Mouth. In the biblical Creation story, the most striking feature is God's creation by the spoken word. On the first day, "God said, 'Let there be light, and there was light' " (vv. 3–5). This is without parallel in Mesopotamian and Egyptian mythology. In *Enuma Elish,* Marduk does "not create the cosmos by utterance, but by gruesomely splitting Tiamat."[19] In the *Atra-Ḥasis Epic,* humankind is created from the flesh and blood of a slaughtered god mixed with clay, but "no hint of the use of dead deity or any other material of a living

one is found in Genesis."[20]

A number of scholars have claimed that creation by word of mouth is best paralleled in Egyptian cosmologies. There are several different traditions, however, that developed over time with significant variations. In the Heliopolis cosmology or theogony, Atum generates the Ennead (nine gods) from himself by the act of masturbation or spitting, "and the two siblings were born—Shu and Tefnut."[21] In another tradition, the Coffin Texts describe Atum as the sun with the name Re-Atum. Sometimes, the two are separated as in "Re in your rising, Atum in your setting."[22] In this sense, Atum, often equated with the sun-god Re, is self-developing and is the originator of the gods and all things.

In the Memphite theology of Egypt, Ptah is compared and contrasted with Atum. Whereas Atum created by "that seed and those hands, (for) Atum's Ennead evolve(ed) through his seed and his fingers, but the Ennead is teeth and lips in this mouth that pronounced the identity of everything and from which Shu and Tefnut emerged and gave birth to the Ennead."[23] Here, the writer achieves his goal of merging the two accounts by saying "that the origin of ennead through the teeth and the lips (of Ptah) is the same as the origin through the semen and hands of Atum."[24] The mouth is, thus, equated with the male organ "from which Shu and Tefnut emerged and gave birth to the Ennead."[25] It was through self-development that Atum or Ptah created the gods. That this teeth and lips here are to be compared to the effortless speech found in the Genesis Creation ignores the parallelism made with Atum and the sexual connotation.

In contrast, there is no hint at self-generation or procreation in the Genesis account. The recurring expression "God said, . . . and there/it was" (e.g., Gen. 1:3, 6, 9, 11) speaks of the effortless, omnipotent, and unchangeable Divine Word of Creation. God's self-existent Word highlights the vast unbridgeable gulf between the biblical picture of Creation and pagan mythology. The Genesis cosmology stresses the essential difference between Divine Being, creation, and created being in order to exclude any idea of emanationism, pantheism, and dualism.

Descriptive Argument. The Genesis cosmology exhibits in various crucial instances a sharply antimythical polemic or argument in its description of created material. This is evidenced in the description of the "deep" (v. 2), the creation of the large aquatic creatures (v. 21), the creative separation of heaven and earth (vv. 6–8), the purpose of the creation of humans as the pinnacle of created beings on earth (vv. 26–28), and creation by Divine Word (v. 3). To this impressive list should be added that the description of the creation and function of the sun and moon (vv. 14–18), whose specific Semitic names were surely avoided, because the same names refer, at the same time, to the sun-god and the moon-god. The use of the terms "greater light" and "lesser light" "breathes a strongly anti-mythical pathos,"[26] or polemic, undermining pagan religions and mythology at fundamental points. The author of Genesis intended the reader to know that the sun and the moon were not gods but were the creation of God for specific functions.

The Creation of Humanity. The magnificent Creation narrative of verses 26–28 speaks of humanity as "the pinnacle of creation."[27] The term for "create" is employed three times in these verses to emphasize the fiat creation of humanity by God. Humans appear as the creature uniquely "blessed" by God (v. 28); they are "the ruler[s] of the world,"[28] including the animal and vegetable kingdoms. All seed-bearing plants and fruit trees are for food (v. 29). This lofty picture of the divine concern and care for humanity's physical needs stands in such sharp contrast to the purpose of creation in ancient Near-Eastern mythology that one is led to conclude that the Bible writer described the purpose of humanity's creation deliberately to combat pagan mythological ideas, while, at the same time, emphasizing the human-centered orientation of Creation.

All the ancient Near-Eastern myths describe the need of humanity's creation as an afterthought, resulting from an attempt to relieve the gods of hard labor and procuring food and drink. This mythical notion is contradicted by the biblical idea that humanity is to rule the world as God's vice-regent. Obviously, this antimythical emphasis cannot be the result of adopting pagan mythical notions; rather, it is rooted in biblical anthropology and the biblical understanding of reality.

In Egyptian cosmologies, "so far no detailed account of the creation of man is known."[29] The primary focus of Egyptian cosmologies is the creation of the Egyptian pantheon of gods; thus, they are better described as theogonies, although the gods themselves represent the elements of nature. A few texts indicate that human-kind came from the tears of Re. "They [Shu and Tefnut] brought to me [Re] my eye with them, after I joined my members together I wept over them. That is how men came into being from the tears that came forth from my eye."[30] The primary emphasis is not on the creation of humanity, which is simply mentioned in passing, but in the restoration of the eye of Re, which had such significant magical and protective powers in ancient Egyptian mythology. In a Coffin Text (7.465, Spell 1130), "I created the gods by my sweat, and mankind from the tears of my eye." It is pointed out that humans are "created like everything else and are called 'the cattle of the god' (Instruction to King Merikare) or 'cattle of Re,' but it is the gods who occupy the center state in the cosmogonies."[31] In the Memphite theology, the creation of humans is not mentioned at all.

The Seven-Day Week and Order of Creation. The complete sequence of Creation in Genesis 1 demonstrates a divine order, so that which was formless and void is formed and filled into a complete ecosystem that will support life. The divine sequence of six lit-eral, twenty-four-hour, consecutive days that culminate in the Sabbath rest is en-tirely absent in ancient Near-Eastern and Egyptian accounts.

Enuma Elish indicates some analogies in the order of creation: firmament, dry land, luminaries, and lastly, humankind. But there are also distinct differences: (1) There is no clear statement that light is created before the luminaries. (2) There is no explicit reference to the creation of the sun (to infer this from Marduk's character

as a solar deity and from what is said about the creation of the moon in Tablet V is difficult). (3) There is no description of the creation of vegetation. (4) Finally, *Enuma Elish* knows nothing of the creation of any animal life in the sea, sky, or earth. A com-parison between Genesis and this account indicates that twice as many processes of creation are outlined in Genesis 1. There is only a general analogy between the or-der of creation in both accounts; "there is no close parallel in the sequence of the creation of elements common to both cosmogonies."[32] Concerning the time for creation, the only possible hint is provided in the *Atra-Ḥasis* account of the creation of humankind. Here, fourteen pieces of clay are mixed with the blood of the slain god and placed in the womb goddess. Af-ter ten months of gestation, the goddess gives birth to seven male and seven female offspring. The birth of humankind after a ten-month gestation is not found in Gen-esis; humanity is created on the sixth day. The link of the Sabbath to a Near-Eastern background has also been futile.

In Egyptian cosmologies, there is no fi-nality of creation. Rather, there is a "one-day pattern of recurrent creation brought about each morning with the sunrise sym-bolizing the daily rebirth of Rê-Amun, the sun-god creator as embodiment of Atum."[33] The cycle of death and rebirth is so central to Egyptian thinking that death itself is seen as part of the normal order of crea-tion. On a funerary papyrus of the Twenty-First Dynasty, a winged serpent on legs is standing on two pairs of legs with the caption: "Death the great god, who made gods and men."[34] This is "a personification of death as a creator god and an impressive visual idea that death is a necessary feature of the world of creation, that is, of the existence in general."[35] A similar image can be seen in the burial chamber of Thutmose III, in which during the eleventh hour of the Amduat, Atum is shown holding the wings of a winged serpent, surrounded on either side by Udjat eyes—the eyes of Re and Horus. The concept of a Sabbath and seven-day sequence is entirely absent.

The Genesis cosmology represents a "complete break"[36] with the pagan mythologies of the ancient Near East and Egypt by undermining prevailing mythical cosmologies and the basic essentials of pagan religions. The description of Creation not only presents the true account, but in so depicting it, the writer chose a great many safeguards against mythology. He used certain terms and motifs, partly related to cosmologically, ideologically, and theologically incompatible pagan concepts and partly in deliberate contrast to ancient Near-Eastern myths, and employed them with a meaning and emphasis expressive of the worldview understanding of reality and cosmology of divine revelation.

The exalted and sublime conception of the Genesis account of Creation presents, at its center, a transcendent God who, as supreme and unique Creator, speaks the world into existence. The center of all creation is humankind as male and female. The Genesis cosmology, which unveils most comprehensively the foundations on which the biblical world reality and worldview rest, knows of no three-storied or triple-decked universe. It provides inspiration's answer to the intellectual question of the who of Creation, which the book of nature points to God as the Creator. It also provides answers to the related questions of how the world was made and what was made. Through action verbs such as "separated" (Gen. 1:4, 7; NASB), "made" (vv. 7, 16, 25, 31), "placed" (v. 17; NASB), "created" (vv. 1, 21, 27; 2:4), "formed" (2:7, 8, 19), "fashioned" (v. 22; NASB), and "said" (1:3, 6, 9, 14, 20, 24, 26) an indication of the how of divine creative activity is revealed. The third intellectual question asks what the transcendent Creator brought forth. The biblical writer himself sums it up in the words "the heavens and the earth, and all the host of them" (2:1).

The biblical Creation account, with the Genesis cosmology, goes far beyond these intellectual questions by addressing itself also to the essential existential question, because it is also the report of the inauguration of the natural and historical processes. It answers what the Divine Creator is able to do. Since the Creator, who is none other than Christ, the Father's creating Agent (John 1:1–4; Heb. 1:1–3), made the cosmos and all that belongs to it, since He is the Maker of the forces of nature and the Sustainer of creation, He can use these forces to bring about His will in the drama of ongoing time, through mighty acts and powerful deeds in nature and history.

Notes

1. Gerhard F. Hasel, "Genesis Is Unique," *Signs of the Times®,* June 1975, 22–26 and "Genesis Is Unique~2" *Signs of the Times®,* July 1975, 22–25. The article was revised and expanded by Michael G. Hasel to include current sources and new information on ancient Near-Eastern and Egyptian parallels.

2. Unless otherwise noted, all scriptural references in this chapter are from the King James Version of the Bible.

3. Gerhard F. Hasel, "Recent Translations of Genesis 1:1: A Critical Look," *The Bible Translator* 22 (1971): 154–168; Hasel, "The Meaning of Genesis 1:1," *Ministry* 49, no. 1 (January 1976): 21–24.

4. Richard J. Clifford, *Creation Accounts in the Ancient Near East and in the Bible* (Washington, DC: Catholic Biblical Association, 1994), 114.

5. Rudolf Bultmann, "New Testament and Mythology," in *Kerygma and Myth,* ed. H. W. Bartsch, vol. 1 (London: Harper & Row, 1953), 2.

6. Albrecht Goetze, "El, Ashertu and the Storm-God," *Ancient Near-Eastern Texts* (1969): 519.

7. Wayne Horowitz, *Mesopotamian Cosmic Geography,* 2nd corr. printing, Mesopotamian Civilizations, bk. 8 (Winona Lake, IN: Eisenbrauns, 2011).

8. S. H. Hooke, "Genesis," in *Peake's Commentary on the Bible,* eds. H. H. Rowley and Matthew Black (London: Thomas Nelson, 1962), 179.

9. David Toshio Tsumura, "The Earth and the Waters in Genesis 1 and 2: A Linguistic Investigation," *Journal for the Study of Old Testament,* supplement series 83 (Sheffield, UK: JSOT Press, 1989), 31.

10. Mary K. Wakeman, *God's Battle With the Monster: A Study in Biblical Imagery* (Leiden: Brill, 1973), 86.

11. Kurt Galling, "Der Charakter der Chaosschilderung in Gen 1.2," *Zeitschrift für Theologie und Kirche* 47 (1950): 151.

12. Tsumura, "The Earth and the Waters," 32, 33.

13. See Gerhard F. Hasel, "The Fountains of the Great Deep," *Origins* 1 (1974): 67–72.

14. The term šĕ'ôl is translated as "grave" (thirty-one times), "hell" (thirty-one times), and "pit" (six times) in the KJV. The rendering "hell" is unfortunate, because the term has nothing to do with torture, torment, or consciousness.

15. Claus Westermann, *Genesis* (Neukirchen-Vluyn, Germany: Neukirchener, 1974), 160.

16. Randall W. Younker and Richard M. Davidson, "The Myth of the Solid Heavenly Dome: Another Look at the Hebrew Term *rāqîaʿ*," *Andrews University Seminary Studies* 49 (2011): 127.

17. Walter C. Kaiser Jr., "The Literary Form of Genesis 1:11," in *New Perspectives on the Old Testament,* ed. J. B. Payne (Waco, TX: Word, 1970), 57.

18. Theodor H. Gaster, "Dragon," *The Interpreter's Dictionary of the Bible,* vol. 1 (1962), 868.

19. Gordon H. Johnston, "Genesis 1 and Ancient Egyptian Creation Myths," *Bibliotheca Sacra* 165 (2008): 187.

20. Alan R. Millard, "A New Babylonian 'Genesis' Story," *Tyndale Bulletin* 18 (1967): 3–18.

21. "From Pyramid Texts Spell 527," trans. James P. Allen, *The Context of Scripture* 1, no. 3:7.

22. James P. Allen, *Genesis in Egypt: The Philosophy of Ancient Egyptian Creation Accounts* (New Haven, CT: Yale University Press, 1988), 10.

23. "From the 'Memphite Theology,'" trans. James P. Allen, *The Context of Scripture* 1, no. 15:21–23.

24. Ragnhild Bjerre Finnestad, "Ptah, Creator of the Gods: Reconsideration of the Ptah Section of the *Denkmal,*" *Numen: International Review for the History of Religions* 23 (1976): 89.

25. James P. Allen, "From the 'Memphite Theology,'" *The Context of Scripture* 1, nos. 15–16: 22.

26. Nahum M. Sarna, *Understanding Genesis* (New York: Schocken, 1970), 9.

27. Ibid., 14.

28. Otto Loretz, "Schöpfung und Mythos," *Stuttgarter Bibelstudien* 32 (Stuttgart: Katholisches Bibelwerk, 1968), 92–98.

29. Jaroslav Černý, *Ancient Egyptian Religion* (Westport, CT: Greenwood, 1979), 48.

30. *Papyrus Bremner-Rhind* (British Museum 10188).

31. Clifford, *Creation Accounts in the Ancient Near East,* 116.

32. Charles Francis Whitley, "The Pattern of Creation in Genesis, Chapter 1," *Journal of Near-Eastern Studies* 17 (1958): 34, 35.

33. Johnston, "Genesis 1," 192.

34. *Papyrus of Henuttawy* (British Museum 10018).

35. Erik Hornung, *Conceptions of God in Ancient Egypt* (Ithaca, NY: Cornell University Press, 1982), 81.

36. Gerhard von Rad, *Genesis: A Commentary* (Philadelphia, PA: Westminster, 1962), 53.

The Myth of the Solid Heavenly Dome

Randall W. Younker
Richard M. Davidson

Most modern biblical scholars assume that the ancient Hebrews had a "pre-scientific," even naive, view of the universe. This understanding is built around the idea that the Hebrew word in Genesis 1, usually translated "firmament" in English Bibles, was actually understood by the ancient Hebrews to be a solid, hemispherical dome or vault that rested upon mountains or pillars that stood along the outermost perimeter of a circular, flat disk—the earth.

Above this solid dome was a celestial ocean ("waters above the firmament"). Attached to the dome and visible to observers below were the stars, sun, and moon. The dome also possessed windows or gates through which celestial waters ("waters above the firmament") could, upon occasion, pass. On the surface of the flat earth were terrestrial oceans ("waters below the firmament") and dry land; below the earth were subterranean waters ("fountains of the deep") and the netherworld of the dead. This understanding of Hebrew cosmology is so common that pictures of it are frequently found in Bible dictionaries and commentaries.

In support of this reconstruction of Hebrew cosmology, supporters bring two lines of argument to bear. The first is textual and linguistic: the context and meaning of certain words support this reconstruction.

Second, this view was common to other peoples of the ancient Near East, especially in Mesopotamia, considered the probable source of Hebrew cosmology. This understanding continued to be accepted throughout the early history of the Christian church and the Middle Ages. It was not, as some argue, until the rise of modern science that the biblical view of cosmology was considered naive and untenable.

History of Interpretation

Babylonian Views of the Heavens. During the latter part of the nineteenth century, scholars commonly suggested that the ancient Hebrews borrowed many of their ideas, including the notion that heaven was a solid hemisphere, from the Babylonians, probably while the Hebrew people were exiled there. The idea that the Hebrews borrowed from the Babylonians was especially common during the pan-Babylonian craze that gripped biblical scholarship for a brief period during the early twentieth century. Closer comparative analysis between Babylonian and Hebrew thought has, however, found so many significant differences between the two that the idea of direct borrowing has been virtually abandoned by subsequent scholarship.

Still, some continue to suggest that the ancient Hebrews borrowed cosmological concepts, including the idea of a solid-domed heaven, from the Mesopotamians. Even this idea, however, had to be scuttled when more recent work by Wilfred G. Lambert could find no evidence that the Mesopotamians themselves believed in a hard-domed heaven; rather, he traces this idea to Peter Jensen's mistranslation of the term "heavens" in his translation of the *Enuma Elish*. Lambert's student, Wayne Horowitz, attempted to piece together a Mesopotamian cosmology from a number of ancient documents, but it is quite different from anything found in the Hebrew Bible.

Horowitz's study suggests that the Mesopotamians believed in six flat heavens, suspended one above the other by cables. When it came to interpreting the stars and the heavens, the Mesopotamians were more interested in astrology—what the gods were doing and what it meant for humanity—than in cosmology. There is no evidence that the Mesopotamians ever believed in a solid heavenly vault.

Greek Views of the Heavens. As early as the sixth century B.C., the ancient Greeks suggested that the heavens might consist of a series of hard spheres. This idea should not be confused, however, with the solid-vault or solid-dome theory suggested by later biblical critics. The critics have envisioned only a hard, hollow hemisphere, resembling half a sphere in the shape of an upside-down bowl. In reality, however, the Greeks argued for a spherical (not flat) earth that was suspended inside a complete, hollow heavenly sphere, which, in turn, was also suspended inside additional outer spheres (a geocentric model). They

believed that these spheres were necessary to explain the movements of the sun, moon, stars, and planets.

It was thought that these celestial bodies were attached to, or embedded in, these large, transparent hard spheres, which carried the celestial bodies along as they rotated in space. A number of different spheres were needed to explain the separate movements of the celestial bodies. Generally, it was believed that there might be at least eight such spheres nested inside each other. The Greeks based the rotations of the spheres (and hence, the celestial bodies) upon their own observations and on the written records of the ancient Babylonians. Aristotle and Ptolemy provide the classic formulations of the Greek celestial-sphere model that influenced all scholars of the early Christian church and the Middle Ages.

Jewish Views of the Heavens. During the Hellenistic period, the Hebrew Bible was translated into Greek. When the translators came to the Hebrew word usually translated as "firmament," they chose to translate it with the word for "something established" or "steadfast." This is not surprising in that the Hebrew text equates the same word with "heavens." The common belief about the heavens at that time (as with Greek views) was that they were solid.

The idea of hard spheres would be picked up by Hellenized Jews as early as the fourth century B.C. The nonbiblical work 1 Enoch discusses a hard firmament with openings through which the sun, moon, and planets move in and out. This work also describes coming to the ends of the earth as far as the heavens; however, there is some dispute about whether 1 Enoch is saying a person can touch the heavens at the ends of the earth or if there is still a chasm that separates the earth from the heavens. The latter seems more likely. The former would support a domed earth, while the latter is in harmony with the Greek idea of the earth being suspended within a sphere.

Another Jewish work, 3 Baruch, recounts the story of men building the Tower of Babel to reach the heavens to see what it is made of (3 Bar. 3:7, 8). Though some have suggested that this supports a dome theory, it can also be understood simply as supporting the idea of a hard heaven, which is not incompatible with the Greek celestial-sphere model. Given the prevailing Greek thought, the latter is more likely.

Early Christianity and the Heavens. Early Christians were following the discussions of the Greek philosophers with interest and speculated on how biblical teaching related to the Greek understanding of the cosmos. They accepted the ideas that the earth was a spherical globe and that the biblical firmament was one of the celestial spheres, but they could not identify which sphere was the biblical firmament, so they tended to add a few spheres to accommodate the Bible to Greek thinking.

Basil of Caesarea and Augustine are among the early church fathers who attempted to harmonize biblical teachings of the cosmos with Greek notions of the celestial spheres. This can also be seen in Jerome's translation of the Bible into Latin (A.D. 405). Jerome used the Greek Old Testament (Septuagint) as one of his sources and was undoubtedly familiar with Greek discussions about the celestial spheres.

Thus, when he came to the book of Genesis and saw that the Greek word used for the Hebrew translated as "firmament" was "something established" or "steadfast," he selected the Latin *firmamentum* to convey the Greek sense of the word. It is from the Latin *firmamentum* that the word *firmament,* used to describe the heavens, came into common usage in English.

It is important to note that the Latin *firmamentum* conveys the Greek concept of hard celestial spheres that was popular at the time; it should *not* be used to support the dome or vault theory. The dome theory, along with the idea of a flat earth, has been almost universally rejected by Christian scholars, both in the early Christian period and throughout the Middle Ages. It should also be noted that though Jerome's translation may be seen as support for the notion of hard celestial spheres, not all Christians accepted this position. Basil, for example, was inclined to believe in a fluid firmament, not a hard sphere. He wrote: "Not a firm and solid nature, which has weight and resistance, it is not this that the word 'firmament' means."[1]

Augustine, on the other hand, was not certain of the nature of the other Greek spheres nor of their composition. In some of his statements, he seems to argue that the firmament of Genesis must be a hard sphere, since it held back the waters above; yet elsewhere in the same essay, he speaks of air and fire as the material essence of the heavens, thereby suggesting soft and fluid heavens.[2]

This unwillingness to commit to a hard-sphere theory is reflected in the common tendency by most Christian scholastics to translate the Hebrew word usually translated as "firmament" as "expansion," or "extension"—the former expressions all convey the meaning of expanse and do not commit one to an understanding of something hard. As Edward Grant notes, "Most Christian authors and Latin Encyclopedists during late antiquity ... thought of the heavens (i.e., celestial spheres) as fiery or elemental in nature, and therefore fluid."[3]

Late Medieval Christianity and the Heavens. The theory of celestial spheres continued to dominate Christian thinking about the cosmos throughout the Middle Ages. The existence of numerous hollow spheres or orbs around the spherical earth was almost universally accepted. However, the actual nature of the spheres was an ongoing topic of debate. Were they hard, fluid, or soft? The debate was a theo-philosophical issue, determined by questions such as the following: Were the hard spheres corruptible (and would a perfect God make something corruptible)? How and in what way were these spheres congruent with the observations of various astronomers?

During the thirteenth century, it seems that more scholastics thought of the spheres as fluid. However, in the fourteenth century, there was a shift toward the majority viewing the celestial hard spheres as being hard. It seems this view was widespread among scholars of the fifteenth and sixteenth centuries as well, although there were also many for whom the precise nature of the composition did not matter.

Therefore, as in early antiquity, Christian biblical and Latin scholars of the early Middle Ages—even into the thirteenth

century—did not view the heavens as hard or fiery. Both prominent Jewish rabbis, such as Abraham ibn Ezra and David Kimchi, and Christian scholars of notoriety, including Thomas Aquinas and Durandus of Saint-Pourçain, preferred to use the word *expanse* during the early part of this period.

Renaissance Views of the Heavens. Three key developments occurred in the late sixteenth and early seventeenth centuries that had significant implications for how the cosmos was viewed. First, the observations by Tycho Brahe of a supernova in 1572 and the discovery of the Great Comet in 1577 seemed to defy the hard-sphere theory. Second, the championing of Copernicus's heliocentric model by Galileo allowed for the possibility of intersecting planetary orbits. Interestingly, although Copernicus's heliocentric model called for a different configuration of the celestial spheres, he still thought the spheres were hard as did Galileo. Nevertheless, the work of Brahe, Copernicus, and Galileo contributed to the eventual rejection of the hard-sphere theory. Thus, by the late seventeenth and during the eighteenth centuries, the idea of hard spheres, which had been popular for three hundred years, was virtually abandoned. Emphasis was again on the notion of soft spheres.

In terms of biblical hermeneutics, however, the Galileo affair led to a third unheralded yet significant development—an essay promoting accommodationism, written by the Benedictine scholar Antoine Augustin Calmet. Calmet had been asked by the church to write an introduction to Galileo's *Dialogue on the Two Chief World Systems* that would set a proper distance between the church's position and that of Galileo.

Calmet was not supposed to endorse Galileo's position. However, he was apparently sympathetic to Galileo's claims and proposed an accommodationist interpretation of the Creation account that suggested the inspired writer, in deference to the ignorance of his audience (the ancient Jews), used language and ideas that would be more easily understood by the original audience. Thus, the heavens were described as a tentlike heavenly vault—perhaps the earliest such claim in which a nonliteral accommodationism hermeneutic was applied. Calmet's ideas would be picked up and promoted by Voltaire. Although a direct connection cannot, at present, be established, Calmet's ideas of what the ancient Jews thought about the cosmos would be very similar to those promoted by nineteenth-century biblical criticism.

Meanwhile, the word translated as "expanse" was almost universal among biblical scholars during the sixteenth and seventeenth centuries. For example, this idea was reflected in the work of the Dominican Santes (or Xantes) Pagnino, one of the leading philologists and biblicists of his day, who was known for his literal adherence to the Hebrew text of Scripture. He consistently translated the word as *expansionem*.

Eighteenth- and Nineteenth-Century Views of the Heavens. Biblical scholars of the eighteenth century continued to endorse *expansionem* as the best translation. An important application of this understanding is found in *The Mosaic Theory of the Solar or Planetary System,* in which Samuel Pye defined the firmament as an expanse or atmosphere of fluid. Significantly, he extends this notion to include also the other planets in the system.

Many examples from the nineteenth century maintained this interpretation of the word translated "firmament." John Murray, a Scottish scholar with a PhD in chemistry, retooled his expertise in ancient history and languages, including Hebrew, to argue that the firmament was a "permanently elastic" substance consisting of a mixture of gaseous matter and vapor that attracted water above it, which was in line with cosmologic views of the time.[4] Not only were his views in line with the current thinking of his time, but *The Truth of Revelation* became one of the early books in the emerging biblical archaeology genre.

Nineteenth-Century Biblical Criticism and the Origin of the Flat-Earth-and-Solid-Dome Theory. It is important to note two interesting and significant nineteenth-century works on the history of science. Historians Jeffery Burton Russell and Christine Garwood respectively debunk the long-held view among modern scholars that ancient philosophers and scientists of the early Christian church, late antiquity, and the Middle Ages believed the earth was flat. After an extensive review of the letters, papers, and books of the major thinkers throughout these periods, Russell and Garwood made the surprising discovery that, apart from a few isolated individuals, *no one* believed in a flat earth—indeed, the consensus throughout this entire period among virtually all scholars and churchmen was that the earth was spherical. Where, then, did the flat-earth understanding of early

Christian and medieval thought originate? They were able to trace its origin to the early nineteenth century when antireligious sentiment was high among many scholars and intellectuals.

This is not to say that there were not skeptics who believed in a flat-earth and domed-heaven prior to this. In fact, this view begins to emerge in the seventeenth and eighteenth centuries. Voltaire promoted this idea in the following about the ancient Hebrews' views of the cosmos: "These childish and savage populations imagined the earth to be flat, supported, I know not how, by its own weight in the air; the sun, moon, and stars to move continually upon a solid vaulted roof called a firmament; and this roof to sustain waters, and have flood-gates at regular distances, through which these waters issued to moisten and fertilize the earth."[5]

However, this was not a widespread view and did not gain a consensus among critical biblical scholars until the nineteenth century.

According to Russell and Garwood, two of the key individuals who helped introduce and popularize this idea in nineteenth-century scholarship were the American author Washington Irving and the Egyptologist Antoine-Jean Letronne. Irving wrote of "the indelible picture of the young Columbus, a 'simple mariner,' appearing before a dark crowd of benighted inquisitors and hooded theologians at a council of Salamanca, all of whom believed that the earth was flat like a plate."[6] Letronne, who was known for his "strong antireligious prejudices," "cleverly drew upon both [his studies in geography and Patristics] to

misrepresent the church fathers and their medieval successors as believing in a flat earth."[7]

In particular, Russell's debunking of the flat-earth myth is significant for understanding the widely held view among biblical scholars that ancient peoples believed that the sky or heaven above them was a metal vault. This attribution of the solid-sky or solid-dome concept to the ancients appears in Western literature at about the same time as the flat-earth myth. The idea of a flat earth becomes an integral component in the reconstruction of the metal-sky or metal-dome cosmology, in which the hemispherical dome necessarily rests or is anchored on a flat earth. Thus, it appears that the biblical critics of the 1850s built their ideas about ancient Hebrew cosmology upon the incorrect flat-earth concept of twenty years earlier. Further, they seem to have confused ancient and medieval discussions of hard celestial spheres with the hemispherical solid-dome or solid-vault and flat-earth myths, which were two quite unrelated concepts.

The flat-earth myth was widely endorsed by critical biblical scholars during the middle of the nineteenth century. At this time, a number of publications emerged that proposed the Bible contained naive views of the cosmos, including the idea that the firmament was a hard dome.

An examination of the whole subject suggests an idea of the meteorology of the Hebrews. "They supposed that, at a moderate distance above the flight of birds, was a solid concave hemisphere, a kind of dome, transparent, in which the stars were fixed, as lamps; and containing openings, to be used or closed as was necessary. It was understood as supporting a kind of celestial ocean, called 'the waters above the firmament,' and 'the waters above the heavens.' "[8]

Other biblical scholars soon picked up on this flat-earth or flat-dome heavenly cosmology. Among the better known was Tayler Lewis, a professor of Greek, an instructor in the "Oriental tongue," and a lecturer on biblical and Oriental literature at Union College in New York State. Likewise, Charles Wycliffe Goodwin, an Egyptologist, argued that the Bible writer believed in a hard-dome heaven. Concerning the Hebrew word translated as "firmament," he wrote, "It has been pretended that the word *rakia* may be translated expanse, so as merely to mean 'empty space.' The context sufficiently rebuts this."[9] Andrews Norton, an American Unitarian preacher and theologian who taught at Bowdoin College and Harvard, asserts that "the blue vault of heaven is a solid firmament, separating the waters which are above it from the waters on the earth, and that in this firmament the heavenly bodies are placed."[10]

Also influential was John William Colenso, an Anglican bishop to Natal, who commented that "if it would be wrong for a Christian Missionary of our day, to enforce the dogmas of the Church in former ages, which we now know to be absurd, and to mislead a class of native catechists, by teaching them that the Earth is flat, and the sky a solid firmament, above which the stores of rain are treasured,—when God has taught us otherwise,—it must be equally wrong and sinful, to teach them that the Scripture stories of the Creation, the Fall,

and the Deluge, are infallible records of historical fact, *if* God, by the discoveries of Science in our day, has taught us to know that these narratives—whatever they may be—are certainly not to be regarded as *history.*"[11]

By this time, the flat-earth-and-domed-heaven cosmology was accepted by both biblical geologists and mainstream historical-critical biblical scholars, in spite of vocal resistance by more conservative and evangelical scholars.

Vapor-Canopy Theory. Around this time, the conservative defense was undermined somewhat by a new theory that returned to the concept of hard spheres—an idea that generally had been abandoned by scientists (Christian or not) during the seventeenth century. The renewed proposal was called the vapor-canopy theory. Specifically, Isaac Newton Vail, drawing on the expression "waters above the firmament" mentioned in Genesis 1:7, proposed that the waters for the Flood came from a canopy of water vapor (or liquid water or ice) surrounding the primeval earth. This theory combined the abandoned hard-sphere theory with the vaulted-heaven interpretation to create a possible model for solving issues for conservative creationist views. It still has its defenders today, although its exegetical foundation is rejected by most evangelical scholars and its science is rejected by both evangelical and secular scientists. Nevertheless, liberal scholars have been delighted to receive support from the more fundamentalist vapor-canopy theorists for their assertion of the naivety of the ancient Hebrews' views of the cosmos.

Pan-Babylonianism and the Solid Dome. The return to the development of the flat-earth-and-domed-heaven theory among mainstream historical-critical scholars received further energy during the pan-Babylonian craze of the late nineteenth to early twentieth centuries. It was suggested that the Hebrews borrowed the hard-dome concept from Mesopotamia during the Hebrew exile. As noted earlier, Jensen played a major role in contributing to misunderstandings about ancient cosmological views. His translation used the word *vault* to describe the Babylonian concept of the heavens, resulting in the notion of "heavenly vault." Jensen's work was very influential for some eighty years.

During this time, a number of pictorial representations of Hebrew cosmologies were constructed, the first of which was published by Giovanni Virginio Schiaparelli in his *Astronomy of the Old Testament* (1903–1905). These cosmologies were patched together from biblical texts taken from different time periods and genres and were based on very literalistic readings. This approach was vigorously opposed by more conservative scholars. William Fairfield Warren argued that the liberal reconstructions would not be recognized by the ancient Hebrews, even if it was drawn out for them on a piece of paper.[12]

Modern Advocates of a Flat-Earth-and-Vaulted-Heaven Hebrew Cosmology. In spite of vigorous opposition to the vault theory by more conservative biblical scholars and the demise of pan-Babylonianism, the idea that the ancient Babylonians and Hebrews believed in a hard hemispherical dome continued to be pushed. Harry Emerson Fosdick was an influential advocate and popularizer during the 1930s, who, like most liberal commentators, continued to accept the view of a naive Hebrew cosmology without really providing careful historical review or in-depth exegetical defense. Liberal views were opposed by evangelical scholars, such as Bernard Ramm. Within Adventist circles, the idea of a naive Hebrew cosmology has been supported by Richard L. Hammill and others.[13]

Of course, even if it can be shown that in the history of Christian scholarship, the dome theory is really a recent nineteenth-century invention tied to incorrect medieval thinking, the question still remains: What did the ancient Hebrews think about the cosmos? Certainly, many nineteenth-century scholars examined the Hebrew text, including, of course, the key word translated as "firmament." In spite of the fact that most biblical linguists prior to the nineteenth century translated it as expanse, rather than understanding it as something solid or hard (like a vault), many nineteenth-century scholars argued that it was a metal substance, thereby supporting the supposition that the ancient Hebrews thought of the heavens above the earth as a solid vault or dome. Therefore, it seems appropriate to take another look at the Hebrew texts and words that mention the heavens and firmament.

A Word Study of the Hebrew Cosmology

It is important to keep in mind that there is no single Hebrew text or passage in which the cosmological elements are brought together to provide a complete, systematic view of the supposed Hebrew cosmology. Rather, scholars have reconstructed the cosmos by piecing together different biblical passages, written at different times, in different genres, for different purposes, none of which were primarily cosmological.

Statistics of Occurrence in the Hebrew Bible and Basic Meanings. The word translated as "firmament" occurs seventeen times in the Hebrew Bible in the *nominal* form: nine times in Genesis (1:6, 7 [three times], 8, 14, 15, 17, 20), five times in Ezekiel (1:22, 23, 25, 26; 10:1), twice in Psalms (19:2; 150:1), and once in Daniel (12:3). In none of these occurrences does it appear in association with any metal. The passages from Genesis, Psalms, and Daniel all refer to the same heavenly reality described in the opening chapter of Scripture. In fact, the only time the nominal form of the word refers to a solid material substance is in Ezekiel 1:22, where the firmament below YHWH's movable throne is said to appear "like the awesome gleam of crystal," but even here, it is important to note that the text does not say it was crystal—only that it had the "gleam of crystal."

The verbal form occurs in the biblical text in its various stems twelve times. In its verbal form, it is explicitly associated with metal five times (Exod. 39:3; Num. 16:38, 39; Isa. 40:19; Jer. 10:9). It is used three times in conjunction with the earth (Isa. 42:5; 44:24; Ps. 136:6), twice with the stamping of feet (Ezek. 6:11; 25:6), and once with the smashing of an enemy (2 Sam. 22:43). Only one time is it possibly associated with the sky (Job 37:18: "Can you, with Him, spread out the skies, strong as a molten mirror?"); however, the term often translated "skies"

in this verse most likely refers to clouds.

Significantly, the verbal form does appear in the same sentence as the word for "heavens" in several verses, all of which have a creation context, but it is not used to refer to the heavens.

The verbal form usually describes a process (after all, it is a verbal form) that enables any given substance to cover or encompass a larger area by becoming thinner. The material acted upon may be any substance that can be spread or expanded by being stretched, hammered, or heated to a state where the material is melted or liquefied. There is, of course, a distinction between stretching and hammering. *Stretching* occurs when the substance is grabbed on its outer edges and pulled away from the center. *Hammering* is when the substance is pounded in the center, forcing the material to move out from the center to the edges. When something is heated to a sufficient temperature, the force of gravity will cause the melted or liquefied material to thin and expand.

The net effect of all three processes is essentially the same, in that the substance will cover a larger area by becoming thinner. In the case of metal, the process makes the material into a thin, flat layer so that it can be used as an overlay. All three of these processes for expanding materials are employed in the Hebrew text, and each is described by the term (with reference to, e.g., various hard metals, molten metal, earth, cloud, dust). The basic meaning of to "expand" in these uses suggests that the noun, which corresponds to the verb and depicts various materials that are expanded, may appropriately be translated as "expanse."

The Heavenly Firmament in Genesis 1 and Elsewhere in the Old Testament. When we look at the use of the word in Genesis 1, the meaning of "expanse" fits the immediate context, and the context also gives clues regarding the nature of this "expanse." First, the function is "to separate the waters from the waters" (Gen. 1:6). As Kenneth Mathews restates this purpose, "God formed an 'expanse' to create a boundary, giving structure to the upper and lower waters (vv. 6, 7). The 'expanse' is the atmosphere that distinguishes the surface waters of the earth (i.e., 'the waters below') from the atmospheric waters or clouds (i.e., 'the waters above')."[14]

That this expanse is not a solid dome is evident from a second clue in the text: not only are the greater and lesser lights placed "in the expanse" on the fourth day of creation (vv. 15, 17), but also the birds created on the fifth day were to fly "in the open expanse of the heavens" (v. 20). Mathews elaborates: "There is no indication, however, that the author conceived of it [*rāqîaʿ*] as a solid mass, a 'firmament' (AV) that supported a body of waters above it.... The 'expanse' describes both the place in which the luminaries were set (vv. 14, 15, 17) and the sky where the birds are observed (v. 20). Thus Genesis' description of the 'expanse' is phenomenological—to the observer on earth, the sun and stars appear to sit in the skies while at the same time birds glide through the atmosphere, piercing the skies."[15]

A third clue in the text is in verse 8, "God called the expanse 'sky' " (NIV). John Sailhamer asks: "Is there a word (in English) or idea that accommodates such a broad use of the term 'expanse'?" He rules out such terms as "ceiling," "vault," or "global ocean," proposing that they "suit neither the use of the term in verse 20 nor the naming of the 'expanse' as 'sky.' Such explanations, though drawn from analogies of ancient Near-Eastern cosmologies, are too specific for the present context. [And we would add that such terms do not represent the ancient Near East cosmologies, as demonstrated above!] Thus it is unlikely that the narrative has in view here a 'solid partition or vault that separates the earth from the waters above.' . . . More likely the narrative has in view something within humankind's everyday experience of the natural world—in general terms, that place where the birds fly and where God placed the lights of heaven (cf. v. 14). In English the word 'sky' appears to cover this sense well."[16]

What is true with regard to the sky in Genesis 1 also holds for the rest of the Hebrew Bible. Although this word and parallel expressions depicting the sky are used in various poetic contexts employing different similes, there is no hint that the sky is a solid dome. C. F. Keil and F. Delitzsch provide a succinct summary regarding its meaning with reference to the sky in Genesis and elsewhere in the Old Testament: "To stretch, spread out, then beat or tread out, means *expansum*, the spreading out of the air, which surrounds the earth as an atmosphere. According to optical appearance, it is described as a carpet spread out above the earth (Ps. civ. 2), a curtain (Isa. xl. 22), a transparent work of sapphire (Ex. xxiv. 10), or a molten looking-glass (Job xxxvii. 18); but there is nothing in these poetical similes to warrant the idea that the heavens were regarded as a solid mass ... such as Greek poets describe."[17]

Water Above. If the expanse is the sky in Genesis 1:6–8, then the mention of the waters that were above the expanse (v. 7) is very likely a reference to clouds. This interpretation is supported by intertextual parallels to Genesis 1 in other Old Testament Creation accounts. Note especially Proverbs 8:28, where what exists above the sky or heavens is explicitly described as the clouds. Many modern translations have rendered it as "clouds" in this verse (KJV, NET, NIV, NJB, NKJV, NLT, RWB, TNIV).

Psalm 78:23 likewise describes the clouds above. Mathews notes that elsewhere in the Old Testament "there is evidence that the Hebrews understood that clouds produced rain and thus, from a phenomenological perspective, 'water' can be described as belonging to the upper atmosphere."[18] Old Testament passages depicting clouds producing rain include Deuteronomy 28:12; Judges 5:4; 1 Kings 18:44, 45; Ecclesiastes 11:3; and Isaiah 5:6. Thus, there is good evidence to conclude that the waters above are equated with clouds in ancient Hebrew thinking (as opposed to a celestial ocean of solid water above a vault).

Keil and Delitzsch present a clear summary of the meaning of "waters above": "The waters under the firmament are the waters upon the globe itself; those above are not the ethereal waters beyond the limits of the terrestrial atmosphere, but the waters which float in the atmosphere, and are separated by it from those upon the earth, the waters which accumulate in clouds, and then bursting these

their bottles, pour down as rain upon the earth."[19]

Windows or Doors of Heaven. It is often suggested that the Hebrews believed there were literal windows or doors in the firmament. However, in Genesis 7:11, it is the windows of the sky, not the windows of the firmament, whence the waters above fall. Windows or doors never appear with the word translated as "firmament" nor with the expression "waters above," which occurs only twice in the Hebrew Bible (Gen. 1:7; Ps. 148:4).

Psalm 78:23 is decisive in understanding the meaning of the terms "windows" and "doors of heaven." In this verse, the term "the doors of heaven" is explicitly associated (by means of poetic synonymous parallelism) with clouds: "Yet He commanded the clouds above and opened the doors of heaven." This verse indicates that "doors of heaven" (and the parallel phrase "windows of heaven") is to be understood figuratively as a reference to clouds. "According to the Old Testament representation, whenever it rains heavily, the doors or windows of heaven are opened."[20] Other Old Testament references make clear that the phrase "windows of heaven" and parallels are figurative expressions.

If the "windows of heaven" refer to the clouds in the sky, then it is reasonable to suggest that the opening of the windows of heaven, mentioned for the first time in connection with the Flood, may imply that there was no rain on the earth (but only a mist that watered the ground, cf. Gen. 2:6, 7) until the time of the Flood. This would be in harmony with the explicit statement of Ellen G. White: "The world before the Flood reasoned that for centuries the laws of nature had been fixed. The recurring seasons had come in their order. Heretofore rain had never fallen; the earth had been watered by a mist or dew."[21]

Day Two of Creation Week: Material and Functional Creation. According to Genesis 1:6–8, on the second day of Creation week, God was involved in both material and functional creative acts. Verses 6a, 7a, and 8 describe the material creation: "Then God said, 'Let there be an expanse in the midst of the waters. . . .' God made the expanse, and . . . called the expanse heaven." Verses 6b, 7b describe the functional creation: " 'Let it [the expanse] separate the waters from the waters.' God made the expanse, and separated the waters which were below the expanse from the waters which were above the expanse." Both material creation (the making of the sky) and the assignment of the function of that creation (to divide the upper atmospheric heavens containing water-bearing clouds from the surface waters of the earth) are an integral part of God's creative activity during Creation week.

A recent interpretation of Genesis 1 published by John Walton seriously challenges the traditional understanding of Creation week. Walton argues that the seven days of Genesis 1 are literal days but that they refer to the inauguration of the cosmos as a functioning temple where God takes up His residence. The six-day Creation week, according to Walton, refers only to functional and not to material creation. The week describes God's establishment and installation of functions.

There is need for a thorough critique of Walton's thesis in another venue. But one of his major theses is that nothing material was created during the six days of Creation. He facilely explains away the other days of Creation but faces a serious obstacle with regard to the second day. He acknowledges: "Day two has a potentially material component (the firmament)."[22] His explanation seeks to sweep away this material component: "No one believes there is actually something material there—no solid construction holds back the upper waters. If the account is material as well as functional we then find ourselves with the problem of trying to explain the material creation of something that does not exist."[23] However, if, as we have argued, the Hebrew word translated as "firmament" does not refer to a solid construction but to the atmospheric heavens or sky, which we still today believe constitutes a material reality (a real location called the "sky"), then material creation was indeed part of day two and was not merely a function established. Taking this into account, Walton's general thesis of no material creation during the six days of Genesis 1 falls to the ground.

Conclusion

The idea that the ancient Hebrews believed that the heavens consisted of a solid vault resting on a flat earth appears to have emerged for the first time only during the early nineteenth century when introduced as part of the flat-earth concept by Irving and Letronne. Scholars who supported this idea argued that the flat earth and vaulted heaven was held throughout the early Christian and medieval periods and was an idea that originated in antiquity, particularly with the ancient Mesopotamians and Hebrews.

However, more recent research has shown that the idea of a flat earth was held neither by the early Christian church nor by medieval scholars. Indeed, the overwhelming evidence is that they believed in a spherical earth, surrounded by celestial spheres (sometimes hard, sometimes soft) that conveyed the sun, moon, stars, and planets in their orbits around the earth. Moreover, research of ancient Babylonian astronomical documents shows that they did not have the concept of a heavenly vault. Rather, this was erroneously introduced into the scholarly literature through a mistranslation of the *Enuma Elish* by Jensen.

A review of the linguistic arguments that the Hebrews believed in the idea of a flat earth and vaulted heaven shows that the arguments are unfounded. The arguments derive from passages that are clearly figurative in nature. One of the great ironies

in recreating a Hebrew cosmology is that scholars have tended to treat figurative usages as literal (e.g., Psalms and Job), while treating literal passages, such as in Genesis, as figurative. The noun form of the word translated as "firmament" was never associated with hard substances in any of its usages in biblical Hebrew—only the verbal form is. Even the latter cannot be definitely tied to metals; rather, it is understood as a process in which a substance is thinned—this can include pounding but also includes stretching. The noun is best translated as "expanse" in all of its usages and has reference to the sky in Genesis 1. The waters above and the windows, doors, or gates of heaven are figurative references to the clouds, which (during the Noahic Flood and, thereafter, would) produce rain. On the second day of Creation, God was involved in both material and functional creation. He made the sky and also assigned its function (to divide the upper atmospheric waters contained in clouds from the surface waters of the earth).

Notes

1. Basil, *Hexaemeron*, Homily 3, translated by Blomfield Jackson, from Nicene and Post-Nicene Fathers, second series, vol. 8, eds. Philip Schaff and Henry Wace (Buffalo, NY: Christian Literature Publishing Co., 1895).

2. Edward Grant, *Planets, Stars and Orbs: The Medieval Cosmos, 1200-1687* (Cambridge: University of Cambridge Press, 1996), 335, 336.

3. Ibid., 336.

4. John Murray, *The Truth of Revelation, Demonstrated by an Appeal to Existing Monuments, Sculptures, Gems, Coins and Medals* (London: Longman, Rees, Orme, Brown, and Green, 1831), 16.

5. Voltaire, *The Works of Voltaire*, eds. Tobias George Smollett et al. (New York: DuMont, 1901), 10:11, 12.

6. Washington Irving, *The Life and Voyages of Christopher Columbus*, ed. John Harmon McElroy (Boston: Twayne, 1981), 50.

7. Antoine-Jean Letronne, "Des opinions cosmographiques des pères de l'église," *Revue des deux mondes* (March 15, 1834): 601–633.

8. John Pye-Smith, *On the Relation Between the Holy Scriptures and Some Parts of Geological Science* (London: Jackson and Walford, 1839), 272.

9. Charles Wycliffe Goodwin, "Mosaic Cosmogony," in *Essays and Reviews*, eds. Frederick Temple et al. (London: Longman, Green, Longman, and Roberts, 1860), 220 n2.

10. Andrews Norton, *The Pentateuch and Its Relation to the Jewish and Christian Dispensations* (London:

Longman, Green, Longman, Roberts, and Green, 1863), 3.

11. John William Colenso, *The Pentateuch and Book of Joshua: Critically Examined*, vol. 4 (London: Longman, Green, Longman, Roberts, and Green, 1863), 288n2.

12. William Fairfield Warren, *The Earliest Cosmologies: The Universe as Pictured in Thought by the Ancient Hebrews, Babylonians, Egyptians, Greeks, Iranians, and Indo-Aryans: A Guidebook for Beginners in the Study of Ancient Literatures and Religion* (New York: Eaton & Mains, 1909).

13. Richard L. Hammill, "Creation Themes in the Old Testament Other Than in Genesis 1 and 2," in *Creation Reconsidered*, ed. James L. Hayward (Roseville, CA: Association of Adventist Forums, 2000), 254, 255.

14. Kenneth Mathews, *Genesis 1–11:26* (Nashville, TN: Broadman & Holman, 1996), 150.

15. Ibid.

16. John H. Sailhamer, "Genesis," in *Expositor's Bible Commentary*, rev. ed., eds. Tremper Longman III and David E. Garland (Grand Rapids, MI: Zondervan, 2008), 1:59.

17. C. F. Keil and F. Delitzsch, *The Pentateuch: Three Volumes in One* (Grand Rapids, MI: Eerdmans, 1976), 1:52, 53.

18. Mathews, *Genesis 1–11:26*, 150.

19. Keil and Delitzsch, *The Pentateuch*, 53, 54.

20. Ibid., 54.

21. Ellen G. White, *Patriarchs and Prophets* (Mountain View, CA: Pacific Press® Pub. Assn., 1922), 96, 97.

22. John H. Walton, *The Lost World of Genesis One: Ancient Cosmology and the Origins Debate* (Downers Grove, IL: InterVarsity, 2009), 94.

23. Ibid.

The Genesis Account of Origins

Richard M. Davidson

Scholars have increasingly recognized that Genesis 1–3 is set apart from the rest of the Bible, constituting a kind of prologue or introduction. These opening chapters of Scripture are now widely regarded as providing the paradigm for the rest of the Bible. John Rankin summarizes the growing conviction among biblical scholars: "Whether one is evangelical or liberal, it is clear that Genesis 1–3 is the interpretive foundation of all Scripture."[1]

The most prominent theme displayed in Genesis 1–3 is that of Creation, which involves various issues of origins. The opening chapters of Genesis are the foundational statement of Scripture regarding Creation. The basic elements in the Genesis account of origins are encapsulated in the opening verse of the Bible, Genesis 1:1:

1. "In the beginning" *the when of origins*
2. "God" *the who of origins*
3. "created" *the how of origins*
4. "the heavens and the earth" *the what of origins*

I. The When: "In the Beginning"

In discussing the when of creation, a number of questions arise for which an answer may be sought in the biblical text. Does Genesis 1; 2 describe an absolute or a relative beginning? Does the Genesis account intend to present a literal, historical portrayal of origins, or is some kind of nonliteral interpretation implied in the text? Does the biblical text of Genesis 1 describe a single Creation event (encompassed within the Creation week), or a two-stage Creation, with a prior Creation described in verse 1, and some kind of interval implied between the description of verse 1, verse 3, and onward? Does the Genesis account of origins present a recent beginning (at least for the events described as the beginning in verse 3, including life on earth), or does it allow for long ages since Creation week?

A. *An Absolute or Relative Beginning?* The answer to the question of an absolute versus a relative beginning in Genesis 1 depends to a large degree upon the translation of the first verse of the Bible: verse 1. There are two major translations—as an independent clause or as a dependent clause.

1. *Independent Clause.* The standard translation of verse 1 until recently is as an independent clause: "In the beginning God created the heavens and the earth." According to the traditional interpretation (dominant until the triumph of historical criticism in the nineteenth century), this verse is taken as a main clause describing the first act of Creation, with verse 2 depicting the condition of the earth after

its initial Creation phase, and verses 3–31 describing the subsequent creative work of God. Such translation or interpretation implies that God existed before matter, and thus, He created planet Earth "out of nothing" at an absolute beginning for Creation.

2. *Dependent Clause.* In recent decades, some modern versions have translated verse 1 as a dependent clause, following the parallels in ancient Near-Eastern creation stories. Verse 1 is taken as a temporal clause, either subordinate to verse 2 ("In the beginning, when God created the heavens and the earth, the earth was a formless void [. . .]"), or subordinate to verse 3 with verse 2 as a parenthesis describing the state of the earth when God began to create ("When God began to create the heavens and the earth—the earth being unformed and void [. . .]—God said [. . .]"). In either case, only verse 3 describes the actual commencement of the work of Creation; when God began to create (v. 1), the earth already existed in the state described in verse 2. For either subordinate clause alternative, Genesis 1 does not address the absolute Creation of planet Earth, and thus, the end result is the same: it gives a relative beginning to creation, allows for the possibility of pre-existing matter before God's creative work described in Genesis 1, and thus, allows for God and matter to be seen as coeternal principles.

Crucial implications of these two main translations—independent and dependent clauses—may be summarized in the following table:

Independent Clause	Dependent Clause
a. *Creatio ex nihilo* (creation out of nothing) is explicitly affirmed.	a. No *creatio ex nihilo* is mentioned.
b. God exists before matter.	b. Matter is already in existence when God began to create, allowing for God and matter to be seen as coeternal.
c. God created the heavens, earth, darkness, the deep, and water.	c. The heavens, earth, darkness, the deep, and water already existed at the beginning of God's creative activity described in Genesis 1.
d. There is an absolute beginning of time for the cosmos.	d. No absolute beginning for time is indicated.

Victor Hamilton, in his commentary on Genesis, summarizes the importance of the proper translation of the opening verse of Scripture: "The issue between these two options—'In the beginning when' and 'In the beginning'—is not esoteric quibbling or an exercise in micrometry. The larger concern is this: Does Genesis 1:1 teach an absolute beginning of creation as a direct act of God? Or does it affirm the existence of matter before the creation of the heavens and earth? To put the question differently, does Gen. 1:1 suggest that in the beginning there was one—God; or does it suggest that in the beginning there were two—God and preexistent chaos?"[2]

The modern impetus for shifting from the independent to the dependent clause translation of verse 1 is largely based on ancient Near-Eastern parallel creation stories, which begin with a dependent (temporal) clause. But such parallels cannot be the norm for interpreting Scripture. Furthermore, it is now widely recognized that verses 1–3 does not constitute a close parallel with the ancient Near-Eastern creation stories. For example, no ancient Mesopotamian creation stories begin with a word like "beginning." Hermann Gunkel, the father of form criticism, affirms: "The cosmogonies of other people contain no word which would come close to the first word of the Bible."[3] Numerous other differences between the biblical and extrabiblical ancient Near-Eastern creation stories reveal that, far from borrowing from such, the biblical writer was engaged in a strong polemic against these other views of origins.

Biblical evidence for the dependent clause interpretation is likewise equivocal. The alleged parallel with the introductory dependent clause of the Genesis 2 Creation account is not as strong as claimed, since verses 4–7, like the ancient Mesopotamian stories, has no word like "beginning" in Genesis 1:1, and there are other major differences in terminology, syntax, and literary and theological function.

Evidence for the traditional view (independent clause) is compelling:

a. *Grammar and Syntax.* Although the Hebrew word translated as "in the beginning" does not have the article and, thus, could theoretically be translated as a construct "in the beginning of . . . ," the normal way for expressing the relationship in Hebrew is for the word to be followed by an absolute noun. In harmony with this normal function of Hebrew grammar, elsewhere in Scripture when the word for "in the beginning" occurs in a dependent clause, it is always followed by an absolute noun, not a finite verb, as in Genesis 1:1. Furthermore, in Hebrew grammar there is regularly no article with temporal expressions like "beginning" when linked with a preposition. Thus, "in the beginning" is the natural reading of this phrase. Isaiah 46:10 provides a precise parallel to Genesis 1:1: the term "from the beginning," without the article, is clearly absolute. Grammatically, therefore, the natural reading of verse 1 is as an independent clause: "In the beginning God created the heavens and the earth."

Syntactically, Umberto Cassuto points out that if verse 1 were a dependent clause, the Hebrew of verse 2 would have normally either omitted the verb altogether or placed the verb before the subject. The syntactical construction that begins verse 2, with "and" plus a noun ("earth"), indicates "that v. 2 begins a new subject" and "therefore, that the first verse is an independent sentence" (independent clause).[4]

b. *Short Stylistic Structure of Genesis 1.* The traditional translation as an independent clause conforms to the pattern of brief, terse sentences throughout the first chapter of the Bible. As Hershel Shanks remarks, "Why adopt a translation that has been aptly described as a [hopelessly tasteless] construction, one which destroys a sublime opening to the world's greatest book?"[5]

c. *Theological Thrust.* The account of Creation throughout Genesis 1 emphasizes the absolute transcendence of God over matter. This chapter describes One who is above and beyond His creation, implying *creatio ex nihilo* and, thus, the independent clause.

d. *Ancient Versions and Other Ancient Witnesses.* All the ancient versions of Scripture render verse 1 as an independent clause. This reading is followed by ancient witnesses, such as Josephus Theophilis of Antioch (A.D. 180) and Pseudo-Justin (A.D. 220–300).

e. *Parallel with John 1:1-3.* The prologue to the Gospel of John is clearly alluding to Genesis 1:1 and commences with the same phrase that begins verse 1 in the LXX the oldest Greek version of the Old Testament. In John 1:1, as in the LXX this phrase "in the beginning" has no article but is unmistakably part of an independent clause: "In the beginning was the Word."

The weight of evidence within Scripture is decisive in pointing toward the traditional translation of Genesis 1:1 as an independent clause: "In the beginning God created the heavens and the earth." The opening verse of the Bible is a distancing from the cosmology of the ancient Near East, an emphasis upon an absolute beginning and implication of *creatio ex nihilo,* in contrast to the ancient Near-Eastern cyclical view of reality and the concept that matter is eternal.

B. *Literal or Nonliteral Beginning?* The question of literal or nonliteral interpretation of the Creation account in Genesis 1; 2 is of major importance both for biblical theology and for contemporary concerns about origins. Many have recognized the intertextual linkage in Scripture between the opening chapters of the Old Testament and the closing chapters of the New Testament. In the overall canonical flow of Scripture, because of the inextricable connection between origins (Gen. 1–3) and end times (Rev. 20–22), without a literal beginning, there is no literal end. Furthermore, it may be argued that the doctrines of humanity, sin, salvation, judgment, Sabbath, and so on, presented already in the opening chapters of Genesis, all hinge upon a literal interpretation of origins.

1. *Nonliteral Interpretations.* Scholars who hold a nonliteral interpretation of Genesis approach the issue in different ways. Some see Genesis 1 as mythology, based upon ancient Near-Eastern parallels as already noted. John Walton has recently advanced the theory of cosmic temple inauguration. According to Walton's interpretation, the Genesis account describes "a seven-day inauguration of the cosmic temple, setting up its functions for the benefit of humanity, with God dwelling in relationship with his creatures."[6] Even though Walton regards the days of Creation as six literal days, for him this Creation is only "functional creation," in other words, assigning functions to the "cosmic temple." He argues that, like the ancient Near-Eastern creation accounts, Genesis 1 says nothing about material creation and no passage

in Scripture is concerned about the age of the earth, and thus, we are free to accept theistic evolution as the means for God's material creation of the cosmos.

Among evangelicals, a still popular interpretation of Genesis 1 is the literary framework hypothesis, which maintains that "the Bible's use of the seven-day week in its narration of the creation is a literary (theological) framework and is not intended to indicate the chronology or duration of the acts of creation."[7] Other evangelical scholars contend that Genesis 1; 2 is essentially theology and, thus, not to be taken literally. A related view argues that the Genesis Creation texts are essentially liturgy or worship. So, for example, Fritz Guy states that "Genesis 1:1–2:3 is first of all an expression of praise, an act of worship, necessarily formulated in the language and conceptions of its time and place. Once the text is deeply experienced as worship, its transposition into a literal narrative, conveying scientifically relevant information, seems not merely a misunderstanding but a distortion, trivialization, and abuse of the text."[8]

Another popular interpretation involves day-age symbolism. There are several day-age theories. First, a common evangelical symbolic view, sometimes called the broad concordist theory, is that the seven days represent seven long ages, thus allowing for theistic evolution (also called evolutionary creation, although sometimes evolution is denied in favor of multiple step-by-step divine Creation acts throughout the long ages). Another theory, the progressive-creationist view, regards the six days as literal days that each open

a new creative period of indeterminate length. Still another theory, espoused particularly by Gerald Schroeder, attempts to harmonize the six twenty-four-hour days of Creation week with the billions of years for the universe as estimated by modern physicists, by positing "cosmic time." The effect of all these day-age views is to have the six days represent much longer periods of time for Creation.

Several evangelical scholars speak of the Genesis account of Creation week in terms of "analogical" or "anthropomorphic" days: "The days are God's workdays, their length is neither specified nor important, and not everything in the account needs to be taken as historically sequential."[9] Still, other scholars see the Genesis Creation account(s) as poetry, metaphor or parable, or vision.

Common to all these nonliteral views is the assumption that the Genesis account of origins is not a literal, straightforward historical account of material Creation.

2. *Evidence for a Literal Interpretation.* There are several lines of evidence within the text of Genesis itself and elsewhere in Scripture that would indicate whether or not the Creation account was intended to be taken as literal.

a. *Literary Genre.* The literary genre of Genesis 1–11 points to the literal historical nature of the Creation account. Kenneth Mathews shows how the suggestion of a parable genre—an illustration drawn from everyday experience—does not fit the contents of Genesis 1 nor does the "vision" genre, since it does not contain the typical preamble and other elements that accompany biblical visions.[10] Steven Boyd shows that Genesis 1:1–2:3 is not intended to be read as poetry or extended poetic metaphor but constitutes the narrative genre of "a literal historical account."[11] Likewise, Daniel Bediako has demonstrated that this passage "constitutes a historical narrative text type."[12] Also, Robert McCabe has concluded that "the framework view poses more exegetical and theological difficulties than it solves and that the traditional, literal reading provides the most consistent interpretation of the exegetical details associated with the context of the early chapters of Genesis."[13]

Walter Kaiser has surveyed and found wanting the evidence for the mythological literary genre of these opening chapters of Genesis and shows how the best genre designation is "historical narrative prose."[14] More recently, John Sailhamer has come to the same conclusion, pointing out the major differences between the style of the ancient Near-Eastern myths and biblical Creation narratives of Genesis 1; 2, prominent among which is that the myths were all written in poetry, while the biblical Creation stories are not poetry but prose narratives. Furthermore, Sailhamer argues that the narratives of Genesis 1; 2 lack any clues that they are to be taken as some kind of nonliteral, symbolic or metaphorical, meta-historical narrative, as some recent evangelicals have maintained. Sailhamer acknowledges that the Creation narratives are different than later biblical narratives, but this is because of their subject matter (creation) and not their literary form (narrative). He suggests that perhaps we should call Genesis 1; 2 "mega-history" to "describe literally and realistically aspects of our world known only to its Creator." As mega-history, "that first week was a real and literal week—one like we ourselves experience every seven days—but that first week was not like any other week. God did an extraordinary work in that week, causing its events to transcend by far anything which has occurred since."[15]

b. *Literary Structure.* The literary structure of Genesis as a whole indicates the intended literal nature of the Creation narratives. It is widely recognized that the whole book of Genesis is structured by the word *generations* in connection with each section of the book (thirteen times). This is a word used in the setting of genealogies concerned with the accurate account of time and history. It means literally "begettings" or "bringings-forth" and implies that Genesis is the "history of beginnings." This use of Genesis 2:4 shows that the narrator intends the account of Creation to be just as literal as the rest of the Genesis narratives.

As Mathews puts it, "The recurring formulaic . . . device shows that the composition was arranged to join the historical moorings of Israel with the beginnings of the cosmos. In this way the composition forms an Adam-Noah-Abraham continuum that loops the patriarchal promissory blessings with the God of cosmos and all human history. The text does not welcome a different reading for Genesis 1–11 as myth versus the patriarchal narratives."[16]

Later in his commentary, Mathews insightfully points out how the structuring of Genesis precludes taking the Genesis account as only theological and not historical: "If we interpret early Genesis as theological parable or story, we have a theology of creation that is grounded neither in history nor the cosmos. . . . The [generational] structure of Genesis requires us to read chap. 1 as relating real events that are presupposed by later Israel. . . . If taken as theological story alone, the interpreter is at odds with the historical intentionality of Genesis."[17]

For critical scholars who reject the historical reliability of all or most of the book of Genesis, this literary evidence will only illuminate the intention of the final editor of Genesis, without any compelling force for their own belief system. But for those who claim to believe in the historicity of the patriarchal narratives, this structure of Genesis, including the appearance of "generations" six times within the first eleven chapters of Genesis, is a powerful internal testimony within the book itself that the account of origins is to be accepted as literally historical like the rest of the book.

c. *Specific Temporal Terms.* Other internal evidence within Genesis that the Creation account is to be taken literally and not figuratively or as symbolical of seven long ages, conforming to the evolutionary model—as suggested by some scholars—involves the use of specific temporal terms. The phrase "evening and morning," appearing at the conclusion of each of the six days of Creation, is used by the author to clearly define the nature of the days of Creation as literal twenty-four-hour days. The references to evening and morning together outside of Genesis 1, invariably, without exception in the Old Testament (fifty-seven times), indicate a literal solar day. Again, the occurrences of the word *day* at the conclusion of each of the six days of creation in Genesis 1 are all connected with a numeric adjective ("one [first] day," "second day," "third day," etc.), and a comparison with occurrences of the term elsewhere in Scripture reveals that such usage always refers to literal days. Furthermore, references to the function of the sun and moon for signs, seasons, days, and years (v. 14) indicate literal time, not symbolic ages.

3. *Biblical References Outside Genesis 1; 2.* Intertextual references to the Creation account elsewhere in Scripture confirm that the biblical writers understood the six days of Creation to be taken as six literal, historical, contiguous, creative, natural twenty-four-hour days. If the six days of Creation week were to be taken as symbolic of long ages, of six visionary days of revelation, only as analogical days, or anything less than the six days of a literal week, then the reference to Creation in the fourth commandment of Exodus 20:8–11, commemorating a literal Sabbath, would make no sense. This is a major argument, not just of Seventh-day Adventists and other Saturday Sabbath keepers![18]

The Sabbath commandment explicitly equates the six days of work followed by the seventh-day Sabbath with the six days of God's Creation work followed by the Sabbath. By equating humanity's six-day workweek with God's six-day workweek at Creation, and further equating the Sabbath to be kept by humankind each week with the first Sabbath after Creation week blessed and sanctified by God, the Divine Lawgiver unequivocally interprets the first week as a literal week, consisting of seven consecutive, contiguous twenty-four-hour days.

As a broader intertextual evidence for the literal nature of the Creation accounts, as well as the historicity of the other accounts of Genesis 1–11, it is important to point out that Jesus and *all* New Testament writers refer to Genesis 1–11 with the underlying assumption that it is literal, reliable history. Every chapter of Genesis 1–11 is referred to somewhere in the New Testament, and Jesus Himself refers to Genesis 1, 2, 3, 4, 5, 6, and 7.

Gerhard F. Hasel, Terence Fretheim, James Stambaugh, among others, have set forth in detail various lines of evidence (including evidence not mentioned here for lack of space), based on comparative, literary, linguistic, intertextual, and other considerations, which lead to the "inescapable conclusion" set forth by Hasel that the designation of the word translated as "day" in Genesis 1 means consistently a literal, natural day of approximately twenty-four hours. "The author of Genesis 1 could not have produced more comprehensive and all-inclusive ways to express the idea of a literal 'day' than the one chosen."[19] Stambaugh has concluded that according to the biblical evidence "God created in a series of six consecutive [approximately] twenty-four hour days."[20]

Though the nonliteral interpretations of biblical origins must be rejected in what they deny (namely, the literal, historical nature of the Genesis account), nevertheless many of them have an element of truth in what they affirm. Genesis 1; 2 is concerned with mythology—not to affirm a mythological interpretation but as a polemic against ancient Near-Eastern mythology. Genesis 1:1–2:4a is structured in a literary, symmetrical form. However, the synthetic parallelism involved in the sequence of the days in Genesis 1 is not a literary artifice created by the human writer but is explicitly described as part of the successive creative acts of God Himself, who as the Master Designer created aesthetically. The divine artistry of Creation within the structure of space and time does not negate the historicity of the Creation narrative.

Genesis 1; 2 does present a profound theology: doctrines of God, Creation, humanity, Sabbath, and so on, but theology in Scripture is not opposed to history. To the contrary, biblical theology is always *rooted* in history. There is no criterion within the Creation accounts of Genesis 1; 2 that allows separation between cosmogony and cosmology, as some have claimed, in order to reject the details of a literal six-day Creation, while retaining the theological truth that the world depends upon God.

Likewise there is profound symbolism and sanctuary or temple imagery in Genesis 1. For example, the language describing the Garden of Eden and the occupation of Adam and Eve clearly allude to the sanctuary imagery and the work of the priests and Levites (Exod. 25–40). Thus, the sanctuary of Eden is a symbol (or better type) of the heavenly sanctuary (Ezek. 28:12–14; Exod. 25:9, 40). But because it points beyond itself does not detract from its own literal reality. Neither does the assigning of functions in this Eden sanctuary exclude the material creation that also took place during the literal six days of Creation. The Genesis Creation account does lead the reader to worship—worship of the true

Creator-God (see the first angel's message in Rev. 14:6, 7), but the account itself is not liturgy or worship.

4. Presuppositions and the Witness of Biblical Scholars. Some biblical scholars, who reject a literal, six-day Creation week, frankly admit that their ultimate criterion for such rejection is on the level of foundational presuppositions, in which the *sola Scriptura* principle is no longer maintained. Rather, some other authority or methodology—be it science, ancient Near-Eastern materials, historical-critical principles (methodological doubt, causal continuum, rule of analogy), and so on—has been accepted in place of the *sola Scriptura* principle. This is true of both liberal-critical and conservative-evangelical scholars.

For example, evangelical scholars Karl Giberson and Francis Collins acknowledge the great weight of the so-called assured results of science with regard to origins in their interpretation of Genesis 1; 2: "We do not believe that God would provide two contradictory revelations. God's revelation in nature, studied by science, should agree with God's revelation in Scripture, studied by theology. Since the revelation from science is so crystal clear about the age of the earth, we believe we should think twice before embracing an approach to the Bible that contradicts this revelation."[21]

Two other evangelical scholars, Richard Carlson and Tremper Longman, freely acknowledge their preunderstanding regarding the relationship between science and theology: "We believe contemporary science addresses questions on *how* physical and biological processes began and continue to develop, while theology and philosophy answer *why* for these same questions."[22] To cite another example, Walton presupposes that to understand biblical culture, including the biblical view of Creation, "The key then is to be found in the literature from the rest of the ancient world."[23] Based upon the supposed nonmaterial functional creation described in ancient Near-Eastern literature, Walton finds the same in Genesis 1; 2 and, thus, is free to accept theistic evolution as taught by science, since the Bible does not speak of material creation.

It is ironic to note that liberal-critical scholars, who frankly acknowledge their historical-critical presuppositions and who do not take the authority of the early chapters of Genesis seriously and, thus, have nothing to lose with regard to their personal faith and the relationship between faith and science, have almost universally acknowledged that the intent of the one who wrote Genesis 1 was to indicate a regular week of six literal days.

In sum, there are a host of scholars, ancient and modern—both critical and evangelical—who affirm that Genesis 1; 2 teaches a literal, material Creation week consisting of six historical, contiguous, creative, natural twenty-four-hour days, followed immediately by a literal twenty-four-hour seventh day, during which God rested, blessed, and sanctified the Sabbath as a memorial of Creation.

C. Single or Two-Stage Beginning? Does the opening chapter of the Bible depict a single week of Creation for all that is encompassed in Genesis 1, or does it imply a prior creation before Creation week and some kind of time gap between verse 1, verse 3, and onward? This issue focuses upon the relationship among verse 1, verse 2, verse 3, and beyond. Several different interpretations of this relationship have been advanced.

1. *Active Gap Theory.* A first interpretation is often labeled as the ruin-restoration or the active-gap view. According to this understanding, verse 1 describes an originally perfect Creation some unknown time ago (millions, billions of years ago). Satan was ruler of this world, but because of his rebellion (described in Isa. 14:12–17), sin entered the universe. Some proponents of the active-gap position hold that God judged this rebellion and reduced it to the ruined, chaotic state described in Genesis 1:2. Others claim that Satan was allowed by God to experiment with this world, and the chaos described in verse 2 is the direct result of satanic experimentation. In any case, those holding this view translate verse 2 as "but the earth had become a ruin and a desolation."

Verse 3 and onward, then, presents an account of a later creation in which God restores what had been ruined. The geological column is usually fitted into the period of time of the first Creation (v. 1) and the succeeding chaos and not in connection with the biblical Flood.

The ruin-restoration or active-gap theory simply cannot stand the test of close grammatical analysis. Verse 2 clearly contains three noun clauses and the fundamental meaning of noun clauses in Hebrew is something fixed, a state or condition, not a sequence or action. According to laws of Hebrew grammar, one must translate "the earth *was* unformed and unfilled," not "the earth *became* unformed and unfilled." Thus, Hebrew grammar leaves no room for the active-gap theory.

2. *Initial Unformed-Unfilled View: No-Gap and Passive-Gap Theories.* The "no-gap" and "passive-gap" theories are subheadings of an interpretation of biblical cosmogony in Genesis 1 that may be termed the "initial unformed-unfilled" view. This is the traditional view, having the support of the majority of Jewish and Christian interpreters through history. According to this initial "unformed-unfilled" view (and common to both the no-gap and passive-gap theories), Verse 1 declares that God created "the heavens and the earth"; verse 2 clarifies that the earth was initially in an unformed and unfilled state; and verses 3 and onward describe the divine process of forming the unformed and filling the unfilled.

This interpretation cohesively follows the natural flow of these verses, without contradiction or omission of any element of the text. However, there are two crucial aspects in this Creation process about which there is disagreement among those who hold to the "initial unformed-unfilled" view. These concern (1) *when* the creation of the "heavens and earth" described in verse 1 occurred—either at the commencement or during the seven days of creation, or sometime before—and (2) *what* is referred to by the phrase "heavens and earth"—a figure of speech for the entire universe or a reference only to this earth and its surrounding heavenly spheres (i.e., our solar system). Depending upon how these two aspects are interpreted, four major possibilities present themselves, two variations of the no-gap theory and two variations of the passive-gap theory.

a. *No-Gap Theory A: Young Universe, Young-Life.* Under the no-gap theory, some see verses 1, 2 all as part of the first day of the seven-day Creation week, and the phrase "heavens and earth" are taken as a figure of speech to refer to the entire universe. This interpretation concludes that the entire universe was created in six literal days some six thousand years ago. This theory may be called the "young-universe, young-life" view and is equated with contemporary young-earth scientific creationism, espoused by many fundamentalists and conservative evangelicals and represented by such organizations as the Institute for Creation Research and Answers in Genesis.

b. *No-Gap Theory B: Young Earth (Not Universe), Young-Life (on Earth).* The other variant of the no-gap theory also sees verses 1, 2 as part of the first day of the seven-day Creation week but takes the term "heavens and earth" to apply only to this earth and its immediate, surrounding atmospheric heavens (and perhaps the solar system). This earth and its surrounding heavenly spheres were created during the Genesis 1 Creation week, and according to this position, nothing is mentioned in Genesis 1 about the creation of the entire universe. This view may be termed the "young-earth (not universe), young-life (on earth)" interpretation and has been suggested by several scholars.

c. *Passive-Gap Theory A: Old-Universe (Including Earth), Young Life (on Earth).* With regard to the passive-gap options, some see verses 1, 2 as a chronological unity separated by a gap in time from the first day of Creation described in verse 3. The expression "heavens and earth" in verse 1 is taken as a figure of speech to refer to the entire universe that was created "in the beginning," before Creation week (which initial creation may be called the *creatio prima*). Verse 2 describes the "raw materials" of the earth in their unformed-unfilled state that were created before—perhaps long before—the seven days of Creation week. Verses 3 and onward depict the actual Creation week (which may be called *creatio secunda*). This view may be termed the "old-universe (including the earth), young-life (on earth)" view and is also widely held by Seventh-day Adventist scholars as well as by a number of other interpreters.

d. *Passive-Gap Theory B: Old-Earth, Young Life (on Earth).* Another variant of the passive-gap position also sees verse 1 separated by a chronological gap from verse 3 but takes the expression "heavens and earth" to refer only to this earth and its surrounding heavenly spheres, which were in their unformed-unfilled state for an unspecified length of time before the events described in Creation week. According to this possibility, nothing is said about the creation of the universe in Genesis 1. This view may be termed the "old-earth, young-life (on earth)" position and is supported by some Seventh-day Adventist scholars.

Even though the position above (no-gap theory A: young universe, young life) is very popular among conservative evangelicals and Christian fundamentalists, Seventh-day Adventist interpreters have generally rejected this option because positing a creation of the entire universe in the six-day Creation week does not allow for the rise of the great controversy in heaven, involving the rebellion of Lucifer-turned-Satan and his angels, described in many biblical passages as a process that clearly took far more than a week to develop (Isa. 14:12–17; Ezek. 28:11–19; Rev. 12:3–12).

Furthermore, it contradicts the clear statement in Job 38:4–7, which reveals that, at the laying of the earth's foundations, the unfallen heavenly beings (the "morning stars" and "sons of God") were already in existence: "Where were you when I laid the foundations of the earth? Tell *Me*, if you have understanding. Who determined its measurements? Surely you know! Or who stretched the line upon it? To what were its foundations fastened? Or who laid its cornerstone, When the morning stars sang together, and all the sons of God shouted for joy?"

The young-universe, young-life view also falters if Genesis 1:1, 2 may be shown to stand outside of the six days of Creation described in verse 3 and onward.

The no-gap theory B, young-earth (not universe), young-life (on earth), is a possibility. Proponents of this view argue that the terms "the heavens" and "earth" in verse 1 are the same terms found later in the chapter and, thus, should be regarded as referring to the same identities: this earth and its surrounding heavenly spheres, not the entire universe. They also point out that the phrase translated as "the heavens and the earth" (v. 1) appears again in virtually the same form at the conclusion of the six days of Creation (2:1) and suggest that Genesis 1:1 and 2:1 introduce and conclude the six days of Creation. Furthermore, the reference in the fourth commandment of the Decalogue to "heavens and

earth" being made "in six days" (Exod. 20:11) is seen as supporting this position. A careful examination of these very points, however, actually favors the passive-gap A view (position c above, old-universe [including earth], young life [on earth]).

3. *Evidence for a Two-Stage Creation of This Earth (the Passive-Gap Interpretation).* These four alternative positions may also be labeled in terms of the number of creation stages represented and what is being created:

No-gap A = single-stage creation (of the entire universe)

No-gap B = single-stage creation (of this earth only)

Passive-gap A = two-stage creation (of the entire universe, including this earth)

Passive-gap B = two-stage creation (of this earth only)

A number of textual considerations and intertextual parallels lead to the two-stage creation (passive-gap) interpretation in general and, more specifically, variation A (the two-stage creation [of the entire universe]), also called the old-universe (including earth), young-life (for this earth) view.

First, as John Hartley points out, "The consistent pattern used for each day of creation tells us that verses 1 and 2 are not an integral part of the first day of creation (vv. 3–5). That is, these first two verses stand apart from the report of what God did on the first day of creation."[24] Hartley is referring to the fact that each of the six days of Creation begins with the words,

"And God said" and ends with the formula "and there was evening and there was morning, day [x]." If the description of the first day is consistent with the other five, this would place verses 1 and 2 outside, and therefore before, the first day of Creation.

Second, recent discourse analysis of Genesis 1:1 at the beginning of the Genesis 1 Creation account indicates that the discourse grammar of these verses points to a two-stage creation. The main storyline does not begin until verse 3. This implies a previous creation of the "heavens and earth" in their "unformed-unfilled" state before the beginning of Creation week and supports either variation of the passive-gap interpretation.

Third, the phrase "the heavens and the earth" in verse 1 is most probably to be taken here, as often elsewhere in Scripture, as a figure of speech expressing the two extremities in order to include all that God has created, in other words, the entire universe. If "heavens and earth" refers to the whole universe, this "beginning" (at least for part of the heavens) must have been *before* the first day of earth's Creation week, since the "sons of God" (unfallen created beings) were already created and sang for joy when the foundations of the earth were laid (Job 38:7). This point supports the passive-gap theory A (position c), as opposed to B (position d).

Fourth, the "heavens and earth" (entire universe) of Genesis 1:1 are to be distinguished from "heaven, earth, and sea" (the three earth habitats) of Genesis 1:3–31 and Exodus 20:11. This means that the Creation action of Genesis 1:1 is outside or before the six-day Creation of Exodus 20:11 and

of Genesis 1:3–31. (This point also supports passive-gap theory A and not B.)

Fifth, the expression "the heavens and the earth" indeed brackets the first Creation account, as noted by those who support the no-gap theory. But what is not usually recognized in that argumentation is that the phrase "heavens and earth" appears *twice* at the end of the Creation account of Genesis 1:1; 2:4. It occurs in Genesis 2:1, but in this verse, it is used to refer to the three habitats found in Genesis 1:3–31. The entire phrase that we find in this verse is "the heavens and the earth, *and all the host of them,*" which is not a figure of expressing totality by expressing the two extremities, as in verse 1, but a reference to the biosphere that is formed and filled during the six days of Creation. There is, however, a figure of speech employing the "heavens and earth" at the end of the Genesis 1 Creation account. It is found in Genesis 2:4: "This is the history of the heavens and the earth when they were created." It is this reference to "heavens and earth" that parallels the phrase in Genesis 1:1 and, like verse 1, refers to the Creation of the entire cosmos, in other words, the universe. This forms a chiastic structure, with an ABBA pattern, in the usage of the phrase "heavens and earth."

A: Genesis 1:1—"heavens and earth," referring to the entire universe.

B: Genesis 1:3–31—"heaven, earth, sea" of planet Earth's three habitats.

B: Genesis 2:1—"heavens and earth

and their hosts" involving earth's three habitats.

A: Genesis 2:4a—"heavens and earth," referring to the entire universe.

This point supports passive-gap theory A and not theory B.

Sixth, Sailhamer points out that the Hebrew word for "beginning," used in verse 1, "does not refer to a point in time but to a *period* or *duration* of time, which falls before a series of events."[25] In the context of verses 1–3, this would seem to imply that (a) the first verse of the Bible refers back to the process of time in which God created the universe; (b) sometime during that process, this earth was created, but it was initially in an "unformed-unfilled" state; and (c) as a potter or architect first gathers materials and, then at some point, later begins shaping the pot on the potter's wheel or constructing the building, so God, the Master Artist—Potter and Architect—first created the raw materials of the earth and then, at the appropriate creative moment, began to form and fill the earth in the six literal working days of Creation week. The text of verse 1 does not indicate how long before Creation week the universe ("heavens and earth") was created. This and the following points could be seen to support a two-stage creation, either variation A or B of the passive-gap interpretation.

Seventh, already in the Creation account of verses 3–31, there is an emphasis upon God's differentiating or separating previously created materials. On the second day, God divided what was already present—the waters from the waters (vv. 6–8). On the

third day, the dry land appeared (which seems to imply it was already present under the water), and the previously existing earth brought forth vegetation (vv. 9–12). On the fifth day, the waters brought forth the fish (v. 20), and on the sixth day, the earth brought forth land creatures (v. 24), implying God's use of pre-existing elements.

Eighth, such a two-stage process of Creation in Genesis 1, like the work of a potter or architect, is supported by the complementary Creation account of Genesis 2. In verse 7, it is evident that God began with the previously created ground or clay and, from this, "formed" the man. There is a two-stage process, beginning with the raw materials—the clay—and proceeding to the forming into man and breathing into his nostrils the breath of life. It is probably not accidental that the narrator here uses the verb "to form," which describes what a potter does with the clay on his potter's wheel. The participial form of the original word actually means "potter," and the narrator may here be alluding to God's artistic work as a Master Potter. In God's creation of the woman, He likewise follows a two-stage process. He begins with the raw materials that are already created—the "side" or "rib" of the man—and from this, God "builds" the woman (vv. 21, 22). Again, it is certainly not accidental that only here in Genesis 1, 2 is the verb for "to architecturally design and build" used for God's Creation. He is a Master Designer or Architect as He creates woman.

Ninth, parallels between Genesis 1; 2; and the account of building the wilderness sanctuary and Solomon's temple seem to point further toward a two-stage creation for this earth. As mentioned earlier, the work of Creation in Genesis 1; 2 is described in technical language that specifically parallels the building of Moses's sanctuary and Solomon's temple. Such intertextual linkages have led numerous Old Testament interpreters in recognizing that, according to the narrative clues, the whole earth is to be seen as the original courtyard and the Garden of Eden as the original sanctuary or temple on this planet. Significantly, the construction of both Mosaic sanctuary and Solomonic temple took place in two stages. First came the gathering of the materials according to the divine plans and command (Exod. 25:1–9; 35:4–9, 20–29; 36:1–7; 1 Chron. 28:1–29:9; 2 Chron. 2), and then came the building process utilizing the previously gathered materials (Exod. 36:8–39:43; 2 Chron. 3; 4). A pattern of two-stage divine creative activity seems to emerge from these parallels that give further impetus to accepting the passive-gap interpretation of Genesis 1.

Last, but certainly not least, God's creative activity throughout the rest of the Bible often involves a two-stage process, presupposing a previous creation. Examples include God's "creating" of His people Israel, using language of Genesis 1:2; God's creation of a "new heart" (Ps. 51:10); His "making" of the "new [i.e. renewed] covenant" (Jer. 31:33); and Jesus's healing miracles involving a two-stage creation (e.g., John 9:6, 7). In particular, the eschatological creation of the new heavens and earth presupposes previously existing materials. Inasmuch as origins parallel end times in Scripture (Gen. 1–3 matching Rev. 20–22),

it is vital to observe the depictions of the end-time new creation described in 2 Peter 3:10–13 and Revelation 20–22 and their parallels with Genesis 1; 2.

After the second coming of Christ, the earth will return to its unformed-unfilled condition, paralleling Genesis 1:22 (see Jer. 4:23; Rev. 20:1, which use the terminology of Gen. 1:2). After the millennium, the earth will be purified by fire (Rev. 20:9, 14, 15; 2 Pet. 3:10, 12), but the "a new heaven and a new earth" (Rev. 21:1; 2 Pet. 3:13) will not be created out *ex nihilo* but out of the purified raw materials, or "elements" (2 Pet. 3:12), remaining from the fire purification process—elements that have been in existence for (at least) thousands of years (vv. 10, 12). If the eschatological creation involved a two-stage process, with God utilizing previously created matter to create the "[re]new[ed] heavens and earth," then it would not be out of character for God to have followed a similar two-stage creation in Genesis 1; 2.

A growing number of recent studies of verses 1–3 have come to support the conclusion of a two-stage creation and the passive-gap interpretation, in particular, the old-universe (including earth), young-life (on earth) variation. Collins's conclusion is illustrative of verses 1–3: "It tells us of the origin of everything [in the universe] in 1:1 and then narrows its attention as the account proceeds. The first verse, as I see it, narrates the initial creation event; then verse 2 describes the condition of the earth just before the creation week gets under way. These two verses stand outside the six days of God's workweek, and—just speaking grammatically—say nothing about the length of time between the initial event of 1:1 and the first day of 1:3."[26]

Those who support the no-gap theory often argue against the passive-gap theory by denying any evidence for such a theory in the biblical text: "There is no textual or contextual basis for supposing that it [Genesis 1:1] introduces a *second* process of creation described in Genesis 1:2–31, separated by an indefinite period of time (as much as 13.7 billion years) from a *first* process of creation mentioned in Genesis 1:1."[27] But at least ten lines of evidence from the text have herein been listed that in fact do support a two-stage creation.

In connection with this argument, it is often conjectured that "the 'gap theory' seems to be motivated by a desire to harmonize Genesis 1 with modern scientific understandings of the size and age of the known universe by interpreting Genesis 1:2–31 as describing only the creation of life on planet Earth."[28] It is suggested that the passive-gap theory is an attempt "to harmonize Scripture and Science. . . . We are being forced to accept the gap by science, not by Scripture."[29]

The Hebrew text of Genesis 1, not science, supports the passive-gap (the old-universe [including this earth], young-life [for this earth]) interpretation of Genesis 1. It need not be dependent upon, or motivated by, the accuracy or inaccuracy of the radiometric time clocks for earth rocks but represents an attempt to be faithful to Scripture, and if some scientific data are harmonized in the process, then all the better. John Lennox has stated it well: "Quite apart from any scientific considerations, the text of Genesis 1:1, in separating the

beginning from day 1, leaves the age of the universe indeterminate. It would therefore be logically possible to believe that the days of Genesis are twenty-four-hour days (of one earth week) *and* to believe that the universe is very ancient. I repeat: this has nothing to do with science. Rather, it has to do with what the text actually says."[30]

4. *Implications for Modern Scientific Interpretation.* The possible openness in the Hebrew text as to whether there is a gap or not between verse 1 and verses 3–31 has implications for interpreting the pre-fossil layers of the geological column. If one accepts the no-gap theory B option (young earth [not universe], young life [on earth]), there is a possibility of relatively young pre-fossil rocks, created as part of the seven-day Creation week (perhaps with the appearance of old age). If one accepts the passive-gap theory A option (old universe [including earth], young life [on earth]) or the passive-gap theory B option (old earth, young life [on earth]), there is the alternate possibility of the pre-fossil raw materials being created at a time of absolute beginning of this earth and its surrounding heavenly spheres during an unspecified time in the past. This initial "unformed-unfilled" state is described in verse 2. Verses 3–31 then describe the process of forming and filling during the seven-day Creation week.

The biblical text of Genesis 1 leaves room for either (a) young pre-fossil rock, created as part of the seven days of Creation (with the appearance of old age), or (b) much older pre-fossil earth rocks, with a long interval between the creation of the inanimate raw materials on earth, described in verses 1, 2, and the seven days of Creation week, described in verse 3 and onward. In either case, the biblical text calls for a short chronology for the creation of life on earth. According to Genesis 1, there is no room for any gap of time in the creation of life on this earth: it came during the third through the sixth of the literal, contiguous, (approximately) twenty-four-hour days of Creation week.

D. *A Recent or Remote Beginning?* Scripture provides no information as to how long ago God created the universe as a whole. But there is strong evidence that the Creation week described in Genesis 1:3–2:4 was recent, sometime in the last several thousand years and not hundreds of thousands, millions, or billions of years ago. The evidence for this is primarily in the genealogies of Genesis 5; 11. These are unique, with no parallel among the other genealogies of the Bible or other ancient Near-Eastern literature. Unlike the other genealogies, which may (and in fact often do) contain gaps, the "chronogenealogies" of Genesis 5; 11 have indicators that they are to be taken as complete genealogies without gaps. These unique interlocking features indicate a specific focus on chronological time and reveal an intention to make clear that there are no gaps between the individual patriarchs mentioned. A patriarch lived x years, begat a son; after he begat this son, he lived y more years and begat more sons and daughters; and all the years of this patriarch were z years. These tight interlocking features make it virtually impossible to argue that there are significant generational gaps. Rather, they purport to present the complete time sequence from father to direct biological son throughout

the genealogical sequence from Adam to Abraham.

To further substantiate the absence of major gaps in the genealogies of Genesis 5; 11, the Hebrew grammatical form of the verb "begat" used throughout these chapters is the special causative form that always elsewhere in the Old Testament refers to actual direct, physical offspring, in other words, biological father-son relationship (Gen. 6:10; Judg. 11:1; 1 Chron. 8:9; 14:3; 2 Chron. 11:21; 13:21; 24:3). In Genesis 5; 11, there is clearly a concern for completeness, accuracy, and precise length of time.

There are several different textual versions of the chronological data in these two chapters: Hebrew text, Greek translation, and Samaritan Pentateuch. The scholarly consensus is that the Hebrew text has preserved the original figures in their purest form, while the Greek translation and Samaritan versions have intentionally schematized the figures for theological reasons. But regardless of which text is chosen, it only represents a difference of a thousand years or so.

Regarding the chronology from Abraham to the present, there is disagreement among Bible-believing scholars whether the Israelite sojourn in Egypt was 215 years or 430 years and, thus, whether to put Abraham in the early second millennium or the late third millennium B.C.; but other than this minor difference, the basic chronology from Abraham to the present is clear from Scripture, and the total is only some four thousand (plus or minus two hundred) years.

Thus, the Bible presents a relatively

recent creation (of life on this earth) a few thousand years ago, not hundreds of thousands, millions, or billions of years. Though minor ambiguities do not allow placement of the exact date, according to Scripture, the seven-day Creation week unambiguously occurred recently. This recent creation becomes significant in light of the character of God. A God of love surely would not allow pain and suffering to continue any longer than necessary to make clear the issues in the great controversy. He wants to bring an end to suffering and death as soon as possible; it is totally out of character with the God of the Bible to allow a history of cruelty and pain to go on for long periods of time—millions of years—when it would serve no purpose in demonstrating the nature of His character in the cosmic controversy against Satan. Thus, the genealogies, pointing to a recent creation, are a window into the heart of a loving, compassionate God.

II. The Who: "In the Beginning, *God*"

The Creation accounts of Genesis 1; 2 emphasize the character of God. While accurately presenting the facts of creation, the emphasis is undoubtedly not so much upon creation as upon the Creator. As Mathews puts it, " 'God' is the *grammatical* subject of the first sentence (1:1) and continues as the *thematic* subject throughout the account."[31]

A. *The Character of God.* In Genesis 1; 2, two different names for God appear, not as supporting evidence for the documentary hypothesis but to emphasize the two major character qualities of the Creator. In Genesis 1:1, 2:4, He is *ʾĕlōhîm*, which is the generic name for God, meaning "All-powerful One" and emphasizing His transcendence as the universal, cosmic, self-existent, almighty, infinite God. This emphasis upon God's transcendence is in accordance with the universal framework of the first Creation account, in which God is before and above creation, and creates effortlessly by His Divine Word. In the supplementary Creation account of verses 4–25, another name for the deity is introduced. He is here also YHWH, which is God's covenant name; He is the immanent, personal God who enters into intimate relationship with His creatures. Just such a God is depicted in this second Creation account: One who bends down as a Potter over a lifeless lump of clay to "shape, form" the man and breathes into his nostrils the breath of life (v. 7); who plants a garden (v. 8); and who "architecturally designs or builds" the woman (v. 22) and officiates at the first wedding (vv. 22–24). Only the Judeo-Christian God is both infinite and personal to meet the human need of an infinite reference point and personal relationship.

Any interpretation of the biblical account of origins must recognize the necessity of remaining faithful to this twofold portrayal of the character of God in the opening chapters of Scripture. Interpretations of these chapters that present God as an accomplice, active or passive, in an evolutionary process of survival of the fittest, millions of years of predation, prior to the fall of humans, must seriously reckon with how these views impinge upon the character of God. Evolutionary creation (theistic evolution) or progressive creationism makes God responsible for millions of years of death, suffering, natural selection, and survival of the fittest, even before sin. Such positions seem to malign the character of God, and this should provide strong reason for pause to the biblical interpreter to consider whether such interpretations of origins are consistent with the explicit depictions of God's character in Genesis 1; 2; and elsewhere in Scripture.

B. *Other Considerations.* A number of other considerations are related to the who of creation, including, among others, the following points, which can be only summarized here:

• No proof of God is provided, but rather, from the outset comes the bold assertion of His existence.

• God is the ultimate foundation of reality. As Ellen White expresses it: " 'In the beginning God.' Here alone can the mind in its eager questioning, fleeing as the dove to the ark, find rest."[32]

• The portrayal of God in the Creation account provides a polemic against the polytheism of the ancient Near East with its many gods, their moral decadence like humankind, the rivalry and struggle between the deities, their mortality, and their pantheism (the gods are part of the uncreated world matter).

• There are intimations of the plurality in the Godhead in Creation, with mention of the "Spirit of God" in Genesis 1:2; the creative Word throughout the Creation account (ten times in Genesis 1); and the "let us" of verse 26, most probably is "a plural of fullness," implying "within the divine Being the distinction of personalities, a plurality within the deity, a 'unanimity of intention and plan' . . . ; [the] germinal idea . . . [of] intra-divine deliberation among 'persons' within the divine Being."[33]

• The who of creation also helps answer the why of creation. With intimations of a plurality of persons within the deity and the character of God being one of covenant love (as YHWH), it would be only natural for Him to wish to create other beings with whom He could share fellowship. This is implicit in the Creation account in which Wisdom (an essence for the preincarnate Christ) is "rejoicing" (literally, "playing, sporting") both with YHWH and with the humans that have been created (vv. 30, 31). It is explicit in Isaiah 45:18: "He did not create it [the earth] to be empty, but formed it to be inhabited."

III. The How: "In the Beginning, God *Created*"

Many scholars claim that the biblical Creation accounts are not concerned with the "how" of creation but only with the theological point that God created. It is true that Genesis 1; 2 provide no technical scientific explanation of the divine creative process. But there is a great deal of attention to the how of divine Creation, and this cannot be discarded as the husk of the Creation accounts to get at the theological kernel of truth that God was the Creator. Though not given in technical scientific language, Genesis nonetheless describes the reality of the divine creative process, using clear observational language. It seems that the events of the six days of Creation "are told from the perspective of one who is standing on the earth's surface observing the universe with the naked eye."[34] The biblical text gives several indicators of the how of creation.

A. *By Uniquely Divine Creativity.* According to Genesis 1, the Hebrew verb used to describe God's creativity is uniquely divine ("create," vv. 1, 21, 27; 2:4). This word describes exclusively God's action; it is never used for human activity. It is also never used with the accusative of matter: what is created is something totally new and effortlessly produced. By itself, the term does not indicate *creatio ex nihilo* (see Ps. 51:12), as has been sometimes claimed. However, in the context of the entire verse of Genesis 1:1, taken as an independent clause describing actual new material creation of the entire universe, *creatio ex nihilo* is explicitly affirmed. By employing this term, the Genesis account provides an implicit polemic against the common ancient Near-Eastern views of creation by sexual procreation or by a struggle with the forces of chaos.

B. *By Divine Fiat.* Creation in Genesis 1 is also by divine fiat: "God said, Let there be ..." (vv. 3, 6, 9, 11, 14, 20, 24, 26). The psalmist summarizes this aspect of how God created: "By the word of the Lord the heavens were made, and all the host of them by the breath of His mouth. ... For He spoke, and it was done; He commanded, and it stood fast" (Ps. 33:6, 9). According to Genesis 1, the universe and this earth are not self-existent, random, or struggled for. The Genesis account is in stark contrast with the Mesopotamian concept of creation, resulting from the struggle between rival deities or the sexual activity of the gods, and it is also in contrast with Egyptian Memphite theology, in which the creative speech of the god Ptah is a magical utterance. In biblical theology, the word of God is concrete; it is the embodiment of power. When God speaks, there is an immediate response in creative action. Part of God's word is His blessing, and in Hebrew thought, God's blessing is the empowering of the one or the thing blessed to fulfill the intended function for which she, he, or it was made. God's creation by divine fiat underscores the centrality of the Word in the Creation process.

C. *As a Polemic.* Specific terminology is used (or avoided) by the narrator, which appears to be an intentional polemic against the mythological struggle with a chaos monster and prevalence of polytheistic deities found in the Mesopotamian creation texts. The word *deep* in verse 2 is an unmythologized masculine rather than the mythological feminine sea monster Tiamat. Again, the names "sun" and "moon" (vv. 14–19) are substituted with the generic terms "greater light" and "lesser light," because the Hebrew names for these luminaries are also the names of deities. As a final example, the term for "sea monsters" in verses 21 and 22 (the name for both mythological creatures and natural sea creatures or serpents) is retained (as the only vocabulary available to express this kind of animal), but this usage is coupled with the strongest term for creation (implying something totally new, no struggle), a term not employed in Genesis 1 since verse 1, to dispel any thought of a rival god.

The how of creation was no doubt penned by the narrator under inspiration with a view toward exposing and warning against the polytheistic Egyptian environment surrounding Israel before the Exodus and the Canaanite environment in which the

Israelites would soon find themselves. But the omniscient Divine Author certainly also inspired this Creation account in order to be a polemic for all time against views of creation that might violate or distort the true picture of God's creative work. The inspired description of God's effortless, personal, and rapid creation by divine fiat protects modern humanity from accepting naturalistic, violent, and random components into one's picture of creation.

D. *Dramatically and Aesthetically.* God is portrayed in Genesis 1; 2 as a Master Designer, creating dramatically and aesthetically. As already noted in the previous section, God, like a Potter, "formed" the man and, like an Architect, "designed or built" the woman. When He made this world, He surely could have created it as completed in an instant, if He had chosen to do so, but He instead dramatically choreographed the Creation pageant over seven days. Note the aesthetic symmetry of the very structure of God's Creation in space and time, similar to the Hebrew aesthetic technique of synthetic parallelism, in which a series of words, acts, or scenes are completed by a matching series.

Introduction (Genesis 1:1)		
Genesis 1:1, 2	"unformed"	"unfilled"
Genesis 1:3–31	**Forming**	**Filling**
	a. light	a^1. luminaries
	b. sky and water separated	b^1. inhabitants of sky and water
	c. dry land and vegetation	c^1. inhabitants of land, animals, and man
Conclusion (Genesis 2:2–3)		
The Sabbath: A Palace in Time		
God is both scientist and artist.		

E. *In the Span of Six Days.* The literal six days of Creation have been addressed under the section of the when of creation, but this concept is also an important component of the how of creation. On one hand, according to Genesis 1, God's method of Creation is not an instantaneous, timeless act in which all things described in Genesis 1; 2 in one momentary flash suddenly appeared. Contrary to the suppositions of Greek dualistic philosophy, which controlled the worldview of early Christian thinkers, such as Origen and Augustine (and still underlies the methodology of much Catholic, Protestant, and modern thought), God is not essentially timeless and unable to enter into spatiotemporal reality. Genesis 1; 2 underscores that God actually created in time as well as in space, creating the raw materials of the earth during a period of time before Creation week and then deliberately and dramatically forming and filling these inorganic, pre-fossil materials throughout the seven-day Creation week. Thus, Genesis 1; 2 serves as a strong bulwark against Greek dualistic thought and calls the contemporary interpreter back to radical biblical realism in which God actually enters time and space, creates in time and space, and calls it very good.

On the other hand, the method of Creation in Genesis 1; 2 is also a powerful witness against accepting the Creation week as occupying long ages of indefinite time, as claimed by proponents of progressive creationism. As mentioned, Genesis 1:3–2:3 clearly refers to the Creation week as seven literal, historical, contiguous, creative, and natural twenty-four-hour days. Furthermore, all life on planet Earth was created during this Creation week (days three through six) and not before. Any attempt to bring long ages into the Creation week, either through some kind of progressive creation or some other nonliteral, nonhistorical interpretation of the Creation week of Genesis 1, is out of harmony with the original intention of the text. Numerous quotations have been cited from both critical and conservative scholars that acknowledge this fact. And Genesis 1 demands an interpretation of rapid creation for the life forms on this planet—plants on day three, fish and fowl on day five, and the other animals and humans on day six. There is no room in the biblical text for the drawn-out process of evolution (even so-called rapid evolution) to operate as a methodology to explain the origin of life during Creation week.

IV. The What: "In the Beginning, God Created the Heavens and the Earth"

A. *"The Heavens and the Earth": The Universe: Genesis 1:1.* Some have taken the phrase in verse 1 "the heavens and the earth" to refer only to this earth and its surrounding heavenly spheres (i.e., the atmosphere and perhaps beyond to include the solar system). This interpretation is following the contextual lead of the usages of the terms "heaven" and "earth" later in Genesis 1 (especially vv. 8, 10) and cannot be absolutely ruled out as a possible way of understanding this phrase. However, significant differences may be noted between the use of the phrase "the heavens and the earth" in the opening verse of Genesis 1, compared to the use of the two terms "heavens" and "earth" separately later in the chapter. In verse 1, both "the heavens" and "the earth" contain the article, whereas when these are named in Genesis 1 (vv. 8, 10), they do not have the article. More importantly, in verse 1, one encounters two terms ("the heavens and the earth"), whereas later in Genesis 1, one finds three terms: "heavens," "earth," and "sea" (vv. 8, 10).

Genesis commentators widely recognize that, when used together as a pair in the Hebrew Bible, the two terms "the heavens and the earth" constitute a figure of speech for the totality of all creation in the cosmos (i.e., what we would describe as the entire universe) and that such is also the case in verse 1. As Sailhamer puts it, "By linking these two extremes into a single expression—'sky and land' or 'heavens and earth'—the Hebrew language expresses the totality of all that exists."[35]

This observation is most likely valid. Thus, verse 1, as already intimated in an earlier section of this study, refers to the creation of the entire universe, which took place "in the beginning" prior to the seven-day Creation week of Genesis 1:3–2:3.

For emphasis, it should be repeated that this still strongly implies *creatio ex nihilo*, creation out of nothing; God is not indebted to pre-existing matter. Also to repeat: the whole universe was not created in six days, as some ardent conservative creationists have mistakenly claimed. Furthermore, if the passive-gap (two-stage creation) interpretation is correct, then the creation of "the heavens and the earth" during the span of time termed "in the beginning," encompassed the whole galactic universe, including the planet Earth in its "unformed and unfilled" condition (v. 2).

B. *"Heaven, Earth, and Sea" (Gen. 1:8–11; Exod. 20:11): The Global Habitats of Our Planet.* By contrast to the spotlight in verse 1 (and again in the matching member of Gen. 2:4a), using the term "the heavens and the earth" in Genesis 1:2, the reference to "the earth" by itself (in fact, placing the noun "the earth" in the emphatic position as the first word in the Hebrew clause) moves the focus of this verse and the rest of the chapter to this planet. The use of the terms "heavens," "earth," and "seas" named in verses 8–11 describes the basic threefold habitat of our planet: sky, land, and water. This threefold habitat was the object of God's creative power during the six days of Creation (vv. 3–31), as He filled these habitats with vegetation, birds, fish, land animals, and humans. At the conclusion of the six days of Creation, the narrator

summarizes the creation of this threefold habitat by indicating that "thus the heavens and the earth, and all the host of them, were finished" (2:1). By adding the term "all the host of them," the narrator makes clear that he is not employing the figure of speech that refers to the entire universe (as in 1:1; 2:4) but has reference to what was created during the six days of Creation week (1:3–31).

Exodus 20:11 likewise refers back to this threefold term, stating that in six days God made "the heavens and earth and the sea"—the habitats of this planet, not the galactic universe. Thus, Genesis 1:1 (followed by 2:4) refers to God's creation of the whole universe, while the remainder of Genesis 1 (summarized by Gen. 2:1) and Exodus 20:11 describe the creation of the three habitats of planet Earth.

Sailhamer calls attention to the distinction between Genesis 1:1 (where the dual term "heavens and earth" refers to the entire universe) and the shift to this earth in the remainder of Genesis 1. Unfortunately, however, he then goes astray when he suggests that the term "the earth" in verse 2, throughout the account of the six-day Creation (some twenty times in Gen. 1:2–2:1) and in the fourth commandment (Exod. 20:11), be translated "the land," and he emphasizes that it refers only to the localized Promised Land for Israel and not to the whole planet's land surface. Likewise, he strays when he maintains that the term "the heavens" in the Genesis 1 account of Creation week refer only to the region above the localized Promised Land.

The context, replete with global (i.e., planet-wide) terms throughout Genesis

1, makes Sailhamer's restricted interpretation of this chapter highly unlikely. It seems extremely arbitrary and, in fact, virtually impossible to limit the descriptions of Creation week in verses 3–31 to the land between the Euphrates and the River of Egypt. How can the dividing of the light from the darkness (v. 3) occur only in the Promised Land? How can the waters be divided from the waters (v. 6) only over the land promised to Israel? How can the waters be gathered into one place called "seas" (v. 10) in the Promised Land? How can the greater light rule the day and the lesser light the night only in a localized area? How can the birds fly across the sky (v. 17) only above the Promised Land? How can the creation of the sea creatures be for the localized area of the future boundaries of Israel? How can the command given to humans to "fill the earth" and their charge to have dominion over "all the earth" be limited only to one localized area? All of this language is clearly global, not just limited to a small geographical area.

That the language of creation in verses 3–31 is global in extent is confirmed in succeeding chapters of Genesis 1–11. The trajectory of major themes throughout Genesis 1–11—Creation, Fall, plan of salvation, spread of sin, judgment by Flood, and God's covenant with the earth—are all global in their scope. Elsewhere has been shown the many occurrences of global terms in the Flood narrative, including several intertextual linkages with Genesis 1.[36] Moreover, after the Flood, the precise command given to Adam is repeated to Noah: "Be fruitful and multiply, and fill the earth" (9:1, 7). Noah was not even in the Promised Land when this command was given, and the following chapter of the Table of Nations (chap. 10) indicates that this command was to be fulfilled globally, not just in a localized area (see especially v. 32, "the nations were divided *on the earth* after the flood"). This global language continues in Genesis 11, where the "whole earth" involves all the languages of the earth (vv. 8, 9). There can be little doubt that throughout Genesis 1–11 these references, and many others, involve global, not localized language, and the creation of "the earth" in Genesis 1:3–31 must perforce also be global in extent.

This conclusion is also substantiated by comparing the Creation account of Genesis 1 to its parallel Creation account in Proverbs 8:22–31. References to "the earth" in verses 23, 26, 29 are in context clearly global in extent (e.g., "foundations of the earth," v. 29), and this is further demonstrated by the parallelism between "the earth" and the clearly global term "world" in verse 26. Thus, Sailhamer's suggestion that "the earth" and "the heavens" should be translated "land" and "sky" in Genesis 1:2 and onward and refer to less than a global creation is unacceptable.

C. *The Two Creation Accounts in Genesis 1 and 2: Identical, Contradictory, or Complementary?* Sailhamer has also mistakenly identified the global Creation week of Genesis 1 with the creation of the localized Garden of Eden in Genesis 2:4 and onward. Contra Sailhamer, it should be recognized that in the complementary Creation account of verses 4–25, the introductory "not yet" verses (vv. 5, 6) continue the global usage of "the earth" of the Genesis 1 account, in describing the four things that had not yet appeared on the surface of the planet before the entrance of sin (thorns, agriculture, cultivation or irrigation, and rain). But then, Genesis 2:7, describing the creation of the man, gives the time frame of the Genesis 2 Creation account, in other words, corresponding with the sixth day of the Creation week of Genesis 1. The rest of Genesis 2 depicts in more detail the activities of God on the sixth day of Creation week and is largely localized within the Garden of Eden.

Others have gone to the opposite extreme than Sailhamer and have posited that Genesis 1; 2 present radically different and contradictory accounts, and that Genesis 2 recapitulates all (or most) of Creation week, rather than only day six. Such a position often betrays a belief in the documentary hypothesis (source criticism) and two different redactors at work in the two accounts. Jacques Doukhan's dissertation and William Shea's literary analysis, among other important studies, provide evidence that Genesis 1; 2 are the product of a single writer and present complementary theological perspectives on the Creation of this world, with Genesis 1 providing a portrayal of the global Creation as such and Genesis 2 focusing attention on humanity's personal needs. Several recent studies discuss in detail alleged contradictions between the Genesis 1 and Genesis 2 Creation accounts and show how the supposed contradictions actually constitute complementarity in presenting a unified and integrated portrayal of Creation.

As referred to earlier, the four things mentioned as "not yet" in verses 4, 5 are not in contradiction with Genesis 1 but simply list those things that had not yet appeared on the surface of the planet before the entrance of sin (thorny plants, agriculture, cultivation or irrigation, and rain). Randall Younker points out that all these items are mentioned in anticipation of Genesis 3, when, after the Fall, such items will come into the picture of human reality.[37] Note that neither of the expressions "plant of the field" nor "herb of the field" used in Genesis 2:5 is found in Genesis 1, while the phrase "herb of the field" appears in Genesis 3:18, thus linking it to after the Fall and referring to cultivated agricultural products eaten by humans as a result of their laborious toil.

Another (and perhaps the major) alleged contradiction between Genesis 1; 2 is the apparent difference in the order of creation between the two accounts. In Genesis 1, the order is vegetation (day 3), birds (day 5), animals (day 6), and then humans, male and female (day 6). Genesis 2 appears to give a different order: man (Gen. 2:7), vegetation (vv. 8, 9), animals and birds (vv. 19, 20), and woman (vv. 21, 22). The two main issues here relate to (1) the different order for the vegetation and (2) the different order for the animals and birds. The apparent contradiction regarding the vegetation disappears when it is recognized that Genesis 1:11, 12 describes how, in response to God's creative word, the earth "brought forth" vegetation, including the fruit trees, while in Genesis 2:8, 9, God "planted" a special garden and, out of the ground, "caused to grow" additional specimens of various kinds of fruit trees that He had already created on day three of Creation week.

At least two possible explanations have been suggested for the apparent contradiction regarding the order of the creation of the birds and animals. The first is simply to translate the form of "formed" as "had formed": "Now the Lord God had formed out of the ground all the wild animals and all the birds in the sky. He brought them to the man to see what he would name them" (v. 19, NIV). This is a legitimate translation of the Hebrew inflection, which refers to completed action but may be translated according to context. With this translation, verse 19 is supplying necessary information to tell the story of Adam's naming of the animals and, at the same time, implying that the creation of the animals had taken place at an earlier time but without giving precise chronological order of this creation.

Another possible explanation for the different order of animals and birds is set forth by Umberto Cassuto, who suggests that, like the planting of the special trees in the Garden of Eden on day six (apart from the general creation of vegetation on the third day), according to verse 19, God is involved in a special additional creation of animals and birds beyond what was created earlier on the fifth and sixth days. However, because of the fivefold use of the term "all or every" in verses 19, 20 ("all the wild animals ... all the birds," NIV), the former explanation is preferable to the latter.

D. *Light, the "Greater" and "Lesser" Lights, and the Stars.* On the first day of Creation God said, " 'Let there be light'; and there was light" (Gen. 1:3). He named the light "day" and darkness "night" (v. 5). However, on the fourth day of Creation week, God ordered into existence "lights in the firmament of the heavens to give light on the earth ... to rule over the day and over the night, and to divide the light from the darkness" (vv. 15, 18). What was the source of the light that illumined our planet before the fourth day?

One possibility is that God's presence was the source of light on the first day of Creation. This is already hinted at in the literary linkage between verse 4 and verse 18. In verse 4, God Himself is the One who "divided the light from the darkness"; while in verse 18, it is the luminaries that are "to divide the light from the darkness." By juxtaposing these two clauses with exactly the same Hebrew words and word order, the reader is invited to conclude that God Himself was the light source of the first three days, performing the function, which He gave to the sun and moon on the fourth day. Another implicit indicator of this interpretation is found in the intertextual linkage between Genesis 1 with Psalm 104, the latter being a stylized account of the Creation story following the same order of description as in the Creation week of Genesis 1. In the section of Psalm 104, paralleling the first day of Creation (Ps. 104:2), God is depicted as covering Himself "with light as with a garment," thus implying that God is the light source of the first days of Creation week. During the first three days, God Himself could have separated the light from the darkness, just as He did at the Red Sea (Exod. 14:19, 20). God Himself being the light source for the first part of the week emphasizes the theocentric (God-centered), not heliocentric (sun-centered) nature of creation, and thus, God anticipates any temptation to worship the sun or moon that might have been encouraged if the luminaries were the first object created during the Creation week.

A second option suggests that the sun was created before the fourth day but became visible on that day (perhaps as a vapor cover was removed). This would explain the evening and morning cycle before day four. Sailhamer correctly points out that the Hebrew syntax of Genesis 1:14 is different from the syntactical pattern of the other days of Creation, in that it contains the verb "to be" plus the infinitive, whereas other days have only the verb without the infinitive. Thus, he suggests that verse 14 should read, "Let the lights in the expanse be for separating" (not as usually translated "let there be lights in the expanse"). Such a subtle but important syntactical shift may imply, Sailhamer suggests, that the lights were already in existence before the fourth day. The "greater" and "lesser" lights could have been created "in the beginning" (before Creation week, v. 1) and not on the fourth day. On the fourth day, they were given a purpose: "to separate the day from the night" and "to mark seasons and days and years."

Sailhamer's suggestion does rightly call attention to a possible difference of syntactical nuancing with regard to the wording of the fourth day but is not without its own difficulties. Most serious is that Sailhamer views verse 16 as not part of the report of creation but as commentary pointing out that it was God (and not anyone else) who had made the lights and put them in the sky. This objection may be overcome if one accepts a variant of this view in which verse 16 is indeed part of the report and not just commentary. According to this variant, the sun and moon were created before Creation week (v. 1), as Sailhamer suggests, but (unlike Sailhamer's view) they were created in their "unformed" and "unfilled" state, as was the earth, and on the fourth day, they were further "made" into their fully functional state (v. 16).

What about the stars? Were they created on the fourth day or before? In the second option mentioned above, the Hebrew syntax of verse 14 may indicate that the sun and moon were already in existence before the fourth day and, thus, could have been created "in the beginning" (before Creation week, v. 1). The same could also be true of the stars. Furthermore, the syntax of verse 16 doesn't require the creation of the stars on day four, and in fact, by not assigning any function to the stars, such as given to the sun and moon, they may be seen as a parenthetical statement added on in this verse to complete the portrayal of the heavenly bodies—"He made the stars also"—without indicating when.

Colin House has argued that in verse 16 the stars are presupposed as already in existence before Creation week and that this is indicated by the use of the Hebrew particle that he finds throughout Genesis to mean "together with." Thus, the Hebrew of verse 16 should read: "The lesser light to rule the night *together with the stars.*"[38] As noted above, several passages of Scripture suggest that celestial bodies and intelligent beings were created before life was brought into existence on this planet (Job 38:7; Ezek. 28:15; 1 Cor. 4:9; Rev. 12:7–9), and this would correlate with the implications that emerge from Genesis 1:16.

E. *Death or Predation Before Sin?* Do the Genesis Creation accounts allow for the possibility that death or predation existed on planet Earth before the Fall and the entrance of sin described in Genesis 3? The active-gap (or ruin-restoration) theory discussed under the when of Creation above allows for long ages of predation and death before the Creation week described in Genesis 1:3–31 cannot be grammatically sustained from the Hebrew text. Verse 2 simply cannot be translated, "The earth *became* without form and empty." As seen above, the text favors a passive gap in which God created the universe ("the heavens and the earth") "in the beginning" before Creation week (v. 1); and the earth at this time was "unformed and unfilled" and "darkness was on the face of the deep." But such description does not imply a negative condition of chaos, as has often been claimed, only that Creation was not yet complete. Furthermore, the terms "unformed and unfilled" in verse 2 imply a sterile, uninhabited waste, with no life, including birds, animals, and vegetation. So not only is there no death on this world before Creation week, there is no life! Verses 1, 2 thus make no room for living organisms to be present upon planet Earth before Creation week, let alone death and predation.

According to Genesis 1; 2, death is not part of the original condition or divine plan for this world. Doukhan's insightful discussion of death in relation to Genesis 1; 2 reveals at least three indicators that support this conclusion.[39] First, at each

stage of Creation, the divine work is pronounced "good" (Gen. 1:4, 10, 18, 21, 25), and at the last stage, it is pronounced "very good" (v. 31). Humanity's relationship with nature is described in positive terms of "dominion," which is a covenant term without a nuance of abuse or cruelty. The text explicitly suggests that animal or human death and suffering are not a part of the original creation situation, as it indicates the diet prescribed for both humans and animals to be the products of plants, not animals (vv. 28–30). This peaceful harmony is also evident in Genesis 2, where animals are brought by God to the man to be named by him, thus implying companionship (albeit incomplete and inadequate) of the animals with humans (v. 18).

A second indicator that death is not part of the picture in Genesis 1; 2 is the statement in Genesis 2:4–6 that at the time of creation the world was "not yet" affected by anything not good. Younker has shown that the four things that were "not yet" in these verses were all situations that came into the world as a result of sin: "(1) the need to deal with thorny plants, (2) the annual uncertainty and hard work of the grain crop, (3) the need to undertake the physically demanding plowing of the ground, and (4) the dependence on the uncertain, but essential, life-giving rain."[40]

Doukhan points to a number of other terms in the Genesis Creation narratives that constitute the use of a descriptive word in anticipation of its being applicable, showing what is "not yet" but will come. Allusions to death and evil, which is "not yet," may be found in the reference to "dust" (v. 7; to which humans will return in death); the mention of the tree of the knowledge of good and evil (v. 17, in anticipation of the confrontation with and experiencing of evil); the human's task to "guard" the garden (v. 15, implying the risk of losing it); and the play on words between "naked" and "cunning" (v. 25; 3:1).[41] Though alluded to before they existed, negative "not good" conditions, including death, are "not yet."

A third indicator that death was not prior to sin and part of the divine plan is that Genesis 3 portrays death as an accident, a surprise, which turns the original picture of peace and harmony (Gen. 1; 2) into conflict. Within Genesis 3, after the Fall, all the harmonious relationships described in Genesis 1; 2 are disrupted: between man and himself (guilt, a recognition of "soul nakedness" that cannot be covered by externals, 3:7–10), between humans and God (fear, v. 10), between man and woman (blame or discord, vv. 12, 13, 16, 17), between humans and animals (deceit, conflict, vv. 1, 13, 15), and between humans and nature (decay, vv. 17–19). Now, death appears immediately (as an animal must die to provide covering for the humans' nakedness, v. 21) and irrevocably (for the humans who have sinned, v. 19). The upset of the ecological balance is directly attributed to the humans' sin (vv. 17, 18). The blessing of Genesis 1; 2 has become the curse (Gen. 3:14, 17).

Tryggve N. D. Mettinger points to the strong contrast regarding death before sin or guilt between the ancient Near-Eastern accounts of theodicy and the Eden narrative in Genesis 2; 3: "What we have in Mesopotamia is a type of theodicy in which death is not the result of human guilt but is the way that the gods arranged human existence. . . . On the other hand, what we have in the Eden Narrative is a theodicy that derives the anomic phenomena from human guilt. Death is not what God intended but is the result of human sin."[42]

A number of commentators have pointed out that one of the major reasons for God's judgment upon the antediluvian world with the Flood was the existence of violence on the earth: "The earth also was corrupt before God, and the earth was filled with violence" (Gen. 6:11). This condition of the earth being "filled with violence" is repeated again in verse 13. The use of the term "violence" undoubtedly includes the presence of brutality and physical violence and, with its subject being "the earth," probably refers to the violent behavior of both humans and animals (note the post-Flood decrees that attempt to limit both human and animal violence, 9:4–6). Divine judgment upon the earth for its violence implies that predation, which presupposes violence, and death, the all-too-frequent result of violence, were not part of the Creation order.

Intertextual allusions to Genesis 1; 2 later in Genesis confirm that death is an intruder, coming as a result of sin and not occurring before the Fall. Doukhan points to the striking intertextual parallels between Genesis 1:28–30 and 9:1–4, where God repeats to Noah the same blessing as to Adam, using the same terms and in the same order. But after the Fall instead of peaceful dominion (as in Creation) there will be fear and dread of humans by the animals, and instead of a vegetarian diet for both humans and animals (as in

Creation), humans are allowed to hunt and eat animals. The juxtaposing of these two passages reveals that the portrayal of conflict and death is not regarded as original in Creation but organically connected to humanity's fall.

Perhaps the most instructive intertextual allusions to Genesis 1 and 2 occur in the Old Testament Hebrew prophets and in the last prophet of the New Testament (the book of Revelation); these messengers of God were inspired to look beyond the present to a future time of salvation, pictured as a re-creation of the world as it was before the Fall. This portrait, drawn largely in the language of a return to the Edenic state, explicitly describes a new/renewed creation of perfect harmony between humanity and nature, where once again predation and death will not exist:

> The wolf also shall dwell with the lamb,
> The leopard shall lie down with the young goat,
> The calf and the young lion and the fatling together;
> And a little child shall lead them.
> The cow and the bear shall graze;
> Their young ones shall lie down together;
> And the lion shall eat straw like the ox.

> The nursing child shall play by the cobra's hole,
> And the weaned child shall put his hand in the viper's den.
> They shall not hurt nor destroy in all My holy mountain,
> For the earth shall be full of the knowledge of the LORD
> As the waters cover the sea. (Isa. 11:6–9)

> He will swallow up death forever,
> And the Lord GOD will wipe away tears from all faces;
> The rebuke of His people
> He will take away from all the earth;
> For the LORD has spoken. (Isa. 25:8)

> I will ransom them from the power of the grave;
> I will redeem them from death.
> O Death, I will be your plagues!
> O Grave, I will be your destruction!
> (Hosea 13:14)

> For behold, I create new heavens and a new earth;
> And the former shall not be remembered or come to mind. (Isa. 65:17)

> "For as the new heavens and the new earth
> Which I will make shall remain before Me," says the LORD,
> "So shall your descendants and your name remain." (Isa. 66:22)

> I am He who lives, and was dead, and behold, I am alive forevermore. Amen. And I have the keys of Hades and of Death. (Rev. 1:18)

> Then Death and Hades were cast into the lake of fire. (Rev. 20:14)

> "And I saw a new heaven and a new earth, for the first heaven and the first earth had passed away. Also there was no more sea. . . . And God will wipe away every tear from their eyes; there shall be no more death,

nor sorrow, nor crying. There shall be no more pain, for the former things have passed away." (Rev. 21:1, 4)

Several studies have carefully examined these and other relevant biblical passages and concluded that "God created the world without the presence of death, pain, and suffering" and that "the 'subjection to futility' spoken of in Romans 8:19–21 began in Genesis 3, not in Genesis 1."[43]

F. *Other Aspects of the What of Creation.* There are numerous other issues related to the what of Creation in Genesis 1; 2, which have been dealt with elsewhere or call for further attention in another venue, and can only be listed here. These include, among others, the following:

1. *The Firmament or Expanse.* The Hebrew word translated "firmament or expense" in Genesis 1 does not refer to a "metallic, hemispherical vault," as many have maintained, based upon what is now recognized as a mistranslation of the parallel ancient Near-Eastern creation story *Enuma Elish* but is best translated as "expanse" in all of its usages, and has reference to the "sky" in Genesis 1. The mention of God's placement of the "greater light" and the "lesser light" in the "firmament or expense" does not betray a wholesale acceptance of ancient Near-Eastern cosmology on the part of the biblical writer, as often claimed. Rather, the account of Genesis 1; 2 seems to provide a polemic against major parts of ancient Near-Eastern cosmology. The "waters above" refer to the upper atmospheric waters contained in the clouds.

2. *Creation "After Its Kind."* The phrase "after its kind" in Genesis 1 (vv. 11, 12, 21, 24, 25) does not imply a fixity of species (as Darwin and many others have claimed); rather, it "refers to a 'multiplicity' of animals and denotes boundaries between basic kinds of animals, but is not linked directly to reproduction."[44]

3. *Imago Dei (Image of God).* Humankind is made in the image of God, after His likeness (vv. 26, 27), which includes, among other considerations, the relational aspects of humanity as in the Godhead, the representation in humanity of the presence of God, and the resemblance of humans to God in both outward form and inward character.

4. *Equality of Man and Woman.* The Genesis Creation accounts (Gen. 1; 2) present the equality of the man and woman without hierarchy before the Fall and present this as the ideal, even in a sinful world.

5. *Marriage.* The Genesis Creation accounts present a succinct theology of marriage (concentrated in the three expressions "leave," "be joined to," "become one flesh" in Gen. 2:24.)

6. *Earth's First Sanctuary.* The Garden of Eden is portrayed as a sanctuary-temple, with Adam and Eve as the priestly officiants.

7. *Creation Care.* A robust theology of creation care (environmental concerns) emerges from a careful study of Genesis 1 and 2.

8. *The Sabbath.* The Sabbath is set forth in Genesis 2:1–3 as a holy institution rooted in and memorial of the six-day Creation.

The remainder of Scripture takes up these and other Creation-related themes. This profound theology of Creation at the beginning of the Bible, developed throughout the biblical canon, calls for us, God's creatures, to praise and worship Him for His wondrous creative works: "Praise the LORD. . . . [He] made heaven and earth, the sea, and all that is in them" (Ps. 146:1, 6); "worship Him who made heaven and earth, the sea, and springs of water" (Rev. 14:7)!

Notes

1. John Rankin, "Power and Gender at the Divinity School," in *Finding God at Harvard: Spiritual Journeys of Christian Thinkers*, ed. Kelly Monroe (Grand Rapids, MI: Zondervan, 1996), 203.

2. Victor P. Hamilton, *The Book of Genesis: Chapters 1-17* (Grand Rapids, MI: Eerdmans, 1990), 105.

3. Hermann Gunkel, *Genesis*, trans. Albert Wolters, 7th ed. (Göttingen, Germany: Vandenhoeck & Ruprecht, 1966), 101.

4. Umberto Cassuto, *The Documentary Hypothesis and the Composition of the Pentateuch: Eight Lectures* (Jerusalem: Magnes, 1961), 20.

5. Hershel Shanks, "How the Bible Begins," *Judaism* 21, no. 1 (1972): 58.

6. John H. Walton, *The Lost World of Genesis One: Ancient Cosmology and the Origins Debate* (Downers Grove, IL: InterVarsity, 2009), 163.

7. Mark E. Ross, "The Framework Hypothesis: An Interpretation of Genesis 1:1-2:3," in *Did God Create in Six Days?* eds. Joseph A. Pipa Jr. and David W. Hall (Taylors, SC: Southern Presbyterian Press, 1999), 113.

8. Fritz Guy, "The Purpose and Function of Scripture: Preface to a Theology of Creation," in *Understanding Genesis: Contemporary Adventist Perspectives*, eds. Brian Bull, Fritz Guy, and Ervin Taylor (Riverside, CA: Adventist Today Foundation, 2006), 93.

9. C. John Collins, *Genesis 1-4: A Linguistic, Literary, and Theological Commentary* (Phillipsburg, NJ: P & R Publishing, 2006), 124.

10. Kenneth A. Mathews, *Genesis 1:1-11:26* (Nashville, TN: Broadman & Holman, 1996), 109.

11. Steven W. Boyd, "The Genre of Genesis 1:1-2:3: What Means This Text?" in *Coming to Grips With Genesis: Biblical Authority and the Age of the Earth*, eds. Terry Mortenson and Thane H. Ury (Green Forest, AZ: Master Books, 2008), 188.

12. Daniel Bediako, *Genesis 1:1-2:3: A Textlinguistic Analysis* (Saarbrücken, Germany: VDM Verlag, 2011), 257.

13. Robert V. McCabe, "A Critique of the Framework Interpretation of the Creation Week," in *Coming to Grips With Genesis*, 211–49.

14. Walter Kaiser, "The Literary Form of Genesis 1–11," in *New Perspectives on the Old Testament* ed. J. Barton Payne (Waco, TX: Word, 1970), 48–65.

15. John H. Sailhamer, *Genesis Unbound: A Provocative New Look at the Creation Account* (Sisters, OR: Multnomah, 1996), 244.

16. Mathews, *Genesis 1:1 -11:26*, 41.

17. Ibid., 110, 111.

18. See, e.g., Henry M. Morris, *Biblical Cosmology and Modern Science* (Grand Rapids, MI: Baker, 1970), 59; Terence E. Fretheim, "Were the Days of Creation Twenty-Four Hours Long? YES," in *The Genesis Debate: Persistent Questions About Creation and the Flood*, ed. Ronald F. Youngblood (Grand Rapids, MI: Baker, 1990), 19, 20.

19. Gerhard F. Hasel, "The 'Days' of Creation in Genesis 1: Literal 'Days' or Figurative 'Periods/Epochs' of Time?" *Origins* 21, no. 1 (1994): 30, 31.

20. James Stambaugh, "The Days of Creation: A Semantic Approach," *CEN Technical Journal* 5, no. 1 (1991): 75.

21. Karl W. Giberson and Francis S. Collins, *The Language of Science and Faith: Straight Answers to Genuine Questions* (Downers Grove, IL: InterVarsity, 2011), 69, 70.

22. Richard F. Carlson and Tremper Longman III, *Science, Creation and the Bible: Reconciling Rival Theories of Origins* (Downers Grove, IL: InterVarsity, 2010), 13.

23. Walton, *The Lost World of Genesis 1*, 12.

24. John E. Hartley, *Genesis* (Peabody, MA: Hendrickson, 2000), 41.

25. Sailhamer, *Genesis Unbound*, 38.

26. Collins, *Genesis 1-4*, 78.

27. Brian Bull and Fritz Guy, *God, Sky and Land: Genesis 1 as the Ancient Hebrews Heard It* (Roseville, CA: Adventist Forum, 2011), 36.

28. Ibid.

29. Marco T. Terreros, "What Is an Adventist? Someone Who Upholds Creation," *Journal of the Adventist Theological Society* 7, no. 2 (1996): 148.

30. John C. Lennox, *Seven Days That Divide the World: The Beginning According to Genesis and Science* (Grand Rapids, MI: Zondervan, 2011), 53 (emphasis added).

31. Mathews, *Genesis 1:1 -11:26*, 113.

32. Ellen G. White, *Education* (Mountain View, CA: Pacific Press® Pub. Assn., 1903), 134.

33. Gerhard F. Hasel, "The Meaning of 'Let Us' in Gen 1:26," *Andrews University Seminary Studies* 13 (1975): 65.

34. Mathews, *Genesis 1:1 –11:26*, 144.

35. Sailhamer, *Genesis Unbound*, 56.

36. Richard M. Davidson, "Biblical Evidence for the Universality of the Genesis Flood," *Origins* 22, no. 2 (1995): 58–73.

37. Randall W. Younker, "Genesis 2: A Second Creation Account?" in *Creation, Catastrophe, and Calvary: Why a Global Flood Is Vital to the Doctrine of Atonement*, ed. John T. Baldwin (Hagerstown, MD: Review and Herald® Pub. Assn., 2000), 69–78.

38. Colin L. House, "Some Notes on Translating— סִיבְכוֹכֵה תֵאֶו [we'et hakôkabîm] in Genesis 1:16," *Andrews University Seminary Studies* 25, no. 3 (1987): 241–248.

39. Jacques B. Doukhan, "Where Did Death Come From? A Study in the Genesis Creation Story," *Adventist Perspectives* 4, no. 1 (1990): 16–18.

40. Younker, "Genesis 2: A Second Creation Account?" 76, 77.

41. Doukhan, "Where Did Death Come From?" 17.

42. Tryggve N. D. Mettinger, *The Eden Narrative: A Literary and Religio-Historical Study of Genesis 2-3* (Winona Lake, IN: Eisenbrauns, 2007), 133.

43. James Stambaugh, "Whence Cometh Death? A Biblical Theology of Physical Death and Natural Evil," in *Coming to Grips With Genesis*, 397.

44. A. Rahel Schafer, "The 'Kinds' of Genesis 1: What is the Meaning of *mîn*?" *Journal of the Adventist Theological Society* 14, no. 1 (2003): 97.

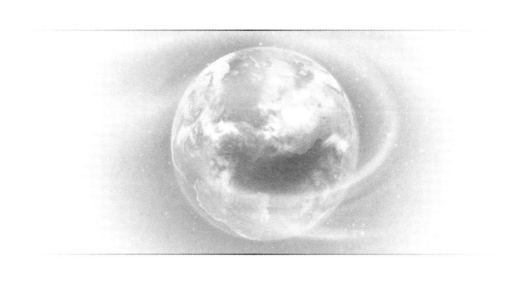

Creation Echoes of Genesis 1 and 2 in the Pentateuch

Paul Gregor

Apart from Genesis 1; 2, creation language is most concentrated in the fourth commandment, especially in Exodus 20:8–11. The first three verses (vv. 8–10) emphasize the command about the seventh day, but the last verse is linked to the first part by a causative clause, indicating the reason for such a demand. It refers to the Creation week when everything was created in six days and on the seventh day God rested (v. 11). The author employed the verb translated "to make," which is in harmony with the Creation story recorded in Genesis 2:2, 3. The same verb is used for the first time during the second day of Creation (Gen. 1:7) in relationship to the creation of the firmament. The same was named "heavens," and it is probable that the fourth commandment (Exod. 20:11) is referring to these "heavens," rather than to the one in Genesis 1:1, which may point to the entire universe.

To Rest

It seems that the vocabulary in Exodus 20:11 corresponds to the Creation account in Genesis 2:1–3 with one exception. While the Genesis account employs one verb translated "to rest," the Exodus account uses another. In Exodus 20:11, the verb is used in a form that appears only thirty times in the Old Testament, and it is mostly employed in theological contexts even though secular contexts are possible. Its subject may vary from things, such as Noah's ark (Gen. 8:4) and the ark of the covenant (Num. 10:36), insects (Exod. 10:14), animals and birds (2 Sam. 21:10), and humans (1 Sam. 25:9), to abstract objects, such as justice (Prov. 14:33), death (Job 3:17, 26; Dan. 12:13), and the Spirit (Num. 11:25; 2 Kings 2:15; Isa. 11:2). The verb used in Genesis 2:1–3 is God's gift given to the human race (Isa. 25:10; 57:2). In these contexts, the verb is to be translated as "to settle down (to rest), to become quiet, and (consequently) to rest."

The verb "to rest" in Genesis 2:1–3 is also used in covenant contexts (Exod. 20:11; 23:12; Deut. 5:14). Obviously, "resting" was extended to the entire human race, animals, and even to nature. God Himself rested on the seventh day (Exod. 20:11) after all His work was completed. This is the only place where the verb translated "to rest" stands as an opposite to work. By implementing the verb in this unique contextual position, the author clearly intended to show that resting should come only as the finale, after the completion of work. This is also evident in Genesis 2:1–3, where the author employed a different verb to indicate the same result.

The verb translated "to rest" in Genesis 2:1–3 appears in its unique form twenty-seven times. In most cases, it is related to the weekly or yearly Sabbath. Its basic meaning is "to cease, come to an end," and it "indicates the pertinent rest and celebration of people (Exod. 16:30; 23:12; 34:21, etc.), animals (23:12), [and] land (Lev. 25:12)."[1]

However, the full breadth of its meaning is evidenced through its wide usage in various contexts. The term is used in the covenant speech just after the Flood. God promised that as long as the earth remained that seedtime and harvest, cold and heat, summer and winter, day and night would not cease (or "rest"). "God decrees that as long as the form of this world exists, the natural processes that carry the life of creation will never come to an end."[2] The promise of God's continual care will not be limited by the human condition but will be granted regardless.

In the same way, the word is used in Joshua 5:12 when manna, which was given to the people on a daily basis throughout the forty years of the wilderness experience, ceases ("rests") on the same day the people of Israel tasted the produce of the land of Canaan. The period in which manna was available to them was completed; it was closed off and came to an end. Again, the cessation of manna was not subject to the human condition. It seems that "to rest" in this usage represents a cessation or a complete stoppage of a process, which has been going on for a certain length of time. The provision of manna came to a conclusion and is not just temporarily interrupted.

Similarly, when the word translated "to rest" is used in relation to the seventh day (Gen. 2:1–3), it is not primarily connected to resting in order to recover but rather indicates that a particular process is completely finished and that there is nothing else to be added to it. Every time when this form of "to rest" is used, it does not require a human condition as a factor for its implementation. Even though it was given to all creation, unfortunately, it seems that the observance of the Sabbath was unique to ancient Israel. It was not an "aversion to labor but the celebrative cessation of a completed work."[3] The seventh day comes as a result of the completion of a six-day cycle, and it is given as a gift from the Creator Himself. He completed His work in six days and rested, and He does not expect less from humankind either. Therefore, the institution of the seventh day does not simply imply a disruption of labor, but the rest has its full meaning only if the tasks set for six days are completed.

The seventh day of the week, requiring rest, represents a literal day that follows six literal days. The only reason for such a request, indicated specifically in the fourth commandment, is that God also finished His work in six days. If the miracle of Creation was not finished within six literal twenty-four-hour days, there is no foundation for keeping the fourth commandment. By connecting the fourth commandment to Creation week, the biblical author made clear that those two are closely related (Exod. 31:17).

Additional Creation Terminology

Creation language plays a pivotal role

not only in the formulation of the fourth commandment, echoes of important concepts and terminology found in Genesis 1 and 2 reappear at crucial places elsewhere in the Pentateuch.

To Dominate. The role of humanity involved "to have dominion" over God's entire creation on this earth (Gen. 1:26). The verb translated "to dominate" is used only twenty-five times in the Old Testament, which complicates its appropriate understanding, and has usually been translated with "to rule, dominate." Apart from Genesis 1:26, 28, the verb can also be found four times in Leviticus and once in Numbers. The remainder of its occurrences appears elsewhere in the Old Testament. Every time it is used in the biblical text, its subject is a human being, a group of individuals, or a nation. Its object could be either human beings or the entire creation of this earth, including plants (Gen. 1:26, 28).

Though its etymology is uncertain, it appears that it is mostly used elsewhere in connection with royalty (1 Kings 4:24; Pss. 8:5, 6; 72:8; 110:2; Isa. 14:2) and, as such, is associated with a variety of meanings. In addition to royalty, the books of Numbers and Leviticus employ the term in a different context. The book of Numbers uses it only once in Balaam's oracle (Num. 24:19). Here, it is used the same as in Genesis 1:26 "to express the speaker's desire, wish, or command where a third person is the subject of the action."[4] This oracle is considered to be a Messianic prophecy, and therefore, the subject is the Messiah Himself. In this case, desire is expressed that the Messiah will "rule" or "have dominion"; in this context, the word has a positive meaning and should refer to a gentle rulership.

The same word is also used four times in the book of Leviticus but in different settings. Three times it is employed in connection to laws of redemption involving Israelites who were sold into servitude. The law provided the same guidelines for all masters, whether they were of Israelite (Lev. 25:43, 46) or of Gentile origin (v. 53). In all three cases, the author's intent "expresses an absolute or categorical prohibition"[5] and is mostly in divine commands.[6] In all cases, it is followed by a noun translated as "harshness" or "severity." Since, in all cases, a strong prohibition is issued, the masters are prohibited to "rule" over their servants with any harshness. In this context, it is obvious that the word translated "to dominate" should be understood as a reference to some type of gentle rule.

The word translated "to dominate" appears for the last time in the Pentateuch in Leviticus 26:17 in the context of covenant making. It is mentioned in the curses section as a caution against disobedience. If the people decided to follow foreign gods, they would not be able to stand against their enemies. A grim warning was issued to the people of Israel with the consequence that "those who hate you shall rule over you." In this context, it is obvious that the word occupies a very important place. Certainly, in this context, it points to a different and harsher type of rulership.

However, this punishment is issued as the first step for insubordination, and it is considered to be the mildest one. Its decisive role in a covenant context does not necessarily imply slavery, which will come as the last resort for the stubborn nation.

Leviticus 26:14–39 includes effectively six steps where God's power and might is exercised in order to bring His disobedient people back to Himself. The divine disciplinary actions show a gradual intensification, resulting eventually in exile. The exile is used here as the last resort and, as such, is placed at the end of the list. Following this line of argument, it is obvious that the first step will be the mildest one; since the word appears in the context of step number one, it should not be understood as cruel, slaverylike dominion by Israel's enemies but rather as a more general indication that other nations will be more successful in everything, including battle, and will dominate Israel.

Bringing all this into the context of the Creation account, the verb "to dominate" seems to bring a clearer understanding of the role God gave to the first humans. The author employed this word skillfully to bring into focus two important elements: (1) the title or office of the first human beings and (2) their obligation toward those who were placed under their care. As noted earlier, the word is closely connected to royalty and, as such, highlights the royal status of the first humans. They are the masters, and all creation is placed under their care and stewardship. As the word indicates, their dominant role must be administered with kindness, care, and compassion for those who are under their superintendence. Further, the word translated as "to dominate" is used here as a bridge to connect Genesis 1; 2. The word used in Genesis 1 introduces generically the role of humans, which is fully explored and understood in the following chapter (Gen. 2:8, 15).

To Put (Definition 1). The biblical author captivates the attention of his readers by introducing the Garden of Eden scene. Genesis 2:8 simply states: "And there he put the man whom he had formed." Interestingly, the author does not specify any justification or purpose for such an action. No explanation is provided as to the rationale of this action. He does not elaborate on this point, since he already provided his readers with such information. The only previous text that deals with such material is located in Genesis 1:26 in the preceding chapter, where humanity was given dominion over all creation.

Some might suggest that the explanation of purpose is found in the following verse (Gen. 2:15), rather than in the previous one (1:26). This is most unlikely for two reasons. First, these two verses are separated by a long description of the garden; and second, in spite of the fact that most English translations use the verb "to put" in both cases, the Hebrew text actually employs two different verbs (one in v. 8 and a different one in v. 15). Therefore, if verses 8 and 15 are related, it should be reasonable to assume that the author would use the same verb. Since he did not, the purpose of verse 8 is located in the previous chapter.

The word translated as "to put" is one of twenty-five verbs most frequently used in the Old Testament and appears in every Old Testament book with the exceptions of Jonah and Ecclesiastes. Since it is widely used, some lexica offer more than twenty-five meanings and many other submeanings. In such cases where a wide variety of meaning does exist for a single verb, its context always plays a crucial role in unlocking its meaning. Among the wide range of its usage, "to put" is used in the context of appointing someone to an office of authority, whether they are taskmasters (Exod. 1:11; 5:14), elders in the community of Israel (18:21), judges (Judg. 11:11), or military commanders (1 Sam. 8:11, 12; 2 Sam. 17:25). It is also used in the context of setting a king upon a throne as a symbol of rulership and an indicator of power (Deut. 17:14, 15; 1 Sam. 8:5; 10:19). Deuteronomy uses the word "to put" four times in this sense, which unmistakably reflects this significance. Furthermore, the language of appointing kings is ultimately connected to the coronation ceremony.

Understanding the meaning of the word "to put" in this context illuminates its significance in the Creation account. The fact that the purpose of Genesis 2:8 is found in 1:26, as earlier established, where rulership and dominion over all creation was given to humanity, brings new light to the understanding of the word "to put" in this context. Genesis 1:26 just serves as an introduction of God's intention to address humanity's role, and 2:8 explains how it was done. God did not just put humans into the Garden of Eden as a missing part in a puzzle or as a misplaced item in its rightful place on a shelf, but rather, He placed humans in order to accept kingship over all creation. On the sixth day of Creation, God introduced the first human beings to the entire creation and performed a coronation ceremony, placing a scepter of dominion into their hands. Since only human beings were created in His image, obviously God had chosen them from among all other living creatures to be granted royal status.

Human beings did not come into this position because they deserved it but because it was given to them. Whenever the verb "to put" is used in this context, its subject (God in this case) is always the one who has "the requisite authority or the competence to achieve the task.... The one who appoints is . . . superior to both the position and the individual appointed."[7] The first humans had to know that their appointment as rulers came from a higher power and that they did not hold ultimate dominion in their hands but were responsible to God, who is the Supreme Authority.

This was also evident in other cultures in which a suzerain king appointed a vassal king. In this setting, the vassal king owed his position and crown to the suzerain king. This is why, in some cases, a vassal king was anointed. This was also evident when kingship was introduced to Israel. At that time, kings were anointed for such positions, and they had to know from the beginning that God was their Suzerain King and Lord to whom they owed everything they had. In this way, the first humans in the Garden of Eden knew right from the beginning not only that they owed their position to their Creator-God but also that, for every decision and every act they made, they were responsible to their Creator-King.

To Put (Definition 2). Though Genesis 2:8 indicates the coronation of the first humans and their role as rulers, verse 15 of the same chapter informs the readers about humanity's responsibilities in this new kingly role. They were given a task in relation to the Garden of Eden, "to till it and keep it." Again, the text (Gen. 2:15) indicates that God "put him in the garden of Eden." As noted earlier, the author opted for bringing an entirely new aspect of function and responsibility for human beings in their role as masters of God's creation.

In spite of the fact that this second definition is not as widely used as the first, its usage in different contexts brings to light its various interpretations and meanings. Among its variants, the verb appears with two slightly different spellings. With one, it usually means "cause to settle down, give rest, bring to rest."[8] Elsewhere, however, as is the case in Genesis 2:15, then it involves a different meaning, such as "leave behind,"[9] referring to either a person (Gen. 42:33; 2 Sam. 16:21; 20:3) or things (Lev. 16:23; Ezek. 42:14; 44:19). In this particular form, the verb may also indicate "permit to remain" or "leave alone," where its objects might include people (Gen. 2:15; 19:16) or things (39:16; Exod. 16:23). When God placed the first couple in the Garden of Eden, He actually left them with a new task. The verb may also implement a notion that He placed them in charge with full authority over His entire creation on earth. God permitted them to remain in this environment as rulers or masters, not to be idle but "to till it and keep it."

To Work, to Serve, and to Keep. The responsibility and title that humanity received did not come without obligations and responsibility. The author employs two very common Hebrew verbs, translated "to till, to work" and "to keep," both in infinitive construct form. The verb translated "to till, to work" appears 287 times in the Old Testament.[10] The verb occurs in six different contexts with a variety of meanings. It may appear without any objects, and in such instances, its meaning is "to work." In this particular context, it appears in the Sabbath commandment where God requires from His people to work six days only (Exod. 20:9; Deut. 5:13). Second, it may be followed by an object and is interpreted as "to work for" or "to serve for." The object of this kind of service may be another human being (Gen. 29:18, 20, 25; 30:26; 31:41) or nation (Ezek. 29:20), or it may be used in a symbolic context (Hos. 12:13). Third, the verb may appear with an inanimate object, such as soil or ground (Gen. 2:5; 3:23; 4:12), vineyards (Deut. 28:39), and flax (Isa. 19:9). In these cases, the verb should be interpreted as "to work, cultivate, develop." Fourth, the verb may also be found in combination with a word most commonly translated as "labor, service." It may involve secular (Gen. 29:27) or cultic service (Num. 3:8; 4:23, 27; 7:5; 8:22; Josh. 22:27). Fifth, the verb may be used with personal objects, in which it is usually interpreted as "to serve." Such service might indicate slavery for an entire life (Exod. 21:6) or only a specified duration of time (Gen. 29:15, 30; 30:26, 29; 31:6, 41). It may also indicate maintaining an alliance (2 Sam. 16:19), or it may reflect vassal relationship (Gen. 14:4; 2 Kings 18:7). Lastly, the verb is also used in the context of serving Yahweh (Exod. 3:12) or other gods (20:5; 23:24; Deut. 5:9).

In addition, the verb translated as "to work, to serve" is also used with pronominal suffixes attached to it, as is the case with Genesis 2:15, and is usually understood as to serve, which involved voluntary (Gen. 29:18; Exod. 7:16) or involuntary service (Deut. 15:12, 18). It sometimes refers to an object mentioned earlier in the text. Objects may vary from humans (Gen.

15:13; 27:29; 29:15, 18; 30:26; Exod. 14:5; 21:6; Deut. 15:12, 18; 20:11), God (Exod. 7:16; Deut. 11:13), or foreign gods (Deut. 4:19; 28:14). In spite of the fact that most English versions translate the word in Genesis 2:15 as "to till, to work," the possibility of implementing the meaning of *servitude* must not be ignored. Indeed, in such a context, it is probable that the Garden of Eden, with all its content, was to be served by the first human beings. This would shed new light on their role in the garden, including their royal obligations.

In addition to serving God's creation in the Garden of Eden, the first couple also accepted another role, namely "to keep it." Here, the author employed one of the most common verbs in the Old Testament and, as such, is present in almost all Semitic languages.

Due to its wide usage, Sauer detected seven different contexts in which the word translated as "to keep it" was employed. Its most frequent subject is human beings (patriarch, king, judge). However, in most cases, its subject is a group of people or the nation of Israel. On the other hand, the object of the word translated "to keep" may be anything of value, whether it is an individual or a possession. In a profane sense, it refers to "protection" and "guardianship" of individuals whether it is a king (1 Sam. 26:15), an ordinary person (19:11; 28:21; 1 Kings 20:39), or even a soul or life (Deut. 4:9; Ps. 71:10). Further, the same meaning is applied when the object is no longer a human being but animals (Gen. 30:31), a way (3:24), a city (2 Kings 9:14), a palace (11:5–7), a house (2 Sam. 15:16), a cave (Josh. 10:18), and property in general (1 Sam. 25:21).

In addition to nonreligious circumstances, the verb translated "to keep" is also frequently used in a variety of religious contexts. It is God who cares and guards His people (Gen. 28:15, 20) and who is also the "keeper of Israel" (Ps. 121:4). The Aaronic blessing uses the same word to express desire where God is portrayed as the One who protects His people (Num. 6:24–26). Furthermore, "to keep" is often used in covenant speeches (Gen. 17:9, 10; Exod. 19:5; Deut. 7:9, 12); and according to Klaus Baltzer, it became a constitutive element of covenant language.[11]

Consequently, it was used in Deuteronomy 5:12 as part of a covenant speech and in the context of the fourth commandment. Here, the word translated "to keep" appears in the infinite absolute form and, as such, "in this use it predominantly expresses divine and/or prophetic commands."[12] To keep the Sabbath simply meant "to preserve its distinctive features by positive action."[13] By observing the Sabbath day, the people of Israel demonstrated obedience to their covenant obligations and expressed their loyalty to God's desire to preserve and guard the seventh day. Since stewardship is deeply embedded in the core meaning of the word "to keep," preservation and guardianship of the seventh day for future generations within the people of God (Deut. 6:7, 8; 11:19) and also for the rest of the world (4:6, 7) is evident.

When the author employs the word translated "to keep" in Genesis 2:15, human beings are the subject, and the Garden of Eden with its entire contents is the object. Guardianship implicates stewardship, which reminded Adam and Eve of the fact that Eden was not their possession but was given to them for safekeeping. In their royal status, they were obliged to serve the garden and to protect it. Protection of the garden does not imply an imperfect world around it, but it refers to the maintenance and, even more so, the preservation of its perfection as it came out of the Creator's hands. Since "to keep" carries in itself a notion of covenant as well, it is possible to recognize that, by protecting the garden and by preserving it, humans entered into a covenant relationship with their Creator and with the entire creation as well. Thus, humans accepted royal status to rule gently by serving the needs of all creation and preserving the Garden of Eden for future generations in a covenant care, which God entrusted them.

As noted earlier, both "to work, to serve" and "to keep" indicate that the object of service and protection should have the same gender and number. The most obvious candidate should be "garden"; however, "garden" is a masculine singular noun and, in this capacity, does not qualify for such a function. It is true that the noun "garden" may also appear as a feminine noun, but in this case, it is clear that the author unmistakably used its masculine form. Since the Garden of Eden was a smaller geographical location that belonged to a larger place (earth), it is possible that the author opted for the feminine form for a reason. Since "earth" is a feminine noun, it is possible that the author tried to indicate that the first couple's service and protection should not be limited only to the Garden of Eden but to the entire planet Earth.

In addition to Genesis 2:15, the verbs "to keep" and "to work, to serve" appear as a pair only once, in Numbers 8:7, and Davidson rightly argues that the first couple received priesthood in the Garden of Eden as well. In this way, they became a royal priesthood with the clear understanding that they were stewards in His service for the better of all who inhabited the Garden of Eden.

To Acquire, to Possess. Melchizedek, the king of Salem, blessed Abraham after his victory over Chedorlaomer and the other three kings from the east and the rescue of his nephew Lot and his family (Gen. 14). In Melchizedek's blessing, the reference to "maker of heaven and earth" (v. 19) is the same phrase used in Abraham's response (v. 22). In spite of the fact that one might expect more common terms denoting "maker," both Melchizedek and Abraham rather employed the word translated "to acquire, to possess" here.

The word translated "to acquire, to possess" is used only eighty-four times in the entire Old Testament. The author of the Pentateuch employs the same word twenty-four times in its various forms. According to most lexicons, the basic meaning of the word is "acquire, purchase, get, possess."[14] Earlier lexicographers indicated its primary meaning as "to found, create,"[15] which is not accepted by current scholars. The word appears in most Semitic languages and, according to Edward Lipinski,[16] has two basic meanings: "acquire" and "retain," with "acquire" being most common.

In most cases, the verb translated "to acquire, to possess" refers to the acquisition of various articles, such as timber and stone (2 Kings 12:13; 22:6; 2 Chron. 34:11), spices (Isa. 43:24), a jug (Jer. 19:1), or a loin-cloth (13:1, 4). It may also refer to property, whether it was a field, a vineyard, a piece of land, a house (Gen. 25:10; 33:19; 49:30; 50:13; Lev. 25:28, 30; 27:24; Josh. 24:32; 2 Sam. 24:21, 24), livestock (12:3), a slave (Gen. 39:1; 47:19, 20; Exod. 21:2; Lev. 22:11; Deut. 28:68), or a wife (Ruth 4:5, 10). The word may also be used to indicate the ransom paid for a prisoner (Neh. 5:8). In all the above cases, it involves monetary payment or other compensation to a third party to obtain the property or things.

The verb may also refer to begetting a child, whether literally or symbolically. In this context, the verb is used only four times in the Old Testament (Gen. 4:1; Deut. 32:6; Ps. 139:13; Prov. 8:22). Out of these four occurrences, only Genesis 4:1 refers to a literal meaning when Eve claimed that she begot her firstborn Cain. It seems that Eve might have been aware of the difficulties of becoming pregnant, since she indicated that this time she became pregnant only due to God's help. If this is correct, then it is obvious that even if God is not a subject here, He played an important role in the process of begetting a child, and as such, He becomes an essential element in understanding the meaning of the verb "to acquire, to possess" in this context. In all other instances where it is used symbolically, the subject is God, and the object is a person (Ps. 139:13), the nation of Israel (Deut. 32:6), and wisdom (Prov. 8:22). So it seems that when God is the subject or when He is involved in the process of begetting, the parental side of the subject (God) is incorporated in the meaning of the verb "to acquire, to possess."

In Genesis 14:19, 22; Leviticus 25:28, 30, 50; Deuteronomy 26:68, the subject is a person, and the object is either property (Lev. 25:28, 30) or an individual (25:50) who needs to be redeemed during the year of jubilee. "To acquire, to possess" also appears once in Zechariah 13:5 with a slightly different meaning: "One who caused to possess."

Obviously, the context of Genesis 14:19, 22 does not leave much room for such an interpretation of the verb "to acquire, to possess," as suggested above ("buyer, one who caused to possess"). On the other hand, the most common interpretation as "maker" or "creator" as found in modern Bible translations is not correct either. Lipinski suggested a new argument that could clarify the enigma concerning the proper meaning in this context.[17] Using extrabiblical material from various inscriptions throughout the ancient Near East, he argues that the best translation of the phrase in Genesis 14:19, 22 is "Elyon, Lord of heaven and earth." If he is correct, then implementation of ownership is quite probable, which might be supported by Zechariah 13:5, where the verb is also used in its participle form. Furthermore, Lipinski indicates that the participle form of "to acquire, to possess" is part of some Hebrew and Aramaic names with the meaning of "Yahweh is the owner" or "Yahweh is begetter."[18] He supports his argument using some Ugaritic parallels where the word is combined with another word that means "the king is the owner."

Since the phrase "heaven and earth" is an object here, it is not difficult to associate this text with the Creation account.

Since God is presented as the One who creates everything, interpreters assumed the understanding of the verb translated "to acquire, to possess" here as "maker" or "creator." Even though this assumption may be correct, it does not utilize the full meaning of the utterance as it was desired by the author. He is not only presented here as a Maker or Creator without any emotions but as the One who is the Lord, Owner, or Possessor, which brings into light His legal obligation toward His creation. Legally, the heaven and earth are His possessions, but this also indicates His obligation to maintain and provide life support for the existence of all creatures, including human beings. This obligation is carefully pointed out by the author, who uses the verb translated as "to acquire, to possess" with this intention. As noted earlier, when God is subject, this verb is found in the context of begetting, bringing parental care into perspective. God is the Lord and Owner of heaven and earth; He acquired their existence; He is the One who cares for all He created with parental love and deep feelings for all His creation.

To Move and Formless. The verb translated as "to move" is used only three times in the entire Old Testament. Apart from Genesis 1:2, it appears in Deuteronomy 32:11 and Jeremiah 23:9. Due to its rare occurrence, its etymology is uncertain, but according to most lexicons, it has two distinctive meanings. It appears only once in Jeremiah 23:9, where it means "grow soft, relax, shake, tremble." Twice it is used to mean "hover, move, flutter." Interestingly, Deuteronomy 32:11 uses the words translated as "to move" and "formless" in the same context,

which is also the case in Genesis 1:2. Both words appear in the Pentateuch only twice, and both times in close proximity to each other.

The author of Deuteronomy 32:11 used the word translated "to move" in Moses's song in which God is the subject and Jacob is the object. Here, God is pictured caring for Jacob (who serves as a synonym for Israel) as an Eagle who "hovers" over its youngsters. In this context, it is clear that verb should be understood as a gesture of tenderheartedness with deep maternal feelings of love and care. Since both occurrences refer to creation of the world (Gen. 1:2) and the Jewish nation (Deut. 32:11), the meaning of the verb translated as "to move" is therefore reserved for gentle movements toward young ones as a sign of protection and assurance. It represents the parental provision of a safe and healthful environment that will ensure the necessary security for the youngster's further development.

When this understanding of the verb is transferred to Genesis 1:2, where the Spirit of God is "to move" over the waters, it is clear that this movement was a show of power, represented by tender love and care. It was a moving force behind God's eternal intentions and serves as a prelude to the imminent creation of everything on this planet. The author intentionally implemented the verb right in the beginning of the Creation account to indicate that not only careful planning preceded the act of Creation but God's love and the tender care He shows as a Parent was present from the very beginning of His creation. It also serves as a promise or indicator that the power of His parental love will find a way to save His children and the entire creation from disaster if anything goes wrong.

In addition to the above mentioned terminology that belongs to the corpus of creation language, there are additional aspects of the Pentateuchal material that have intertextual connections with the Creation narratives, which were covered by other publications and, as such, do not need to be elaborately dealt with here. It seems that Phyllis A. Bird states correctly that "canonically, the understanding of human nature expressed or implied in the laws . . . may be viewed as commentary on the creation texts."[19]

Conclusion

The author of the Pentateuch was extremely careful and selective in the choice of certain words to demonstrate certain important issues and effects of God's power of creation. It is reasonable to argue that the intention of the author was to indicate God's parental love right from the beginning as the driving force, resulting in the perfect creation of this planet and everything contained in it.

Most obviously, humanity was given a different role and function. God intended that the first humans were to rule responsibly over the entire creation, bearing in mind that they were accountable for their actions to their Creator. With this understanding, they accepted their royal role of protecting and preserving the Garden of Eden by rendering service to the entire creation. Furthermore, they received the gift of the Sabbath, which provides a covenantal rest as a perpetual sign of the Creator's authority and ownership as Suzerain King.

Notes

1. Fritz Stolz, "שׁבת šābat," in *Theological Lexicon of the Old Testament,* 3:1298.

2. Eernst Haag, "שׁבת šābat," in *Theological Dictionary of the Old Testament,* 14:382.

3. Kenneth A. Mathews, *Genesis 1-11:26* (Nashville, TN: Broadman & Holman, 1996), 179.

4. Page G. Kelley, *Biblical Hebrew: An Introductory Grammar* (Grand Rapids, MI: Eerdmans, 1992), 131.

5. Ibid., 173.

6. This is evident in Exodus 20 where the same device is used in eight of the Ten Commandments.

7. S. Meier, "שׂים," in *New International Dictionary of Old Testament Theology & Exegesis,* 3:1238.

8. Horst Dietrich Preuss, "נוּח nûaḥ," in *Theological Dictionary of the Old Testament,* 9:278.

9. J. N. Oswalt, "נוח," in *New International Dictionary of Old Testament Theology and Exegesis,* 3:57.

10. Claus Westermann, "'ebed," in *Theological Lexicon of the Old Testament,* 2:820, 21.

11. Klaus Baltzer, *Covenant Formulary in Old Testament, Jewish, and Early Christian Writings,* trans. David E. Green (Philadelphia: Fortress, 1971), 44–47.

12. Bruce K. Waltke and M. O'Connor, *An Introduction to Biblical Hebrew Syntax* (Winona Lake, ID: Eisenbrauns, 1989), 593.

13. Moshe Weinfeld, *Deuteronomy 1-11,* Anchor Bible, vol. 5 (New York: Doubleday, 1991), 302.

14. W. L. Holladay, *A Concise Hebrew and Aramaic Lexicon of the Old Testament* (Grand Rapids, MI: Eerdmans, 1971), 320.

15. S. P. Tregelles, *Gesenius' Hebrew and Chaldee Lexicon to the Old Testament Scriptures* (London: Chapman & Hall, 1905), 735.

16. Edward Lipinski, "הָנָק qānâ," in *Theological Dictionary of the Old Testament,* 13:59–62.

17. Ibid., 62, 63.

18. Ibid., 63.

19. Phyllis A. Bird, "Bone of My Bone and Flesh of My Flesh," *Theology Today* 50, no. 4 (January 1994): 255.

Creation in the Psalms: Psalm 104

Richard M. Davidson

tectonic paradigm shift in modern critical scholarship has occurred in the last few decades. And it has come to view Creation, and not just salvation history, as foundational to the rest of the Old Testament. Much attention has rightly been given to the Creation accounts in Genesis, since in the theological ground plan of the Old Testament, Genesis 1–3 has been considered the introduction to the canon, and the whole rest of the canon regularly harks back to and builds upon this Edenic pattern. Not nearly as much study has been given to the numerous references to Creation in the Psalms, which, by their sheer volume, surpass that of Genesis 1–3. References or allusions to Creation appear in more than fifty of the 150 psalms.

The psalmists usually allude specifically to Creation in expressions of other concerns. Creation motifs usually highlight numerous aspects of divine activity, such as the election of Israel, the Exodus, the deliverance of the psalmist from trouble, and God's ongoing providence and preservation of His Creation. But one psalm—from beginning to end—has as its subject God's Creation of the world: Psalm 104.

A close look at Psalm 104 may shed light upon the issues of the origins of the heavens and earth.

Questions of Introduction

There is no superscription for Psalm 104 in the Hebrew Bible. The Greek and Latin versions, however, give as the heading "A Psalm of David." This is no doubt due to the words "bless the LORD, O my soul," at the beginning and end of Psalms 103 and 104. Psalm 103 contains the superscription "A Psalm of David."

These are the only two psalms with the phrase "bless the LORD, O my soul." And other common features link the two psalms. The last stanza of Psalm 103 ends with an evocation of God's cosmic rule, and Psalm 104 begins with this same evocation. There are also a striking number of verbal connections scattered throughout the two psalms. "Such links suggest a common authorship for these two psalms, and this impression gets even stronger when their subject-matters are taken into account."[1]

In the final canonical arrangement of the Psalter, where these psalms are placed back to back, it seems very likely that they are meant to stand together as Davidic psalms. The omission of the inscription for Psalm 104 may be for theological reasons, to link this psalm even more closely with the previous one, revealing the continuity of theological themes between the two.[2]

Some have seen a link between Psalm 104 and "The Hymn to Aten" composed in the fourteenth century B.C. reign of

Amenophis IV, a hymn honoring the sun disk Aten as the supreme and sole creator. The composer of Psalm 104 may have been acquainted with "The Hymn to Aten" and utilized some of its imagery in his composition. But the parallels between the two compositions are few and imprecise: only seventeen of the 149 lines of "The Hymn to Aten" show any similarities with Psalm 104. Furthermore, the focus of the two compositions is different. Hence, even if the composer of Psalm 104 knew of the Egyptian hymn and borrowed some of its phraseology, he pressed the imagery into his own original composition. And the language he did borrow may well have been with polemical as well as aesthetic intent.

Scholars have recognized this psalm as one of the most, if not the most, intricately and exquisitely crafted literary productions in the entire Psalter. "The psalm is remarkable for the movement and vividness of the images that crowd into the picture of creation. In this respect it is probably unsurpassed in literature. Someone has said that it would be worth studying Hebrew for ten years if as a result of that study the student could read this psalm in the original."[3]

"Psalm 104 was composed with unabashed joy and freedom of expression," writes scholar William Brown, "and yet it exhibits a theological sophistication scarcely matched by any other psalm. Here, rigorous thinking and rapturous wonder find a compelling convergence. The world, as grand and manifold as it is, is inscribed with coherence and conviviality."[4] Such theological depth is especially apparent as the psalmist insightfully interprets the Creation narratives of Genesis.

Psalm 104 as Inner Biblical Interpretation of Genesis 1–3

If the Genesis Creation narratives were written by Moses (fifteenth century B.C.), as assumed in this study, and if Psalm 104 was written by David (tenth century B.C.), as argued above, then Psalm 104 is clearly dependent upon Genesis 1–3 and not vice versa. There is general consensus that Psalm 104 "is a poetic retelling of the Genesis story, and it therefore falls under the rubric of 'inner biblical interpretation.' "[5]

There is wide recognition among Old Testament scholars that Psalm 104 not only interprets the Genesis Creation accounts but also follows the same basic order as the days of Creation in Genesis 1. Walter Zorn writes, "A summary of the Creation account is contained in the psalm, similar to the record in Genesis chapter one. . . . Following the order of Creation as given in Genesis, he [the psalmist] shows how God, in successive stages, was preparing for the welfare and comfort of his creatures."[6]

Franz Delitzsch classifies this psalm as a "Hymn in Honour of the God of the Seven Days."[7] He then summarizes its contents: "The Psalm is altogether an echo of the . . . history of the seven days of Creation . . . in Gen. i.1–ii.3. Corresponding to the seven days it falls into seven groups. . . . It begins with the light and closes with an allusion to the divine Sabbath."[8]

Jacques B. Doukhan's dissertation on the literary structure of the Genesis Creation story contains a penetrating analysis of the literary structure of Psalm 104 and its parallels with the Genesis Creation accounts. Doukhan's delineation of the seven days of Creation week as portrayed in Psalm 104 builds upon both thematic and termino-logical correspondences. Thematically, the following outline emerges: [9]

Day One: motif of light (Ps. 104:2a)

Day Two: creation of firmament, refer-ence to waters above (vv. 2b–4)

Day Three: appearance of the ground: for-mation of the earth plants (vv. 5–18)

Day Four: luminaries to indicate seasons and time (vv. 19–23)

Day Five: first mention of animals in terms of creatures; allusion to birds; sea and living beings in it (vv. 24–26)

Day Six: food for animals and man; gift of life by God for animals and man (vv. 27–30)

Day Seven: glory of God; allusion to the revelation on Sinai (vv. 31, 32)

Doukhan shows that there are also the-matic connections between Psalm 104 (in the sections dealing with humankind) and the second Genesis Creation account (Gen. 2:4b). He also points out how each of the seven sections of Psalm 104 shares signif-icant, common wording with its corre-sponding section of the Genesis Creation narrative (1:1–2:4a). [10]

In his article on Creation in the *Handbook of Seventh-day Adventist Theology,* William Shea exams the correspondences between the Creation week of Genesis 1:1–2:4a and Psalm 104 and presents an outline similar to that of Doukhan and others. Shea points out that Psalm 104, in following the order of events of the six days of Creation, often "utilizes an anticipation of what would come about from those days; it looks for-ward to their potential, their function, and their benefit." [11]

Delitzsch expresses it the other way around, stressing the psalmist's focus upon the present condition of the world: "The poet sings the God-ordained present condition of the world with respect to the creative beginnings recorded in Genesis i.1–ii. 3." [12] In light of the use of the word translated as "create" in Psalm 104:30 with regard to God's continued preservation of His Creation, it is not inappropriate to speak of Psalm 104 as describing both the original Creation and the preservation of Creation by YHWH, the sovereign Creator. Thus, the poetic depiction of the events of Creation includes not only completed ac-tion but also ongoing action.

The psalmist presents the Creation ac-count in dialogue with real life in the here and now. It is assumed that he not only penetrates the meaning of the Genesis Cre-ation narratives but he interprets. Yet, as a poet inspired by the Spirit, he is capable of supplying new insights into issues of or-igins that may not be found explicit, or at all, in the Genesis Creation accounts.

Psalm 104 and Issues of Origins

Day One (Ps. 104:1, 2a). In the first section of Psalm 104 (following the introductory "bless the LORD, O my soul"), the psalmist praises God with the motif of light found in the first day of Creation week (Gen. 1:3–5): "O LORD my God, You are very great; You are clothed with splendor and maj-esty, covering Yourself with light as with a cloak." Whereas in Genesis 1:3 God says, "Let there be light," Psalm 104 gives more detail regarding that light.

Shea points out how this statement in verses 1, 2a solves an unanswered question arising from the Genesis Creation account re-garding the source of light in Creation before the appearance of the sun and moon on the fourth day: "From His radiant glory the light of Creation issues. Psalm 104 provides an answer to the long-standing question about the source of the light on the first day of Creation: The light that surrounded the person of God provided light for the earth."[13] As God Himself provides the light on the first day, He makes a theological statement that Creation is ultimately not human centered or centered in the sun but centered in God (theocentric). The theocentric nature of Creation is a dominant theme throughout the entire psalm.

Day Two (Ps. 104:2b–4). Verses 2b–4 describes the creation of the firmament, with focus upon the waters above (separated from the waters below, described in the next section), corresponding to the second day of Creation week (Gen. 1:6–8). With poetic similes and metaphors, the psalmist depicts YHWH as the One who is "stretching out [the atmospheric] heavens like a curtain, laying the beams of His upper chambers in the waters, making the clouds His chariot, walking upon the wings of the wind, making the winds His messengers, flaming fire, His ministers."[14] By repeated use of participles in Psalm 104:1–4, the author places emphasis upon the Doer ("The one who . . .") and not so much upon the deeds. The phraseology of "stretching out the heavens like a curtain" highlights the ease with which God creates (in contrast to the other accounts of Creation by struggle and conflict). It also gives further support to the conclusion that the Hebrew word usually translated "firmament" in Genesis 1 does not refer to a solid dome, as many modern scholars have asserted.

The language of this section, as well as other portions of the psalm, have been seen by some scholars to parallel the portrayals of the Canaanite storm god, Baal, the "Rider of the Clouds," in Ugaritic literature. If such parallelism exists and the psalmist consciously employs language from Ugaritic poetry (as seems probable for such psalms as Ps. 29), the motivation of the psalmist is not only to employ vivid poetic imagery to describe YHWH but also to insist that it is YHWH, not Baal, who is the true "Rider of the Clouds" and the One who controls the elements of nature, including the atmosphere and the storms.

Day Three (Ps. 104:5–18). Verses 5–18 corresponds to the third day of Creation week (Gen. 1:9–18), which involved the gathering of the waters under heaven within divinely ordained boundaries, the appearing of the dry ground, and the formation of vegetation on the earth. Psalm 104:5–6a switch to the completed action and set the background for the events of day three by referring to the origin of the "unformed-unfilled" state of the earth described in Genesis 1:1, 2 (prior to the events of the first day): "He [has] established the earth upon its foundations, So that it will not totter forever and ever. You [have] covered it with the deep as with a garment." As a Master Builder, God has established the earth and its foundations with such permanence that "it will not totter forever and ever." The word translated as "deep" in Psalm 104:6a is the same as in Genesis 1:2: "Darkness was over the surface of the deep." The fact that the deep here is compared to a piece of clothing fits with the literal understanding of the term in Genesis 1.

Psalm 104:6b–9 then vividly and elaborately describe the divine command and activity in causing dry land to appear, which in Genesis 1:9 is depicted by a single brushstroke: "God said, 'Let the waters below the heavens be gathered into one place, and let the dry land appear'; and it was so." The poetic description of the divine fiat and action heighten the vividness by a sense of immediacy: "The waters stood above the mountains. They fled at Your blast, rushed away at the sound of Your thunder,—mountains rising, valleys sinking—to the place You established for them. You set bounds they must not pass so that they never again cover the earth" (NJPS).

Although the waters of the deep in Psalm 104 are not mythologized as a chaos monster with whom YHWH must struggle, nonetheless there is a hint of the tremendous power behind their waves as they envelop the earth. God's command described by the neutral verb "said" in Genesis 1:9 is intensified in Psalm 104 to a divine "rebuke" of the waters. In response to the divine rebuke, the waters "fled," or they "hurried away." Such language may actually constitute a polemic against Canaanite mythology, affirming that YHWH, unlike the storm god in the Canaanite combat myth, did not have to struggle to subdue the sea; the sea obeyed his voice!

Psalm 104 also provides details about earth's topography as it came forth from the Creator's hands: there were mountains! According to verse 6, mountains existed under the surface of the watery deep, even in the "unformed-unfilled" condition of the earth described in Genesis 1:2. According to Psalm 104:7, 8, dry land appeared as a result of new activity of mountain uplift and valley depression: the waters "fled at Your blast, rushed away at the sound of Your thunder,—mountains rising, valleys sinking—to the place You established for them" (NJPS). What may be inferred from Genesis 1—four rivers coming from a common source flow in four different directions imply that they must begin from an elevated place like a mountain—is made explicit in Psalm 104:8. Leupold graphically sets forth the implications of this verse: "We can scarcely conceive the stupendous upheavals and readjustments that took place at that time and on so vast a scale. But none of this movement was left to blind chance. . . . Everything was continually under perfect divine control."[15]

This section of Psalm 104, as viewed in the context of what precedes and what follows, refers primarily to the third day of Creation and not to the Genesis flood. Other biblical references associate Creation with the formation of mountains (Prov. 8:25, 26; Ps. 90:2). The phrase stating that the waters "will not return to cover the earth" should probably also be interpreted as primarily referring to Creation, inasmuch as other clear references to Creation have parallel language of God setting boundaries for the sea (Prov. 8:29; Job 38:10, 11). But since the psalm was written after the worldwide Flood recorded in Genesis 6–9 (when Creation was returned to its "unformed-unfilled" state as at the beginning of the third day of Creation), the psalmist may also be alluding to the Genesis flood in his assurance that the waters "will not return to cover the earth," in parallel with the clear reference to the Flood in Isaiah 54:9.

Patrick D. Miller Jr. perceptively notes

that in the psalmist's description of Psalm 104:5–9, "The Creation of the earth thus occurs in two stages, both of which are the Lord's doing: the covering of earth with the deep and the movement of these waters to places where they may function in a constructive way (see vv. 10–13)."[16] This may provide further support for a two-stage Creation described in Genesis 1, with the Creation of earth in its "unformed-unfilled," water-covered state occurring "in the beginning" before Creation week (Gen. 1:1, 2) and the causing of dry land to appear occurring on day three of Creation (vv. 9, 10).

The poetic interpretation of the third day of Creation week places special emphasis upon the water involved in God's creative activity, including not only the primordial deep that existed prior to Creation week (Gen. 1:1–3) and the gathering of the water together within boundaries so that dry land might appear on day three proper (Ps. 104:9, 10) but also the water that God employs to moisten the earth in His continuing preservation of His Creation. Verses 10–12 describe the water in the form of springs that God continually "sends forth" to "give drink to every beast of the field" (v. 11) and provide habitat for "the birds of the heavens" (v. 12).

Verse 13 depicts the rain water from "His upper chambers" by which God is "watering the mountains." The reference to rain does not imply that rain was created during Creation week—the Genesis Creation account specifically precludes this (Gen. 2:5, 6). Rather, the verses of this section of Psalm 104 describe God's preservation of the world or providence after Creation week (and the rain that came at the time of the Flood and

after) for the purpose of satisfying the needs of His creatures: "The earth is satisfied with the fruit of His works" (v. 13).

These verses may, like previous ones in the psalm, also contain an implicit polemic against central tenants of Canaanite religion. The Hebrew poet insists that it was YHWH who freely and graciously provided the water necessary for the earth's fertility, without need for humans to arouse and stimulate Him by means of sexual orgies on the high places as in the fertility cults.

Verses 14–17 move to a description of vegetation that was created on the third day of Creation week. Verse 14 describes the two main kinds of vegetation created by God: "The grass to grow for the cattle, and vegetation for the labor of man, so that he may bring forth food from the earth." This harks back not only to the description of God's Creation of vegetation on the third day in Genesis 1:11, 12 but also alludes to the vegetarian diet provided for the land creatures that were created on the sixth day (vv. 29, 30): "every green plant" for the nonhuman species (v. 30, NASB) and "every plant yielding seed . . . and every tree which has fruit yielding seed" for humans (v. 29, NASB). The post-Fall benefit of God's Creation of vegetation for humans is displayed as the psalmist refers to the delicacies of wine, oil, and bread that strengthen and gladden the heart of man (Ps. 104:14, 15). There are three evidences of God's bountiful provision for human needs. In these verses, the psalmist emphasizes what was already implicit in Genesis 1, namely the purposefulness of God's creative activity in providing for and bringing joy to His creatures.

Psalm 104:16, 17 turn from the edible vegetation to the majestic "trees of the LORD." God's care for the trees is underscored as they "drink their fill," and these mighty trees, including the cedars of Lebanon and the fir trees, in turn demonstrate purposefulness in providing habitat for the birds. Verse 18 concludes this section with one more look at the majestic high mountains and cliffs, again underscoring the purposefulness of their creation: the mountains are "for the wild goats"; the cliffs are "a refuge for the [coneys or rock badgers]."

Walter Harrelson summarizes this divine purposefulness for the creatures described in this section of the psalm: "God made fir trees for the storks to nest in, and he made storks to nest in the fir trees. He made high, inaccessible mountains for the wild goats to run and jump upon, and he made wild goats to do the jumping and cavorting. He created the vast expanse of rock-covered earth in eastern Jordan for rock badgers to live and play in, and he created rock badgers for the rocks. Storks and goats and rock badgers do not serve mankind. They do what is appropriate to them, and God provided a place that is itself fulfilling its function when it ministers to the needs of its special creatures."[17]

Day Four (Ps. 104:19–23). The next section of Psalm 104:19–23, provides a poetic interpretation of the fourth day of Creation week as described in Genesis 1:14–19. The psalmist does not feel the need that Moses did in Genesis 1 to use the circumlocution "greater light" for the term "sun" and "lesser light" for the term "moon"; apparently, he was not worried that he might be misunderstood to describe deities when he gave the actual names for the celestial bodies (Ps. 104:19). The psalmist also does not follow the order in which the celestial bodies are presented in Genesis 1. Instead, he first refers to the moon and then the sun: "He made the moon for the seasons; the sun knows the place of its setting" (v. 19). In the verses that follow, it is the night that is first described (vv. 20, 21), followed by the day (v. 22). This seems to be the poet's way of highlighting the evening-morning sequence of the days in Creation, without explicitly stating as much.

As in Genesis 1:14, for the psalmist, the moon exists for the purpose of marking "seasons" (Ps. 104:19). But beyond this purpose, the night, over which the moon rules, is purposeful in the post-Fall condition of the world to provide time for animals to prowl and seek their food: "You appoint darkness and it becomes night, in which all the beasts of the forest prowl about. The young lions roar after their prey and seek their food from God" (vv. 20, 21). The night is for the animals, but the day is for the purpose of providing time for humans to labor: "When the sun rises they [the animals] withdraw and lie down in their dens. Man goes forth to his work and to his labor until evening" (vv. 22, 23). The reference to human "labor" may hark back to the description of human labor in the Garden of Eden (Gen. 2:15) and, particularly, to the depiction of human labor outside the garden (3:23), showing that the psalmist was providing a poetic interpretation of Genesis 2; 3 as well as Genesis 1.

Although the composer of Psalm 104 is selective in his use of materials from the

Genesis Creation accounts, it does not appear accidental or arbitrary that he omits any reference to the stars in dealing with the Creation on the fourth day. The grammatical structure of Genesis 1:16 implies that the stars were not created on the fourth day but already existed before the commencement of Creation week. By not mentioning the stars in this section of the Psalm, the poet seems to lend further support to that conclusion.

Day Five (Ps. 104:24-26). As will be pointed out below, this psalm not only follows the sequence of the days of Creation but also reveals a chiastic symmetry among these days. Verse 24 is central to that chiasm, in which the psalmist exuberantly extols YHWH for His works of Creation: "O Lord, how many are Your works! In wisdom You have made them all; the earth is full of Your possessions." This verse looks both backward and forward in the psalm (note the word *works,* which harks back to v. 13 and forward to v. 31), and may be seen as a transition between day four and day five. It links YHWH's Creation with wisdom; in a later inspired Creation poem (Prov. 8), this Wisdom will be set forth as a hypostasis for the divine Son of God, the pre-existent Christ. The Hebrew expression translated by NASB and some other versions as "Your possessions," in the context of this psalm, should probably be rendered "your creatures" (i.e., the ones created)—or better, "your creations"—again, highlighting the dominant Creation theme of the psalm.

Though Psalm 104:24 is the central verse in the psalm, pointing both backward and forward, at the same time, it has language that may be linked specifically to day five of

Creation (and beyond). As Doukhan points out, "Up to now the animals are mentioned merely in connection with the Creation of the earth (as inhabitants) and the Creation of the luminaries (as their indications of daily life); only from day five on, are the animals concerned as created."[18]

Verses 24–26 focus on the fifth day of Creation week in Genesis 1, during which God made the birds of the air and the inhabitants of the sea (Gen. 1:20–23). The Creation of the birds is not explicitly mentioned in this section, perhaps because they have already been referred to (twice) in connection with the description of the purpose of the vegetation of the third day (Ps. 104:12, 17). There is, however, probably a subtle allusion to the birds in the echo between the rare Hebrew term for "possessions, creature, Creation" in verse 24 and a similar-sounding, rare Hebrew term for "to make a nest" in verse 17. This echoing allows the psalmist in verse 24 "by means of the alliteration, [to] refer to the idea the former word conveys. This is common practice in Hebrew poetry."[19] Without actually mentioning the birds in verse 24, the psalmist is able to allude to them (and their building of nests) by means of the alliterative echo between verses 17 and 24.

The main emphasis of this section is upon the creatures of the sea. Verse 25 provides an overview: "There is the sea, great and broad, in which are swarms without number, animals both small and great." The poetic representation in this verse is short, but paucity of poetic lines is offset by their length. Verse 25 constitutes the longest metrical line of the psalm.

Along with the fish comes the somewhat

surprising mention of ships, human-made vessels, in contrast with the works of God: "There the ships move along" (v. 26a). However, the mention of ships is not so surprising when one realizes that the focus of this section is upon the things that move along "there," that is, in the sea. The psalmist, describing the ongoing benefits of the Creation week, does not hesitate to fill in the picture of the teeming life in the sea by noting the movement of the ships.

In the next breath, the psalmist describes the sea creature Leviathan (v. 26b). Although elsewhere in Scripture, Leviathan is described in terms that are likely redeployed from mythology as a rebellious sea monster that has to be conquered and destroyed by God (74:14; Isa. 27:1), in this psalm, Leviathan is depicted as one of the giant sea creatures that God "formed to sport in it [the sea]" (Ps. 104:26b). This is reminiscent of the picture of Leviathan found in Job 41. It is a creature "formed" by God. Genesis 2:7, 19 indicates that God "formed" Adam, the large land animals, and the birds. Now, from Psalm 104:26, we learn that at least one of the sea creatures was also "formed" by God. Furthermore, this verse tells us the purpose of God's creating Leviathan, namely "to sport or play" in the sea! This alludes to a theology of divine play, which is further elaborated in Proverbs 8, with Wisdom (the Son of God) mediating between creatures and YHWH in their joyous play. This insight into the joyous and celebrative attitude of God while creating expands the understanding of His character from what might be learned only from the Creation accounts of Genesis 1; 2.

Day Six (Ps. 104:27-30). Land animals and human beings, created on the sixth day according to Genesis 1:24–31, have already been mentioned in earlier verses of Psalm 104, where the poet describes God's provision for their food. In this section, the psalmist refers back to that depiction: "They all wait for You to give them their food in due season. You give to them, they gather it up; You open Your hand, they are satisfied with good" (vv. 27, 28). The word for "good" harks back to the repeated refrain in Genesis 1; 2 that what God created was "good" and in particular to the sixth day of Creation, where the term is used by God twice (Gen. 1:25, 31). It may also allude to Genesis 2:18, in which Adam's existence without a partner was described as "not good," and therefore by implication, God's supplying him with a partner is "good."

A crucial aspect of the sixth day emphasized by the psalmist in this stanza of Psalm 104 is God's giving life to humans and land animals by filling them with His breath, as described in Genesis 2:7 (of Adam) and in the Flood narrative (of other land creatures as well). In this same passage, he also alludes to the post-Fall state of the world in which death occurs as God withdraws his Spirit or breath from His creatures, and they return to dust (Gen. 3:19): "You hide Your face, they are dismayed; You take away their spirit, they expire and return to dust. You send forth Your Spirit they are created; and You renew the face of the ground" (Ps. 104:29, 30).

The term translated as "created," which describes the activity unique to God in effortlessly bringing into existence something totally new, is used in Genesis 1; 2 particularly (although not exclusively) to describe the Creation of humans during the first Creation week (Gen. 1:27). But Psalm 104:30 shows that every human, as well as every other creature on earth, who has been born since that first Creation week, is the product of God's continuing creative work. Though Genesis 1 gives special place to humans in the Creation account as having dominion over the animals, and other psalms (such as Ps. 8) underscore this role of humans vis-à-vis the animal kingdom, Psalm 104 emphasizes the similarity of all of God's creatures having the breath of life. All are ultimately dependent upon God for their life and sustenance.

This stanza ends on a note of hope: "You [YHWH] renew the face of the ground" (v. 30b). This phraseology is a reversal of the curse of Genesis 3:19 ("By the sweat of your face you will eat bread, till you return to the ground") and of the destruction at the time of the Flood ("Thus He blotted out every living thing that was upon the face of the land" [Gen. 7:23]). In His ongoing providential care for His creation, God continues to renew the face of the ground, in other words, "replenish all the living of the earth" (NLT).

Day Seven (Ps. 104:31-35). Though numerous scholars have recognized that Psalm 104 follows the same basic order as the six days of Creation in Genesis 1, there is little attempt to connect the last five verses with the Genesis Creation account. If the first thirty verses of Psalm 104 have a clear parallel, section by section, with the sequence of the six days of Creation, why is there little recognition of the possibility that the last section of Psalm 104 might parallel the seventh day of Creation, the Sabbath?

What has been largely, if not entirely, overlooked by many recent commentators has been emphasized in Delitzsch's classic nineteenth-century Old Testament commentary. As noted earlier, Delitzsch labels this psalm as a "Hymn in Honour of the God of the Seven Days"[20] and summarizes its contents as "altogether an echo of the . . . history of the seven days of creation . . . in Gen. i.1–ii.3. Corresponding to the seven days it falls into seven groups. . . . It begins with the light and closes with an allusion to the divine Sabbath."[21] In the final section of Psalm 104, verses 31–35, Delitzsch finds a clear allusion to the Sabbath: "The poet has now come to an end with the review of the wonders of the Creation, and closes in this seventh group . . . with a sabbatic meditation."[22]

This "sabbatic meditation" begins with the poet's wish: "Let the glory of the LORD endure forever; let the LORD be glad in His works" (v. 31). The psalmist "wishes that the glory of God, which He has put upon His creatures, and which is reflected and echoed back by them to Him, may continue for ever, and that His works may ever be so constituted that He who was satisfied at the completion of His six days' work may be able to rejoice in them."[23]

Especially significant in linking this final stanza of the poem to the Sabbath is the close relationship between the reference to the poet's rejoicing in YHWH (v. 34) and the reference to YHWH's rejoicing in creation (v. 31): "Between 'I will rejoice,' ver. 34, and 'He shall rejoice,' ver. 31, there exists a reciprocal relation, as between the Sabbath of the creature in God and the Sabbath of God in the creature."[24]

There is also an eschatological implication of the sabbatical meditation, in the poet's linkage of rejoicing in creation with the destruction of the wicked: "When the Psalmist wishes that God may have joy in His works of Creation, and seeks on his part to please God and to have his joy in God, he is also warranted in wishing that those who take pleasure in wickedness, and instead of giving God joy excite His wrath, may be removed from the earth . . . ; for they are contrary to the purpose of the good Creation of God, they imperil its continuance, and mar the joy of His creatures."[25]

Two Seventh-day Adventist scholars have called special attention to the Sabbath allusion in Psalm 104:31–35. In his doctoral dissertation, Doukhan points out the thematic and terminological parallels between Genesis 1:1–2:4a and Psalm 104. He notes the thematic correspondence of the glory of God in Creation and the allusion to the revelation on Sinai in Psalm 104:32, and then he draws the implication: "This reference to Sinai in direct association with the very concern of creation points to the Sabbath."

Doukhan also points to the fact that both the introduction and conclusion of Psalm 104 (vv. 1, 33, and nowhere else in the Psalm) bring together the two names employed for God in Genesis 1; 2: Elohim and YHWH. This may imply the poet's recognition of the unity and complementarity of the two accounts of Creation in Genesis 1; 2.[26]

The other Adventist scholar to call attention to the Sabbath allusion in Psalm 104 is Shea: "In Genesis the account of Creation week goes on to describe the seventh day. The psalm has something similar. On the Sabbath we recognize that God is our Creator; we honor Him in the commemoration of Creation. That is the first thing mentioned in Psalm 104:31. When God finished His Creation, He said that it was 'very good.' In Psalm 104 He rejoices in His works (verse 31)."[27]

Shea's major contribution to the Sabbath theology of Psalm 104 may be in drawing out the significance of what is described in verse 32: "He looks at the earth, and it trembles; He touches the mountains, and they smoke." Shea comments: "This is the picture of a theophany, the manifestation of God's personal presence. This is what happens on the Sabbath when the Lord draws near to His people and makes Himself known. Struck with reverential awe, they render Him worship."[28]

As Shea points out, that worship is depicted in the final verses of the psalm: "Human beings bring worship and honor and glory and praise to God (verse 33). This is not a onetime occurrence: The psalmist promises to carry on this activity as long as life lasts. The praises of the Lord are on the lips of the psalmist continually. Silence is another part of worship. In verse 34 the psalmist asks that silent meditation upon the Lord may be pleasing to God. Finally, this reflection upon worship ends with rejoicing (verse 35)."[29]

There appears to be sufficient evidence that Psalm 104 not only refers to the first six days of Creation week but also, in its final stanza, alludes to the seventh-day Sabbath of Genesis 2:1–4a. Significant insights into the Sabbath emerge from Psalm 104:31–35, including themes of God's glorification and rejoicing in His created works (v. 31), the presence of God (v. 32) leading to reverential awe and exuberant singing and praise in worship (v. 33), meditation upon and joy in the Lord (v. 34), and the wish-prayer for an eschatological end of the wicked who refuse to praise God (v. 35).

Chiastic Symmetry Among the Days of Creation

The inspired composer of Psalm 104 not only structures his composition in the sequence of the days of Creation but also sets forth a symmetrical arrangement among these days. Though many scholars have

recognized the symmetrical arrangement of the Genesis Creation days, the psalmist's close reading of the Genesis Creation account has also apparently detected a chiastic pattern among these days, the structure of which he employs in his composition. Recognizing this chiastic structure goes far in explaining what elements of the various days of Creation were highlighted by the psalmist to poetically display the chiasm, while also remaining faithful to the six-day flow of Genesis 1. The chiastic structure of Psalm 104 may be schematically diagramed like this:

A. Introduction (Ps. 104:1a): "Bless the Lord O my soul"
  B. Day One (vv. 1b, 2a): praise and theophany; "Yhwh, my God"
    C. Day Two (vv. 2b–4): emphasis upon the wind, spirit, or breath
      D. Day Three (vv. 5–18): emphasis upon the deep, sea waters, and springs
        E. Day Four (vv. 19–24): moon, sun, and climactic exultation
      D'. Day Five (vv. 25, 26): emphasis upon the sea and its moving things
    C'. Day Six (vv. 27–30): emphasis upon the spirit or breath
  B'. Day Seven (vv. 31–35a): theophany and praise; "Yhwh, my God"
A'. Conclusion (v. 35b): "Bless the Lord, O my soul." Coda: "Hallelujah"

A Theology of Psalm 104 and Its Adjacent Psalms

Two Major Theological Themes. Two terms that stand out in bold relief in Psalm 104 are translated as "works or made" (Ps. 104:4, 13, 19, 24, 31) and "satisfy" (vv. 13, 16, 28). These constitute the two main theological points of the psalm: God's initial "works" of Creation and His continual "satisfying" or providing for His creation. Though other biblical Creation accounts (such as Genesis 1) focus upon God's initial Creation, Psalm 104 is virtually unique in emphasizing God's continuing creation.

"Here," writes Harrelson, "we confront a picture of Creation different from any

Creation stories or motifs in the entire Hebrew Bible, so far as I can see. God the creator works continually at the task of Creation. . . . All life depends at every moment upon the quickening spirit of God. There is no life without the divine breath. . . . [The psalmist in Psalm 104] is portraying a direct dependence of all things, all life, upon the active presence of God, in every moment, for all time."[30]

Psalm 104 uniquely and powerfully joins both initial and continuous work of divine Creation. As Miller remarks: "Surely no text of Scripture speaks more directly and in detail about the Creation and about what God did and does in creation and in the sustaining of creation than does this psalm."[31]

Historicity and Literality of the Genesis Creation Narratives. After affirming the theological importance of Psalm 104 as a Creation text, Miller joins others who have argued that, since the psalm is written in poetry, it should not be interpreted literally (as really having happened as described): "Here [Psalm 104], however, there is no external report vulnerable to literal and scientific analysis. One cannot analyze Psalm 104 that way. It is poetry, and we know not to interpret poetry literally."[32]

Hebrew poetry does indeed contain an abundance of imagery, which must be recognized and interpreted as such. But it is incorrect to conclude that, after taking into account the obvious imagery involved, Hebrew poetry should not be interpreted literally. Quite the contrary, in the Hebrew Bible the poetic genre does not negate a literal interpretation of the events described (e.g., Exod. 15; Dan. 7; and some 40 percent of the Old Testament, which is in poetry). In fact, biblical writers often wrote in poetry to underscore what is literally and historically true. The poetic representation of the seven days of Creation in Psalm 104 does not negate the literality and historicity of the Genesis Creation week any more than the poetic representation of the Exodus in Psalms 105; 106 negates the literality and historicity of the Exodus events or the poetic representation of the Babylonian captivity in Psalm 137 negates the literality and historicity of the Exile.

Purposefulness, Beauty, and Joy of Creation. Psalm 104 not only assumes and builds upon the literality of the Genesis Creation accounts, but it reaffirms and amplifies the sense of orderliness and purposefulness that emerges from Genesis 1 and 2. Everything is created "in wisdom" (Ps. 104:24), in an orderly way, and has its purpose. The psalm also underscores and develops the sense of beauty and pleasure that God's orderly, purposeful Creation brings, not only to His creatures but to God Himself. This is already implied in Genesis 1 as God proclaims His works good and beautiful (the meaning of the Hebrew *ṭôb*), but it comes into full expression in the exquisitely wrought turns of phrase and plenitude of imagery in Psalm 104, climaxing with the exclamation: "Let the LORD be glad in His works" (v. 31). This aesthetic, pleasurable quality of God's Creation also contains an element of joy (note the threefold use of "glad" in vv. 15, 31, 34b) and even playfulness (in reference to the Leviathan of v. 26).

Post-Fall Perspective. At the same time, Psalm 104 often describes God's created world from the perspective of how it functions after the Fall. Notice, for example, the reference to rainfall from God's upper chambers (v. 13), in contrast to the mist that rose from the ground in pre-Fall Eden (Gen. 2:5, 6); the existence of predatory activity on the part of animals (Ps. 104:20, 21), in contrast to the vegetarian diet of all animals in Genesis 1:29, 30; the cultivation of the earth by humans at labor (Ps. 104:14, 23; cf. Gen. 3:18), which may be in contrast to the pre-Fall tending and keeping of the trees and plants in the Garden of Eden (2:8–15); and the existence of sinners and wicked who need to be consumed (Ps. 104:35; cf. Gen. 3), in contrast to a perfect world without sin in pre-Fall Eden (Gen.

1; 2). These references of the psalmist are not to be taken as contradicting the picture presented in Genesis 1; 2; they are in keeping with the psalmist's poetic strategy to blend the depiction of the seven days of Creation week with a view of God's preservation of Creation in its present condition after the Fall. The psalmist does not teach death and predation before sin, as some have claimed.

Human Interdependence and Integration With the Rest of Creation. One especially surprising theological feature of the psalm comes in its depiction of humans within the scheme of Creation. Unlike Psalm 8, which builds upon Genesis 1:26–28 and emphasizes humanity's God-given dominion over the rest of Creation, Psalm 104 emphasizes that all sensate beings, whom God has created, share this world together.

"There is a clear distinction between humankind and the different animals, but they are talked about in parallel ways as creatures of the world God has made. Humankind assumes not a central or special place but an integral part of the whole. . . . There is thus no language of domination, no *imago dei* that sets human beings apart from or puts them in rule over the other beasts. . . . While bypassing all the complex issues of the interrelationships among these 'creatures,' the psalm assumes a world in which they are all present, all in their place, all doing their work, and all provided for by God's goodness."[33]

Psalm 104 does not deny the model of dominion that is highlighted in Genesis 1 and Psalm 8, but it stresses what has been called by some the model of "integration." Harrelson goes even further than

integration when he describes the intrinsic importance of other created things apart from humanity: "I know of no more direct word in the Bible about the independent significance of things and creatures on which man does not depend for life. . . . God has interest in badgers and wild goats and storks for their own sakes. He has interest in trees and mountains and rock-cairns that simply serve nonhuman purposes."[34] *God* cares for *His* earth!

Ecological Concerns. Though there is great potential elsewhere for a full development of the ecological concerns of Psalm 104, it must be noted here that the psalm describes the interdependence of natural phenomena in such a way as to highlight what we would today speak of in ecological terms.

Psalm 104 "is informed by a basic ecological sense of the interdependence of things. Water, topology, and the change of seasons and day and night form an intricate system in which creatures live. . . . What has been rent asunder in the modern view of the world, with consequences for motivation and conduct only recently grasped, is held together here—knowledge of the world and knowledge of God. To intervene in the flow of water, the habitat of birds and animals, the topography of the earth, is to breach an intricate divine ecology into which human life itself is integrated."[35]

Recent studies on Creation care frequently reference Psalm 104. It affirms fundamental biblical principles of environmental concern, for example, the goodness of God's creation; God's active and unceasing sustaining of the world's existence at both macro and micro levels; His generous and loving care for both humans and the rest of the animals, birds, and fish; the God-focused purpose shared by humans with all creation (Ps. 104:27, 28); God's establishment of the relationship between the earth and the water (vv. 5–9); and His provision of water for all creatures after the Fall (vv. 10–13), even for sea creatures, such as Leviathan (vv. 25, 26), and for the trees (v. 16).

The reference to sinners and wicked in verse 35 also may call attention to ecological concerns. Although such general terms may have in view any acts of sin and wickedness committed after the Fall described in Genesis 3, the overall context of this psalm invites a view of these sins against the picture of God's good creation.

Theological Connections With Adjacent Psalms. Earlier mention has been made of how both Psalms 103 and 104 (and only these two psalms in the Psalter) begin and end with the same exclamation on the part of the psalmist ("Bless the Lord, O my soul") and contain many other verbal connections, all pointing to the likelihood of a common authorship. Here are underscored major thematic connections implied by the juxtaposition of these two psalms.[36]

Psalm 104 expresses poetic praise to YHWH as Creator and Preserver of creation. Psalm 103 expresses thanksgiving to YHWH for His compassion, mercy, and forgiveness. Thus, the celebration of God's creation and His steadfast love belong together. Both God's creation and preservation and His mercy and forgiveness are aspects of YHWH's manifold "works." Creation cannot be separated from salvation history.

There is also strong linkage of terminology

between Psalms 104 and 105. Both psalms end with the Hebrew word translated "praise the Lord." Most striking are the three key terms that occur *in the very same order* at the end of Psalm 104 (v. 33, 34) and at the beginning of Psalm 105 (v. 2, 3): "sing," "meditation or meditate," and "rejoice." This is the only place in the entire Bible where such combination of terms is repeated in the same sequence.

These linkages invite theological connections between the two psalms. Psalm 105 and its complement Psalm 106 carry forward the theme of salvation history found in Psalm 103 on the national level, as they encompass the high points in Israel's entire history as a nation. As they bring book four of the Psalter to a close, they call for praise of YHWH for His "wonderful works" (Pss. 105:2, 5; 106:7, 22). The creation of Psalm 104 is enfolded in the bosom of salvation history that surrounds it in Psalm 103; 105; 106. Both creation and salvation or judgment are revelations of the same wonderful, gracious, good God. Both call forth spontaneous praise from the worshiper: "Bless the Lord, O my soul. Hallelujah!" This call to praise may be viewed as one of the main, if not the main, purposes of all these psalms.

Synthesis and Conclusion

In conclusion, it may be helpful to synthesize significant details of Psalm 104 that reaffirm, amplify, or further contribute to questions of origins set forth in Genesis 1; 2.

The When of Creation. Under the question of when, Psalm 104 affirms the absolute beginning of Creation as a direct act of

God, in parallel with the interpretation of Genesis 1:1 as an independent clause. The psalm explicitly indicates, for example, that the word for "deep"—which is described in connection with the "unformed-unfilled" condition of the earth in Genesis 1:2—is created by God: "You covered it [the earth] with the deep as with a garment" (v. 6).

Psalm 104 also assumes the seven-day Creation week, as the entire psalm systematically moves through the activities of each day in Genesis 1, including the Sabbath on the seventh day. This Creation week is assumed to be literal, even though the interpretation of Genesis 1; 2 is given in poetic form. The evening-morning rhythm of each day also seems implied by reference to the creation of the moon before the sun and to the night before the day (Ps. 104:19–23).

Verses 5–9 seem to lend support to a two-stage Creation for the raw materials of this earth (land and water): the first stage before the beginning of Creation week, during which time the foundations of the earth were laid, mountains formed, and all covered by the watery deep; and the second stage on the third day of Creation week, during which time mountains rose and valleys sank, allowing dry land to appear from amid the receding "deep," forming earth and seas.

As with Genesis 1, Psalm 104 places the appointment of the sun and moon for seasons in the midst of Creation week, not at the beginning, and clarifies what is not explained in Genesis about the source of the light before day four, namely, the light with which God clothed Himself (vv. 1b, 2a). The lack of reference to the stars in verses 19–23, which describe the celestial luminaries, may imply what is suggested also in Genesis 1, namely, that the stars were not created during the Creation week but were already in existence before that time.

By blending into a seamless whole the account of Creation week with the present conditions of the earth after the Fall, moving effortlessly and almost unnoticeably from the time of origins to the present, the psalmist may be implying relative temporal continuity between the past and present, in other words, a relatively recent and not remote creation. There is no implication, however, of a process of (theistic) evolution linking past and present.

There is an eschatological perspective within the when of Creation. Verse 5 gives the promise that the earth and its foundations "will not totter forever and ever." There is assurance that this planet will never cease to exist. Furthermore, from the perspective of time after the Flood, the psalmist indicates that the waters, which once covered the earth but were assigned their boundaries, "will not return to cover the earth" (Ps. 104:9). Verse 30 seems to point beyond the present life-death cycle to the future: "You send forth Your Spirit, they are created; and You renew the face of the ground." As Deissler correctly observes, "God's final ordering word does not apply to death but to life.... The final verse [v. 30] corroborates this future-oriented view, which points to the renewal of the present while the old is not destroyed but transformed."[37] The language of verses 24–30 actually may imply the (eschatological) resurrection of marine and terrestrial creatures.

With regard to Genesis 1:1, it has been suggested that the Hebrew term for "in the beginning" was deliberately chosen by Moses to rhyme with the term for "in the end" in Genesis 49:1, in order to illustrate the eschatological perspective of the Torah from the very first verse. In similar fashion, the psalmist in Psalm 104 depicts a perfect world created by God and ends his poetic meditation with the wish-prayer: "Let sinners be consumed from the earth and let the wicked be no more" (v. 35). He looks forward to the day when all who have marred the perfect Creation will be gone, and the earth can once again fully reflect God's original intention in its Creation.

The Who of Creation. As to the who of Creation, the psalmist reaffirms that God the Creator is both Elohim of Genesis 1 and YHWH Elohim of Genesis 2; 3 (see the use of both names for God in Gen. 1; 24; 31; 45). For the psalmist, both Genesis Creation accounts (Gen. 1; 2–3) belong together and are part and parcel of the same narrative. The Creator is both the all-powerful, transcendent One (the meaning of Elohim) and the personal, immanent, covenant Lord (the implications of the name YHWH). As in Genesis 1–3, the God of creation is presented in the psalm as One of moral goodness, full of tender care for the creatures He has made, in contrast to the deities of nations surrounding Israel who are often depicted as cruel and capricious. YHWH is presented as One God (beside whom there is none other), but at the same time, there is mention of YHWH's Spirit being sent forth (Ps. 104:30; cf. Gen. 1:2), perhaps an intimation of more than one person of the Godhead.

The How of Creation. Regarding the how of Creation, Psalm 104 reaffirms the statements in Genesis 1; 2 that God "creates" (Ps. 104:30; cf. Gen. 1:1, 21, 27; 2:4a), a term that describes exclusively God's action and refers to effortlessly producing something totally new, in contrast to the common ancient Near-Eastern views of creation by sexual procreation or by a struggle with the forces of chaos. The psalm also uses other verbs for creation found in Genesis 1; 2: "to make" (Ps. 104:4, 19, 24; cf. Gen. 1:7, 11, 12, 16, 25, 26, 31; 2:2, 3, 4, 18; plus, the related noun "works" in Ps. 104:13, 24, 31; not found in Gen. 1; 2), "to form [like a potter]" (Ps. 104:26, used for God's forming the sea creature Leviathan, whereas in Genesis it refers only to the first human and to the larger land animals; Gen. 2:7, 8, 19), and "to plant" (Ps. 104:16, of the cedars of Lebanon; cf. Gen. 2:8 and God's planting of the garden).

The psalmist adds other picturesque verbs for God's creative activity not found in the Genesis Creation account, such as "to stretch out" (the heavens, Ps. 104:2), "to lay beams" (of His upper chambers, v. 3), "to found, establish" (the foundations of the earth, v. 5, and the place for the mountains and the valleys, v. 8), "to cover" (the earth with the deep, v. 6), and "to appoint" (darkness, v. 20). In at least one verse (v. 7), YHWH is described as creating by divine fiat: "At Your rebuke they fled, at the sound of Your thunder [or voice; cf. Psalm 29] they hurried away."

Whereas in Genesis 1; 2, God is depicted as a Potter, an Architect or Builder, and a Gardener, in Psalm 104, God is all of these and many more. A whole host of metaphors are evoked to depict God's creative work:

"Close and emphatic are the metaphors," writes Hans-Joachim Kraus. "Yahweh creates the world like a master builder: he 'lays the beams' of his heavenly dwelling. Like a family father, he stretches the tent roof. Like a field general, he thunders at the primeval waters—they flee. Like a farm manager, he leads the quickening waters to the living beings and the fields. Like the father of a household, he distributes his goods and gifts. And all of this is done with sovereign, world-transcending power, profound wisdom, and gracious goodness. The conception of the heavenly king stands behind the whole psalm."[38]

The primary principle underlying how God created, both in Genesis 1; 2; and Psalm 104, is that of separation. This involves the entire process of bringing order to the cosmos and establishing the roles and functions of that which was created. In Genesis 1; 2, the term "separate" occurs in verses 4, 6, 7, 14, and 18. There is separation between the following contrasts in both Genesis 1; 2; and Psalm 104: day and night (Gen. 1:5, 14; Ps. 104:19–23), upper and lower waters (Gen. 1:6–8; Ps. 104:3, 6–13), earth and sea (Gen. 1:9, 10; Ps. 104:5–9), grass and trees (Gen. 1:11, 12, 29, 30; Ps. 104:14–17), greater and lesser light (Gen. 1:16–18; Ps. 104:19), birds and fish (Gen. 1:20–22; Ps. 104:17, 25, 26), God and human (Gen. 1:27; Ps. 104:33–35), male and female (Gen. 1:27; not in Ps. 104), humans and animals (Gen. 1:28–30; Ps. 104:14, 20–23), and weekday and holy Sabbath time (Gen. 2:1–3; implied in Ps. 104:31–35).

Psalm 104 gives a hint that is not mentioned in Genesis 1 as to the mechanism God used to accomplish the gathering of the water into one place and the appearing of dry land on the third day: "The mountains rose; the valleys sank down" (Ps. 104:8). As the mountains rose out of the deep, the water ran off into the sunken valleys, thus producing the dry land (earth) and surrounding waters (seas). Is there some allusion here to what is now referred to as plate tectonics involving the pre-Cambrian crust and continental drift?

The descriptions of divine Creation in Psalm 104, as in Genesis 1; 2, serve as a polemic against the views of creation among Israel's neighbors. While borrowing picturesque imagery reminiscent of Canaanite Baal the storm god, YHWH (not Baal) is the One who rides on the clouds. It is clear from Psalm 104 that YHWH, unlike Baal, did not need to struggle in cosmic combat against a sea deity in creation; He simply spoke and the wind and waves (which He himself had created) obeyed Him! In the psalm, "the reliability of earth is permanent and need not be repeated in annual cycle or crisis times; and resulting creation is unified ontologically with no remnant of cosmic dualism."[39] It is YHWH, not Baal, who provides water to fertilize the earth, and this is freely given by a gracious Creator, not coaxed by humans via sympathetic magic in the fertility cult rituals. Whereas "in Canaanite mythology Leviathan is a powerful primeval dragon. . . , here it is a sea creature formed by the Creator, obedient as a pet, with whom Yahweh jests and plays."[40]

While utilizing phraseology akin to that used in the Egyptian hymn to Aten, the deified sun disk, Psalm 104 does not describe the sun as a deity. In fact, the sun is mentioned only in one verse of the psalm (v. 19), and "it figures as a mere creature, a cogwheel in the well-ordered cosmos designed by YHWH. YHWH is master of the sun as he is of the storm."[41] Such depiction of the sun by the psalmist represents an explicit polemic against not only "The Hymn to Aten" but all sun worship in whatever form it may appear. By recognizing God as the source of light from the beginning of Creation, the psalmist indicates what Genesis 1 also makes clear, namely, that Creation is not sun centered but theocentric, God centered.

One of the primary contributions of Psalm 104 as to the how of creation is its emphasis upon the aesthetic quality of the creative process. In Genesis 1:1–2:4a, the Creation week is structured in a symmetrical way, similar to Hebrew poetic block parallelism, a parallelism not in matching poetic lines but in the creative acts of God Himself, who as the Master Designer creates aesthetically. As noted above, Psalm 104 captures this aesthetic dimension of the divine Creation in various ways, including the chiastic structure of the psalm, the unsurpassed use of vivid imagery, and the language of joy, pleasure, and even play.

The What of Creation. With regard to the what of Creation, Psalm 104 seems to limit its description to the earth and its surrounding heavenly spheres (the moon and sun) and does not discuss the creation of the universe as a whole (in contrast to what may be implied by the term "the heavens and the earth" in Gen. 1:1). As with Genesis 1:3ff., the psalm is focused upon the global habitats of our planet: the atmospheric heavens, the earth (dry land), and the seas.

Whereas in Genesis 1, the Creation narrative describes what is created in general categories (such as the "trees bearing fruit with seed" of vv. 11, 12, "every winged bird" of v. 21, and the "cattle and creeping things and beasts of the earth" in vv. 24, 25), in Psalm 104, the psalmist gives specific examples of species within these general categories (such as the "cedars of Lebanon" in v. 16, the "stork" in v. 17, and the "wild donkeys," "wild goats," "*shephanim* [conies or rock badgers]," and "young lions" in vv. 11, 18, and 21). Both Genesis 1 and Psalm 104 underscore the wholeness of Creation, as they refer to the "all," which God has made (Gen. 1:31; Ps. 104:24, 27).

In his poetic depiction of what was created, the psalmist brings together information both from Genesis 1:1–2:4a and Genesis 2:4b–25 (the latter describing in more detail what was created on the sixth day mentioned in Gen. 1). For example, his poetic description of humans encompasses the provision of food for their diet by God (Ps. 104:14), mentioned in Genesis 1:29, and refers to their formula of creation involving dust plus the breath or spirit of God (vv. 29, 30), mentioned in Genesis 2:7. The psalmist blends into a beautiful whole the various facets of creation delineated in Genesis 1; 2.

In this psalm, God's work of creation is not limited to Creation week; the acts of God in preserving and renewing His creation are viewed as continuing, for example, verse 30, where the Hebrew verb for "create" is used for God's bringing into existence humans and animals in the here and now.

The Why of Creation. The what of Creation

in Psalm 104, especially in its climactic allusion to the Sabbath, actually moves from the question of what to the question of why, only hinted at in Genesis 1; 2. In Genesis 2:1–3, God sanctifies the seventh day, and elsewhere, Scripture indicates God making something holy by His presence (e.g., the burning bush, Exod. 3:2–5; the sanctuary, 25:8; 40:34–38). This implies that Sabbath is a time when God enters into an intimate personal relationship with His creatures and a time when His creatures can worship Him with joy and praise. The climax of Creation in Genesis 1 and 2 is thus a call to praise and worship. In Psalm 104, creation more explicitly calls the reader to the same response as in Genesis 1 and 2: joyful worship and praise of the Creator. How appropriate that this psalm concludes with the first Hallelujah found in the Psalter!

Notes

1. Paul E. Dion, "Yhwh as Storm-God and Sun-God: The Double Legacy of Egypt and Canaan as Reflected in Psalm 104," *Zeitschrift für die alttestamentliche Wissenschaft* 103 (1991): 44.

2. In the discussion that follows, I will usually speak of the author as the psalmist, although, for reasons stated previously, I am convinced that this psalmist is probably David himself.

3. *Seventh-day Adventist Bible Commentary* (Hagerstown, MD: Review and Herald® Pub. Assn., 1977), 3:863.

4. William P. Brown, "The Lion, the Wicked, and the Wonder of It All: Psalm 104 and the Playful God," *Journal for Preachers* 29, no. 3 (2006): 15.

5. Adele Berlin, "The Wisdom of Creation in Psalm 104," in *Seeking out the Wisdom of the Ancients: Essays Offered to Honor Michael V. Fox on the Occasion of His Sixty-Fifth Birthday*, eds. Ronald L. Troxel et al. (Winona Lake, ID: Eisenbrauns, 2005), 75.

6. Walter D. Zorn, *Psalms*, vol. 2, The College Press NIV Commentary (Joplin, MO: College Press, 2004), 264, 266.

7. Franz Delitzsch, *Commentary on the Old Testament: Psalms*, vol. 3 (Grand Rapids, MI: Eerdmans, n.d.), 125.

8. Ibid., 127, 128.

9. Jacques B. Doukhan, *The Genesis Creation Story: Its Literary Structure*, Andrews University Seminary Doctrinal Dissertation Series, vol. 5 (Berrien Springs, MI: Andrews University Press, 1978), 84–87.

10. Ibid., 86.

11. William H. Shea, "Creation," in *Handbook of Seventh-day Adventist Theology*, Commentary Reference Series, vol. 12, ed. Raoul Dederen (Hagerstown, MD: Review and Herald®, 2000), 430.

12. Delitzsch, *Commentary on the Old* Testament, 127.

13. Shea, "Creation," 430.

14. Author's translation to reflect the series of participles in this passage.

15. H. C. Leupold, *Exposition of Psalms* (Grand Rapids, MI: Baker, 1969), 726.

16. Patrick D. Miller Jr., "The Poetry of Creation: Psalm 104," in *God Who Creates: Essays in Honor of W. Sibley Towner*, eds. William P. Brown and S. Dean McBride Jr. (Grand Rapids, MI: Eerdmans, 2000), 91.

17. Walter Harrelson, "On God's Care for the Earth: Psalm 104," *Currents in Theology and Mission* 2, no. 1 (February 1975): 20.

18. Doukhan, *The Genesis Creation Story*, 85.

19. Ibid.

20. Delitzsch, *Commentary on the Old Testament*, 125.

21. Ibid., 127, 128.

22. Ibid., 136.

23. Ibid.

24. Ibid.

25. Ibid.

26. Ibid., 89, 90.

27. Shea, "Creation," 431.

28. Ibid.

29. Ibid.

30. Harrelson, "On God's Care for the Earth," 21.

31. Miller, "The Poetry of Creation," 96.

32. Ibid.

33. Ibid., 99.

34. Harrelson, "On God's Care for the Earth," 20.

35. James Luther Mays, *Psalms* (Louisville, KY: John Knox, 1994), 334.

36. Scholars have recently begun to recognize the

theological sophistication of the final editor(s) of the Psalms, as psalms with similar theological content are grouped together. See, e.g., J. Clinton McCann, ed., *The Shape and Shaping of the Psalter* (Sheffield, England: JSOT Press, 1993).

37. Alfons Deissler, "The Theology of Psalm 104," in *Standing Before God: Studies on Prayer in Scripture and in Tradition With Essays in Honor of John M. Oesterreicher*, eds. Asher Finkel and Lawrence Frizzell (New York: KTAV, 1981), 37.

38. Hans-Joachim Kraus, *Psalms 60–150: A Commentary*, trans. Hilton C. Oswald (Minneapolis: Augsburg, 1989), 304.

39. Mays, *Psalms*, 333.

40. Deissler, "The Theology of Psalm 104," 35.

41. Paul E. Dion, "Yhwh as Storm-God and Sun-God," 58.

The Creation Theme in the Book of Psalms

Alexej Murán

Although Creation is not considered the most significant theme in the book of Psalms, it is clearly present. As an overall look at the Creation theme, the major focus will be on Creation as a supportive theme in the Psalms. The psalmists often speak about the Creator and creation and use Creation imagery or Creation language.

To classify a "Creation psalm" is difficult, since Creation is rarely a main theme. There is one exception: Psalm 104, which is considered to be a Creation psalm by most scholars. Therefore, Psalm 104 requires separate study and was addressed in the previous chapter.

Classification of Themes
Related to Creation

In examining the use of Creation as a supportive theme in the book of Psalms, twelve different primary themes stand out. These can be further divided into three groups.

Themes in the first group pertain to the knowledge of God. This is the most prominent use of the Creation theme in the book of Psalms. In this group, Creation is the reason to praise God; it describes who God is; more specifically, it portrays His power; and finally, it shows that God as a Creator is also the Sustainer of His creation.

The second group is a continuation of the theme of God as sustainer, but it specifically deals with humans rather than the general creation. It begins with a description of human existence, clarifying the difference between God and humanity. The second point portrays a God who is different from His creation and, at some points, seemingly distant from His creation. After understanding the difference between being human and the seemingly distant Creator, Creation shows that it is safe to trust in God who is ready to bless His creation.

The third group delves further into the relationship between God and humankind. It is based on the law of God, which according to a supportive Creation theme, was established at the beginning by God, the Creator. After a description of the law, the Creation theme gives God the right to judge as the One who created everything and as the One who set the rules in place, so everything would work in perfect order. Creation is also used to identify the wicked; however, it also shows that salvation and restoration emanate from God, who has the power to save.

The book of Psalms includes several other minor themes linked to the Creation theme, such as joy or miscellaneous instructions about creation. It should be pointed out that the main theme of Creation in the book of Psalms is never the actual Creation process, with the only arguable exception being Psalm 104. In the same way, Creation is never used as a major theme throughout Psalms, again with the possible exception of Psalm 104. There are psalms (such as 8 or 29) that include major Creation references; however, the main purpose of these large sections is not the actual Creation process but one of the previously mentioned themes.

Twelve Themes Associated With Creation

1. *Praise of God.* God's praise is *the* central theme of the book of Psalms. Though it is not necessarily found in every psalm, it is the most recurring theme in the entire book. There are eight different Hebrew terms in the psalms that express the idea of praise. Combined, they occur 186 times. The poets not only exhorted the people but every living thing to praise the Lord. The praise of God is closely related to the book of Psalms as well as to creation. There is solid evidence to suggest that the praise of God is the central reason for the Creation theme in the book of Psalms. In fact, some scholars argue that, outside Genesis 1; 2, Creation always appears in the setting of praise.

The praise of God may not always be a direct and immediate result of a Creation reference, but it can be implied or found in the larger context of the psalm. One example of a reference with the lack of specific praise of God is found in Psalm 119:73. In this verse, the psalmist calls on God the Creator to give him understanding of the law. The immediate result of the Creation reference is the Creator's ability to teach the writer His laws. The rest of this section in this acrostic psalm (which organizes

every eight successive verses in a sequence based on the Hebrew alphabet) does not include any other references to the praise of God. In the introductory section, however, the psalmist says that learning God's law results in the praise of God (Ps. 119:7). Therefore, the psalmist's call on the Creator to give him understanding of the law should eventually result in praise. Only in a few other psalms can the praise of God be seen in this extended connection with Creation. On the other hand, there are hymns of praise, which "summon the theme of Creation in admiration for Yahweh,"[1] as well as kingship psalms, which use the Creation motif to underline the fact that God is the Creator who should be praised and worshiped. The following examples show how Creation is placed within the context of praise.

• *Psalm 100.* This is the only psalm with the title "psalm of thanksgiving." Its structure is very similar to that of Psalm 95:1–7. It begins with a call to praise and then gives a reason for the praise, followed by another call and reason to praise. It is possible to interpret this as a reference to the creation of a nation; because of its close relationship with Psalm 95, however, it should also be understood in the context of the creation of humans.

In both psalms, references to Creation are found in the middle of two calls to praise God. Because of this central placement, the Creation reference is connected to both calls to worship, emphasizing that God is the maker of heaven and earth. Also, both psalms include the theme of thanksgiving. In Psalm 100, it is found in the second appeal, and in Psalm 95, it is part of the first appeal. Therefore, the praise of the Creator includes not only the admiration of His power but also the thanksgiving for His work. Worshiping the Creator is also a joyous occasion. Both psalms make reference to joyful singing or noise, as, for example, "joyful singing" (Ps. 100:2) and making a "joyful noise" (95:2, KJV), which are used in the opening appeal of each. This is an exuberant time when created beings give praise to their Creator. Both psalms exhibit a universal perspective and include the entire creation in their call to worship. Universality is an important feature of the Creation references in the book of Psalms.

• *Psalm 148.* This psalm contains the most detailed call for all creation to praise God. It begins with an appeal to the heavenly realms and to the sun, moon, and stars. In the psalms, this is always the order in which creation is presented. Heaven and things relating to heaven are mentioned first, followed by the earth. Praise always begins with a look at the sky, and the heavens are the first to "telling of the glory of God" (Ps. 19:1). They are to praise God just as all earthly things should praise God. The reason is stated in Psalm 148:5: "For He commanded and they were created." The realization that the heavens, which often cause people to stand in awe, are just a creation of God is part of worship. He is the Creator not only of the earth but also of the heavens.

Continuing with verse 7, the psalmist turns to the earth. There, he follows the sequence of the Creation week in Genesis 1, beginning with water, dry land, trees, animals, and finishing with men and women, old and young. Mentioning the old with the young seems to evoke a sense of post-Edenic life. Most of the time, creation is presented from the perspective of a sinful world. Therefore, almost every reference to creation will include a reference or an allusion to the life and death cycle.

Creation extends praise to every created being. "The creator holds everything that he has made in a relationship to himself, with a commitment of his faithful love. In this relationship all created beings are called to look to him in trust and praise."[2] God is not only the God of Israel who delivered them from Egypt but also the God of all creation.

References to Egypt and the creation of Israel are also used as a reason for praise, but this praise is limited to the nation of Israel. When God is called the Creator of all, however, He should be praised not only by one group of people or only by a single nation but by all. Therefore, one of the reasons for using Creation references in connection with the praise of God is to include every created being in the call to praise the Creator of heaven and earth, making its effects universal.

• *Psalm 33.* This psalm of praise includes clear reference to creation as the first motivation for praise (Ps. 33:4–9). After the appeal to praise God with singing and the playing of instruments, the psalmist provides the reason for this joyful call: because "the word of the LORD is upright" (v. 4). "The first motivation for praising Yahweh is grounded in his essential character."[3] God's word is faithful, loving righteousness and justice, showing His loving-kindness to the earth. The description of the word continues with its power to create. This description comprises four parallel lines (vv. 6, 9).

6.   By word—heavens
      By breath of His mouth—host

9.   He spoke—it was done
      He commanded—it stood

The word of the Lord has power, and all the Creation that the psalmist sees is the result of this word.

• *Psalm 92.* Psalm 92 is the only psalm clearly associated with the Sabbath. The superscription calls it "a Psalm, a Song for the Sabbath day." Its connection to Creation has been recognized by many scholars. It brings out two aspects of Sabbath worship and, at the same time, two aspects of the Creator: creation and redemption, corresponding to the two versions of the fourth commandment. As a concluding day of the six-day Creation, God's rest on the seventh day signifies the completeness of God's "very good" creation. At the same time, it is the seventh day that points to the restoration of God's creation through His redeeming act, clearly seen in the history of Israel and foreshadowing the final eschatological restoration.

The first section (Ps. 92:1–4) opens with joyous praise and thanksgiving. It is a call of praise, which correlates to the theme of the day that God has consecrated and blessed. In the final verse of this section (v. 4), the writer declares the reason for his gladness to be "what You have done" and "the works of Your hands." In other psalms, this Hebrew expression points back to Creation. The work of the Creator brings joy and gladness to the psalmist, who expresses his adoration through praise and worship.

The second section (Ps. 92:5–9) begins with the theme of Creation, repeating the praise of God's works. It is the understanding of these works that separates the intelligent from the fools. These "senseless" men (v. 6) become "the wicked" (v. 7). Verse 7 introduces a new topic and a second Sabbath theme, which is redemption. At this point, the Creator also becomes the redeemer. In spite of the rapid expansion of the iniquity, the Creator is the Redeemer of His creation.

The last section (vv. 10–15) elaborates on the theme of God as redeemer and sustainer of His creation. The psalmist describes the power and willingness of God to help His creation and points to the eschatological restoration. As a result of the second theme of the Sabbath, in the last line of this Psalm, the writer returns again to praise.

2. Who Is God? The Creation theme can also be used as a means to reveal who God is. Knowledge of who God is often directly related to the praise of God. The psalms presented in the previous section would then fall into this category. They specified who God is, and as a result, they call all Creation to praise Him. "Who is God," in this case, is limited only to the primary understanding of God as the Other, the Creator, the One who is in contrast to everyone and everything else. More specific characteristics of God will be discussed in the different themes below.

The contrast between the Creator and creation is the primary purpose of the

Creation reference in showing who God is. God is in heaven, unlike His creation, which is associated with the earth. God is not dependent on food, sun, or other resources to exist. As the Creator, He existed prior to Creation.

• *Psalm 113.* Most of these psalms begin and end with a call to praise the Lord; their primary theme is the praise of God. Their many references to creation in comparison with other psalms are a direct result of a close relationship between the praise of God and creation.

Psalm 113 is connected with the song of Hannah. Parallels between these two songs are striking, particularly considering the fact that both use imagery of God as Creator. Psalm 113 contains several allusions to creation, beginning with a glance toward the heavens. Often in the book of Psalms, the phrase "the glory of God is above the heavens" is found in the context of creation, and so in this case, we can assume that verse 4 is also alluding to creation. The first clear reference to creation, however, begins with the question, "Who is like the LORD?" (v. 5). "The poet declares God's incomparability, a theme expressed in the question. Everything builds up to this question, and what follows answers it, without naming God."[4] "Patterns of the basic 'who-is-like' formula recur throughout the Old Testament (e.g., Exod. 15:11; Deut. 3:24; Ps. 35:10; Isa. 40:12ff.; 46:5) as a part of theological affirmations and in personal names. Both usages serve as reminders of the LORD's uniqueness. There is no one like Yahweh!"[5]

The following verses describe who God is through the use of Creation language.

"He is enthroned on high" is a phrase often connected with El Elyon; He is the Maker of heaven and earth. This high place is not in the mountains; in fact, it is not even in the heavens. The Lord is portrayed as being above the heavens looking down on them (Ps. 113:6). He is the Creator of the earth but also the heavens. The coupling of heaven and earth shows that "God is so exalted that there is no difference between the two in their relative distance to Him."[6] This incomparability "theme appears always in hymnic contexts and frequently in the Psalms."[7]

Verses 7–9 show two cases of the Creator God coming down to finite humans. God is also the One who "raises the poor from the dust" (v. 7), alluding to Genesis 2:7, in which God formed humankind out of this same substance. God also places this human with the rulers and princes. In a similar way, God placed humanity to be the ruler over the rest of the creation (Gen. 1:28). The imagery of God as Creator ends in Psalm 113:9 with a barren woman who becomes a mother. In the Creation story, God is blessing all living beings with a blessing of an "multiply" (Gen. 1:28). In the same way, the God of creation gives children to a barren woman. These two cases imply "that Yahweh achieves where other gods cannot penetrate."[8]

In this psalm, God is both "transcendent and imminent; He is above the highest, and yet stoops to the lowest."[9] He is a God who, as the Creator, is above His creation, but at the same time, He is concerned with His creation. "Psalm 113 provides a natural theological entrance into two corollary truths about God, His transcendence and

His immanence."[10] God the Creator is always the One who is far, but at the same time, He is very close.

• *Psalm 90.* This is a psalm ascribed to Moses. Because the meter is not uniform, its form is difficult to reconstruct. As noted by Cas J. A. Vos, however, "Despite textual and critical problems, the psalm is highly artistic in its composition."[11] He divides this psalm into four sections:

1, 2	The invocation of God
3–10	The petitioner expressing need
11–16	Prayer asking for God's intervention
17	Prospect of future salvation

The primary purpose of this psalm is to illustrate God's greatness. Even though it should also be understood as a prayer for God's mercy, it begins with the recognition of who God is. It seems that the recognition of God and understanding *who* He is takes priority over the resolution of the need.

The psalm begins with an invocation in which the psalmist contrasts the eternal nature of God with the limits surrounding humans. They return to dust, from which they were created (Gen. 3:19), but He is eternal. "The glorification of His eternal power vaults into the sphere of precreation."[12] Reference to the "birth of mountains" not only indicates that God is their Creator but shows that God was present at the time they were created. He was present before everything was created. The contrast between the Creator-God and the mountains seems to dethrone the mountains of their supposed divine powers.

"The poet seeks to convey the thought that God is the most ancient of all and preceded all other Creations."[13] This can be observed in the structure of Psalm 90: 1, 2.

    a. You are Lord
      b. *Time:* "throughout all generations"
        c. *Place:* "mountains"
        c. *Place:* "earth and the world"
      b. *Time:* "everlasting"
    a. You are God

These verses express "the sovereignty and eternity of the God of Israel."[14] As with most psalms involving Creation themes, however, the psalm "does not deal with Israel in any particular way; it treats the human condition as a whole, is general in nature, striking a universal note."[15]

3. *God's Power.* God is almighty; He is different than the gods created by humankind. Even though humans were given the honor and privilege to rule the earth, God is the Maker of them; He is much greater and even indescribable to us. So how are we able to comprehend this greatness of El Elyon? The psalmists often use the Creation theme to present a clearer picture of the vastness, greatness, and power of God. As already demonstrated, this greatness can be seen in His eternal nature and in His contrast to creation. In addition to being different and eternal, He is also powerful enough to create and rule His creation. When God's power is described, it is often in the context of His love and support for His creation.

• *Psalm 74.* Psalm 74 is a lament describing the absence and silence of God. The center of this psalm of Asaph contains allusions to creation (vv. 12–17), which recall "God's power in Creation and the Exodus."[16]

Furthermore, this power is closely related to the salvation of God. "The hymnic glorification in the framework of a prayer song includes an appeal to God and at the same time trust in Yahweh's salvific power."[17]

Creation is mixed with allusions to the Exodus, a common technique in the psalms. Creation and Exodus often go together as a single theme. They both result in the creation of people. Many scholars have tried to distinguish between these two themes; however, as Hans-Joachim Kraus correctly pointed out, this is not necessarily a question of "either-or." Both of these themes became part of Israel's experience and became part of who God is. He is not the God of one or the other but the God of all creation and the God of the Exodus.

In verses 12–17, the song of petition is interrupted by a description of God's might. Also, the structure of the psalm changes from plural "us" to singular "my." It is clearly distinguished from the rest of the psalm. While being forsaken by God, the people hold on to His creative power. This section is characterized by the repetition of the word translated "you." It starts with the expression "God is my King." This shows an intimate relationship between God and His creation.

The first image of a powerful God is associated with water. God by His strength divides the seas (v. 13a) and breaks the heads of the sea monsters (v. 13b). In Ugaritic literature, these are personified by the sea god Yam. In this psalm, God is not struggling with this "god" but, by His power, crushes it. He also crushes Leviathan, an animal used predominantly as a symbol of immense power. God is the conqueror of

"primeval forces."[18]

Verse 14 returns to the imagery of water. All the rivers and springs are subject to God's power. He as the Creator is stronger than any part of His creation. The last two verses describe lights (v. 16), marking boundaries for the earth, and the seasons (v. 17). "The sequence between light and darkness reflects the Hebrew usage of placing the evening at the beginning of the new day."[19] These are the works of God's hands, the result of His power. "The ultimate of God's supreme might is depicted in His ability to manipulate and control nature."[20] They operate according to the boundaries set by the Lord.

- *Psalm 89.* The psalm of Ethan the Ezrahite includes at least six clear references to creation. The section most evidently tied to the theme of the power of God is found in Psalm 89:9–13. These verses describe the power of God's arm and right hand. They are both in construct form with the noun, often translated as "strength," "power," or "might." This powerful hand of God rules over the surging sea (v. 9), scatters the enemies (v. 10)—everything is created by Him (vv. 11, 12). Therefore, creation is a symbol of His power. In line with other psalms, these references to creation are preceded by the question "who is like You?" (v. 8). As George J. Zemek has observed, the "who-is-like" formula is often used in the Old Testament and reveals God's uniqueness.[21] In this psalm, God's power is a reason for humanity to praise God while, at the same time, also marking the source of the blessing.

4. *God as Sustainer.* The power of God is not the only reason for praise and trust.

Even though He is all-powerful and able to do as He wishes, it is not these attributes alone that draw the people to turn to Him. Knowing only His power would result in fear. However, the power of God is closely associated with God's ability to sustain His creation. Knowing God as Sustainer causes people to fear Him because of His love. With His ability to create, He must also possess the ability to sustain that which He has created. Psalm 104 is not included in this chapter, but it should be pointed out that it is one of the best examples of the amalgamation of creation and God's work of nurturing His creation. The following examples will include the psalms where creation is found in the context of an image of God providing for His creation.

• *Psalm 65.* Psalm 65 is David's song of praise. Without ceasing, it praises God for His works. Beginning with praise and followed by the blessing of the elected, both themes often go together with creation. This psalm can be divided into three parts:

a. *God in the temple (vv. 1–4)*
b. *God of the world (vv. 5–8)*
c. *God of the earth (vv. 9–13)*

The structure of this psalm echoes the author's priorities regarding his relationship with God, His praise, followed by the forgiveness of sins, God's acts of redemption, and ending with God as the cosmic farmer. The first reference to creation is found in Psalm 65:6, a description of God's power, connecting the previously examined theme with a new theme that begins in verse 9. The break between verses 1–8 and 9–13 is also shown by looking at the meter. Whereas verses 1–8 are based on a three plus three meter, verses 9–13 have an uneven form.

Verses 9–13 allude to day three of Creation week (Gen. 1:9–13). Considered to be the best *"Harvest Song* ever written,"[22] it describes everything "in terms of excess."[23] It begins with the provision of water, similar to the separation of water in Genesis 1:9, 10. Psalms 65:9 speaks about "God's stream," which is a poetical reference to "the mythical source for rain."[24]

This is followed by references to grain, pastures, and meadows. In the Genesis Creation account, God commanded and the newly created land produced vegetation, plants, and trees. In Psalm 65, God provides food for people and animals. The entire ecosystem works in harmony because of His willingness to care for His creation. It is not the result of chance but of divine love. "God is the very sustainer of life."[25] These references to agriculture "emphasize Yahweh's role in assuring a bountiful harvest and in bringing joy to replace tears."[26] The God of creation is depicted as a caring God, who seems to be working in order for living beings to survive.

• *Psalm 147.* Psalm 147 includes four clear references to creation. In verses 8 and 9, God is described as provider for His creation. Similarly to Psalm 65, the main reference is to the third day of Creation and is placed in the post-Flood world with references to rain. All the creation references, which are associated with the sustaining acts of God, are connected with the post-Flood world. God who provided at the time of Creation is the God who is still providing at the time of the post-Flood world. He provides food not only for Israel or humans but also for the cattle and young ravens (Ps. 147:9). This reference to other living beings is also a common feature of other Creation references. God the Creator is not exclusively the God of Israel, but He is the God of all creation. Therefore, unless clearly stated, all references to God as Creator should be understood in the universal sense. This fact, in connection with the sustaining acts of God, is clearly seen in Psalm 145:15, 16, where all living things are looking to God for their food.

5. *Who Are We?* The second major group of four themes focuses on the relationship between the Creator and creation. These themes are often interchangeable and, at times, overlap with the previous four themes. Who we are is closely linked to who God is. Trust in God is directly connected to knowing God as Sustainer.

• *Psalm 8.* Psalm 8 is often referred to as a "song of creation."[27] It comes very close to being a Creation psalm, with most verses dedicated to Creation; however, its main focus is the praise of God. The psalm has the following structure:

a. The praise of God (v. 2ab)
   b. Creation that gives praise to God (vv. 2c, 3)
      c⁰. The fragility of humanity (vv. 4, 5)
      c¹. The greatness of humanity (vv. 6, 7)
   b. Creation that serves humanity (vv. 7, 8)
a. The praise of God (v. 9)

The artistry of this direct address to God is hidden in the contrast between two questions ("how" and "what") as they relate to creation and to each other. "*how* majestic is Your name" underlines God's awesome power displayed in His creation. The theology of name dominates this psalm. In this context, "Lord" "really means, 'He who causes to be.' "[28] "*What* is man" (v. 4) highlights the insignificance of humanity but, at the same time, their importance in God's eyes.

Enveloped by the praise of God in verses 1, 2, 9, the main section (vv. 3–8) describes the Creation account with humankind as its central figure. The praise begins with a look to the sky. Description of these great heavenly bodies underlines the marvel over God's involvement and interest in humanity. Humankind is weak and small in comparison to the rest of creation. The Hebrew term usually translated as "humankind" denotes "weakness and frailty."[29]

The psalms often describe the insignificance of humanity, but this particular psalm goes beyond that by adding the idea of importance, which is a result of humanity's relationship to God. It is not a result of work or achievements but represents God's gift of power over creation. Without God, humankind is insignificant, physically inferior to many other created beings, yet with God, they are elevated to the role of a ruler.

Following the marvel over humanity's dominion, the writer provides a list of created beings subjected to humankind. These are presented in the reverse order of the Genesis Creation account, a stylistic feature that further highlights the central role of humanity in creation. Without verses 1, 2, 9, this psalm would seem to be an elevation and a tribute to humankind; however, the introduction and conclusion use the theme of Creation and the description of humanity to further stress the praise of God.

• *Psalm 139.* Psalm 139 is a highly personal depiction of the intimacy between David and his Creator. James Luther Mays calls it "the most personal expression in Scripture of the Old Testament's radical monotheism."[30] This psalm in verses 13–16 points to the amazing way God created humans. It is written as a confession of the psalmist. He is expressing his amazement over his own intricate body. Reference to the mother's womb implies the post-Creation creative work of God, but the depths of the earth seem to be placed in the same position, perhaps alluding to God's formation of Adam out of the dust of the ground. God is forming the human body in a mother's womb but also in the depths of the earth. This seeming contradiction is a result of the poetic language. This section includes references to the formation of a skeleton, allusions to veins and arteries, and descriptions of an embryo before it becomes a fully developed body.

The most important aspect of this text is its confirmation that a plan existed before creation. This is the central point of this section. God saw and had a plan before He began creating. Therefore, humans are not an accident but a result of God's careful plan. This awe over the intricate design of the human body is interrupted by a spontaneous expression of praise in verse 14. Excitement over God's amazing work could also be the reason for the variation of the meter. It may "correspond to emotional fluctuations on the poet's part."[31] As previously indicated, praise is a direct response to creation. When psalmists consider the works of God's hands, their first response is in praise.

• *Psalms 90; 113.* Both of these psalms have already been analyzed in connection with the question of who God is; however, they also show who people are in contrast to God. The main feature of these psalms is their description of a short life and their association with dust and ashes. This theme of a short life is the result of sin. God created people to live in the Garden of Eden, but after sin entered the world, their connection with the Creator and the source of life was severely damaged. Looking back at Creation from the perspective of a sinful state of being, life is limited by the substances out of which people were created. Even though the result of Creation was "very good," sin caused a return to the pre-Creation state. In spite of humanity's diminished longevity, both psalms allude to the hope that the Lord will bless them through their children and through His presence. These psalms illustrate an important feature of Creation, which is found in Genesis 3. Because the psalmists viewed the Creation from the perspective of a sinful world, they often mix the perfect world of Genesis 1; 2 with the decaying world of Genesis 3.

6. *God's Remoteness.* As concluded above, God is very different from His creation. He is not limited by space, sustenance, or even time. This sometimes leads to a seemingly large chasm between God and humanity. The theme of a distant God is predominantly found in the lament psalms. In these psalms, the writers express their feelings regarding the lack of God's presence,

manifest in their lives.

• *Psalm 89.* As already noted, Psalm 89 includes a reference to creation in support of the theme of the power of God. This psalm is composed in seven stanzas. It begins with praise of God for His faithfulness, but it ends with a lament over suffering and pain. Toward the end of this psalm, Ethan turns from praise to the realization that God is punishing the people for their wickedness. This punishment is seen as God's rejection, anger, and renunciation of the covenant. The climax is found in verse 49, "which sums up the whole: 'Where are your former deeds of loyalty which you swore to David in your faithfulness?' "[32]

Verses 46–48 are separated from the rest of the text by the use of the term *selah.* They begin with a question regarding the length of God's anger. It is a call to God to return to His people. Ethan then asks God for the reason of his creation. Why would God create humans? Even though this psalm is closely connected to the covenant and the covenant people, when the Creation theme is expressed, it has a very universal tone. The people are called "sons of man" (v. 48) and not sons of Abraham or sons of Israel.

This appeal to God to give the psalmist a reason for his existence comes from the understanding that God originally had a plan for humanity. The result of sin, however, was a gap between God and His creation. This culminated in the apparent "absence" of God. This theme of an absent God is found in numerous psalms, often in relationship with God's creation. In this psalm, it is used as an appeal to God to act and remember His creation. It seems as if the writer is afraid that he is not going

to experience God's deliverance. For him, "the human perception of God's goodness ends with their death without exception."[33] Even in distress and with feelings of separation, the psalmist admits that he is a created being.

7. *Trust in God.* Another important hint to creation is found in connection with the theme of trust. It is often combined with the salvation theme and salvation history. Trust in God is one of the main themes in the psalms, but it is often a result of creation.

• *Psalm 146.* Psalm 146 is the first of the final section of Hallel psalms. Its overall theme is the praise of God, but in the middle, it elaborates on a theme of trust. This trust then turns into help, which comes from the Creator, which then prompts the praise of God.

"The structure of Psalm 146 reflects the pattern of the hymn."[34] It begins and concludes with calls to praise the Lord, but it also includes instructions and reasons for the praise. It can be divided into two major groups, each being subdivided into two sections:

> a. Praise and trust (vv. 1–4)
> > b. Whom to praise (vv. 1, 2)
> > > c. Whom not to trust (vv. 3, 4)
> a. Trust and praise (vv. 5–10)
> > > c. Whom to trust (vv. 5–9)
> > b. Whom to praise (v. 10)

Another way to divide this psalm is to recognize the first and final verses as an *inclusio,* which would then make the middle section a call to trust the Lord. In a way, this psalm "is framed between a prelude and a postlude declaring the poet's intention to praise the Lord."[35]

Hallel's Introduction (vv. 1, 2)
  a. Whom not to trust (v. 3a)
    b. Why are they? (vv. 3b, 4)
  a. Blessing over those who hope in
      the Lord (v. 5)
    b. Who is he? (vv. 6–9)
Hallel's Conclusion

From this outline, it can be observed that the author uses an introverted parallelism. "The body of the hymn thus gives instruction about the wrong and right way [to praise the Lord] (cf. Psalm 1). The wrong way is putting trust in human leaders; the right way is to trust the Lord for help and hope."[36] This conclusion can then be tied to the Creation reference, which further assures the reader of the trustworthy source of help.

The interesting feature of this psalm is its use of the possessive pronoun used in connection with God. There is a move from *my* God" to "*his* God" and eventually to "*your* God." The last verse of this psalm states that God is a God for "all generations." Therefore, through the careful use of different pronouns, this psalm clearly applies to every person, not just a specific group of people. This key feature associated with the Creation theme was already observed in other psalms.

○ *Verses 1, 2: Call to Praise the Lord.* The psalm begins with a double exhortation to praise the Lord. The psalmist is urging himself to praise God. This call is immediately followed by an assurance that the author or the singer will praise the Lord. It is a promise to praise the Lord as long as the person remains alive. This theme of life and death is then expanded upon in the following section.

○ *Verses 3, 4: Whom to Distrust.* As pointed in the structure of this psalm, verses 3 and 4 are an admonition and an explanation as to whom not to trust. Verse 3 begins with words "do not trust in princes," followed by "in mortal man." Several translations add "nor" between princes and mortal man. This conjunction is not found in the Hebrew text and was redacted from the LXX addition of the word translated as "and." However, these two phrases should be viewed as a parallel thought, which is developed in the following verses. The princes and the mortal men are the same group of people. They are only "mortal man who cannot save" (JPS). Therefore, just as the author, these princes have a life that will come to an end. The following are the reasons not to trust in mortal man: (1) There is no salvation in him. (2) His spirit departs. (3) He returns to earth. (4) His thoughts perish.

This psalm is clearly saying that even the princes with all their riches and glory are but humans, who rely on their power from the Lord, just as any other "mortal man." Calling the Creation story "Israel's myth of human beginnings," James L. Crenshaw points to the connection between verses 3 and 4 and the Genesis Creation account. However, it is not only found in chapter three but also in the delegation of power over the earth to humans.

○ *Verses 5–9: Source of Happiness.* This section begins with the word *happy,* its last occurrence in the book of Psalms. This happiness is based on help and hope. God is the helper, but He is also the object of hope, bringing together the present and the future aspects of God's blessing. This section is written in an apparent structure. After the two-line introduction, there are five lines, four of which begin with the word *who*. They describe God as the maker of heaven, earth, and the sea, who keeps faith, executes justice, and gives food. "Permanence and power alone are not the grounds for trust. Trust is also founded on character, so the Lord's character is epitomized in a phrase (6c)."[37]

These who lines are followed by five lines beginning with "the LORD" and concluding with two additional lines. The first section describes God as the Creator, Almighty, All-powerful Judge, and Sustainer. The second part speaks about a God who is concerned with prisoners, the blind, strangers, the fatherless, and widows. It can be divided into the following descriptions of God's character: (1) frees the prisoners, (2) opens the eyes of the blind, (3) raises those who are bowed down, (4) loves the righteous, (5) preserves the strangers, (6) supports the fatherless, (7) supports the widow, (8) frustrates the way of the wicked.

The Lord loves the righteous, but at the same time, He hates the wicked. "The Lord would not be God if He did not deal with evil and evil-doers."[38] God prevents the way of the wicked from reaching its goal. "Ten lines are devoted to detailing the Divine compassion for men, but one line is enough to indicate His attitude towards the wicked."[39] This section is focused on the goodness of the Creator toward His creation, but it includes a description of the way the Creator deals with a corrupted creation.

○ *Verse 10: Conclusion.* The first half of this verse is a summary of the whole psalm. The Lord is a King to all creation in contrast to the princes in verse 3. "The kingship of the Lord (Ps. 146:10) is shown to involve his creating of all, his frustrating of the wicked, and above all, his salvation, healing, and care of all the humble in their need."[40] The last verse concludes with another hallelujah statement. This praise of God is a direct result of the previous verses.

8. *Divine Blessing.* Blessing and creation go together not only in the book of Psalms but also in the rest of the Hebrew Bible. In the Garden of Eden, God pronounced the first blessings over animals, over humans, and even over a time. When this creation blessing is applied to humans, it often results in an increase of descendants, clearly relating to the original Genesis blessing. Furthermore, this blessing prompts the praise of God from whom all these blessings flow. Specific texts that stand out use what scholars call "a cultic-blessing formula." The following texts are included in this category: Psalms 115:14–16; 121:1, 2; 124:8; 134; 146:5, 6a.

• *Psalm 115.* Psalm 115 is part of the first of the Hallel psalms, which include Psalms 113–118. It describes people who seem to be in a state of distress. Even though their adversaries may appear to be stronger, this psalm presents a major and paramount difference (i.e., their God, "Maker of heaven and earth," Ps. 115:15). The psalm begins with a comparison between God and the other gods. The result is a call for Israel, the house of Aaron, and those who fear the Lord to trust God, making this psalm and the following blessing all-inclusive.

The second half of the psalm (v. 12–16) is a blessing that includes a cultic-blessing formula.

○ *Verses 12, 13: Confidence in God's Blessing.* These two verses give assurance that the God of the heavens is a God who cares for His Creation by blessing it. This includes Israel, the house of Aaron, and those who fear the Lord. The assumption that this last group is very broad is deduced from the clarification that this includes the small together with the great. The original blessing pronounced by God during the Creation week was not in any way associated with Israel or the land of Israel, since at that time, neither of them existed. This point, however, stands on the understanding of the origin of the following blessing.

○ *Verses 14–16: Theme of Creation.* Verses 14–16 are joined by their recollection of the Creation story. Scholars generally agree that this is a priestly blessing. Most scholars rely on Norman C. Habel's proposition that verse 15 is a Canaanite cultic phrase of blessing. It cannot be denied that there are similarities between earlier inscriptions found in and around the land of Israel, but what Habel missed is the connection of this phrase to Genesis 1; 2, which are pre-Israel and pre-Canaan accounts of Creation. The blessing begins with the promise of children. This was important during the postexilic period, since the people were few in number. However, if this blessing is compared with the Genesis Creation account, it is easy to notice that God the Creator pronounced the same blessing over His creation. This Creation blessing was not exclusively for humans (Gen. 1:28) but included fish and birds of the air (v. 22).

Psalm 115:15 describes God as "Maker of heaven and earth." In the Genesis story, God "made" the expanse (Gen. 1:7), the two great lights (v. 16), animals (v. 25), and humans (v. 26). The Creation story in Genesis 1 ends with a statement that "all that He had made" was very good. Psalm 115:15 summarizes this by stating that God is the maker of everything. He is the Creator. "This is not a god who cannot do anything, like the gods described in verses 4–7, but the God who made the heavens and the earth (v. 15)."[41] In the Old Testament, the combination of "heaven and earth" is often used as another way of saying "everything." Beginning with Genesis 1:1, this phrase "heaven and earth" is used as the object of God's creation. What this first statement in the Bible is saying is that God is the Creator of everything, and as such, He is referred to in Psalm 115:15.

The last verse of this Creation blessing is referring back to Genesis 1:28. Not only is this blessing promising fruitfulness in inhabiting the earth, but it also speaks about humans as rulers of the earth. Psalm 115:16 makes a distinction between heaven and earth by asserting that heaven is the space where the Lord rules, while earth is the place where humanity functions as ruler. The first half of this verse is referring back to verse 3. In it, the Lord is found to be in heaven, possibly emphasizing His authority. He is able to do "whatever He pleases" (v. 3). In contrast to Him, people are given the earth.

9. *God's Law.* Together with the praise of God, God's law is one of the major themes of the book of Psalms. It often goes together with God's privilege to judge, the

description of the wicked, and the theme of salvation and restoration. Together, these four themes comprise the final focus of this study. After looking at God's power portrayed in the past and His interaction with humankind in the present, this last section highlights the message of hope and joy in the future. In spite of the present troubles, through the law and God's implementation of this law in combination with His love and mercy, the psalmists look at life confidently and positively.

• *Psalm 119.* The acrostic Psalm 119 is the longest poetic composition focusing upon law. In addition to numerous allusions to creation, it has two clear references to creation. The first is found in verse 73 and the second in verses 90, 91. Both are placed in the context of the law, but their primary theme is different.

Verse 73 is a confession that God's hands formed the psalmist. This entire section underscores "the intimate relation between the poet and God."[42] This is not the first time a similar statement has been made, but this is the only time this phrase is put within the context of the law in the book of Psalms. It should be remembered that the creation of humanity is not presented in a negative way, as in Psalm 89 or Job 10:8. Because God is the Creator, the psalmist is asking for understanding of the law. This request for understanding is the result of God's ability to give it. "The great Creator is the best Teacher."[43] "The poet of this psalm finds joy in remembering his having been made and fashioned by the God who now corrects him."[44] Because God established the law and created the psalmist, He is able to help the writer understand the

law, and this fact brings joy to the writer. Martin S. Rozenberg concludes that God created humans, so He could "learn and practice God's laws as a guide in perfecting the world."[45]

Psalm 119:89 begins a section with a statement that the word of the Lord is settled in the heavens forever. In the following verse, the psalmist uses a Creation reference. The Lord "established the earth" and it "stands." The verb translated as "stand" is repeated in the next line. It says that "they" stand according to God's ordinances or judgments. At creation, God placed His laws that stand forever and are a guide for all creation. These laws are "enduring, like heaven and earth."[46] It is interesting to notice that when creation is connected to humanity, it often results in an ephemeral predicament; however, when creation is seen in connection with God or His law, it is emphasizing the eternal quality of both.

10. *God as Judge.* God is not only the Creator but also the originator of the law. He established the rules, and as such, He has the authority to judge those who do not live according to His rules. In this category, the Creation references give God the authority to judge His creation. God has the right to judge, not because He was given this right from some other entity but because He established everything. Furthermore, God's judgment is often associated with joy and, as such, is viewed very positively by the psalmists.

• *Psalm 96.* As in most of the psalms, God's judgment is seen as a positive thing. All creation, including the heavens, seas, trees, and fields, is to rejoice because God is coming to judge the world. The first reference to God as Creator is found in verse 5. In this verse, God is contrasted with other gods. He is not like them; He is not an idol, because He "made the heavens."

There is no mention of earth. It is as if the psalmist is talking only about the heavenly realm. In this sphere, often associated with the divine dwelling place, only God reigns; He is the One who created it. The second reference to creation is found in verse 10. This time, the heavens are omitted, and God is described as the One who established the world. It begins with the statement "the Lord reigns," followed by the observation that "the world is firmly established." The whole verse, then, has the following structure:

Imperative: Say among the nations
    a. The Lord reigns
    b. He created the world
    b. His creation will last
    a. His reign will be just

God is the Ruler and Judge. He is the Ruler, because He created everything, and as Creator-King, He has the right to judge all creation. In this verse, the first two and the last two statements go together, and at the same time, the first and the last are connected, just as the middle is also connected. God reigns as the Creator, and at the same time, His creation "will not be moved," because He will judge it. God the King is also God the Judge, who created a lasting, unshakable, and unmovable world.

11. *Who Are the Wicked?* Because the psalms were written in a context tainted by sin, they reflect the presence of sin and sinful nature. The psalmists, who often struggled to keep the law, frequently ask for forgiveness and, at the same time, are subject to the results of sin in this world. However, in contrast to the psalmists—who in spite of their sinful state, fear God—there are those who are called *wicked*. Especially "cursing" psalms often depict a loathsome and shocking picture of their destiny. The psalmists ask for forgiveness, yet they call for punishment of the wicked. Who are these wicked people? In addition to saying that the wicked are in opposition to the psalmist, the author often assumes that the reader knows the characteristics of the wicked. Several psalms clarify who the wicked are, and some use the Creation theme in their argument.

• *Psalm 73.* This psalm shows the personal inner struggle of the writer due to the effects of the wicked. It is not necessarily because they oppress him, but as this psalm clearly shows, because the psalmist is envious of them. It concludes with a theme of praise and victory over the wicked.

Verse 9 includes a short categorization of the wicked by using an allusion to creation. Wicked people do not consider God as the Creator. They seem to disregard His law and even His power as the Creator. This is strengthened by questioning His power. Other psalms also include similar questions in connection with God as the Creator. Therefore, in the book of Psalms, rejecting creation and God's work of creation is a sign of wickedness.

12. *God as Savior and Helper.* References to creation often appear in the larger context of salvation; however, these two themes are usually not combined in the immediate context. In most instances, creation

and salvation in the Psalms are connected through another theme. There are some occurrences when God's help and creation are put together, though usually in the larger context of blessing.

• *Psalm 121.* Psalm 121 is the first of the so-called Songs of Ascent or pilgrimage psalms that employ the phrase "who made heaven and earth." This rare phrase is used three times in these psalms. The main themes of the Songs of Ascent are of the greatness of God, His creative power, His help, and His act of sustaining His creation.

The major theme of Psalm 121 is help through creation. By this, the writer shows that the Lord has the power and willingness to help His people. "The notion of watching over someone . . . pervades Psalm 121, echoing numerous references to divine protection."[47]

The writer of this psalm uses the poetic strategy of an unanswered question. Progression holds the tension of the psalm until the end. "The tension created in verse 1b by this question is not completely resolved in verse 2. It is only fully answered in verses 3–8."[48] Therefore, verses 3–8 are, in a way, an expansion of the answer given in verse 2. Verses 3–8 describe a progression from uncertainty to certainty, from anxiety to confidence. The development of the psalms can be divided into three parts:

a. The Lord, "who made heaven and earth."
b. The Lord is the sustainer of Israel.
c. The Lord will sustain you.

Divine protection and the sixfold repetition of the word for "to keep, to preserve"

provide the overall unity of this psalm. It begins in first person singular form. Both verses 1, 2 include "my" help. In verse 3, the voice changes to second person singular. It seems that a different speaker is addressing the first person. Most commentators see the setting of this psalm as a dialogue between "a father and his son going up to Jerusalem for the pilgrim festival, . . . or a priest blessing a pilgrim going back home from the feast, . . . or a group of pilgrims encouraging one another en route."[49]

○ *Verses 1, 2: Introduction of the Trust in the Lord.* The psalm begins with the image of mountains. The reader, however, has no clear idea where these mountains are located. This is followed by the even stranger phrase "from where shall my help come," which can be taken as a question or a statement. In parallel to that stands verse 2, beginning with the statement that "help comes from the Lord." Moreover, this Lord "made heaven and earth." Before going further, it should be established which mountains the psalmist is referring to.

There are three major ways of interpreting the reference to these mountains. First of all, there is a literal explanation. In this view, the mountains referred to in Psalm 121 are real mountains surrounding Jerusalem, which must be crossed to gain access to the city. There are numerous dangers on the way as the people cross these treacherous routes.

The second view sees the mountains as a symbol for a place where God lives. In this interpretation, the second half of verse 1 is not taken as a question but as a statement, to which the next line connects. In this way, the psalm has an ascending structure, in which one theme is developed in the next sentence.

The last major interpretation views the mountains as a metaphor for a dwelling place of other gods. "The hilltops were the seats of ancient sanctuaries, inherited from the Canaanites, which were strongly condemned (Lev. 26:30; Ps. 78:58)."[50] It was quite common that the nations built their "high places" and sanctuaries on the mountains. Psalm 121:2 avers a negative response. It looks to the right source of help—namely the Lord.

Another possible explanation of this quandary comes by combining the first and last view. In this way, the mountains are a symbol of other gods but, at the same time, are literal mountains with no source of help. Yet, they are a place where the Lord will continue His protection. This use of the plural form for the mountains in the blessing and help context is further supported by Genesis 49:26, in which the blessing surpasses or swells over the mountains. In other words, mountains are used as a contrast to the greatness of the coming blessing. As Habel notes, they are not the "source of divine aid and blessing (Gen 49:26)."[51] Similarly, Psalm 121 uses mountains in contrast to the real blessing.

The negative understanding of the relationship between mountains and the question in verse 1 is further supported by the use of introverted parallelism in verse 2:

a. Contemplation of creation: The hills
  b. Question: Where does my help
      come from?
  b. Answer: From the Lord
a. Contemplation of creation: The Creator[52]

Both verses are joined together by a poetic device "in which a word in the last part of a stich ('my help') is repeated in the first part of the following stich."[53]

The phrase "who made heaven and earth," in this case, is put in contrast to the mountains. Mountains are only part of Creation, but the help comes from the Creator. God's character can be seen in His creation, but help and blessing come only from the original source—He "who made heaven and earth." This formula is therefore used as a synonym for "almighty." It is the El Elyon of Melchizedek, who is powerful enough to help and to protect.

○ *Verses 3, 4.* Verses 1, 2 are linked by the use of the first person singular form and by another example of the poetic device in which "the last part of a stich is repeated in the first part of the following stich." This same technique is also used in verses 3 and 4, strengthening the argument for an inverted parallelism in verses 1 and 2.

a. He will protect you from slipping.
  b. He will not sleep.
a. He will keep Israel.
  b. He will not sleep.

○ *Verses 5-8.* The conclusion of this psalm is the description of God's protection through the use of the repetition of the four Hebrew letters usually transliterated YHWH or JHVH. "The deliberate placement of the Name Yahweh ... serves to direct the emphasis to Yahweh's actions."[54] Verse 5 begins this conclusion by stating who God is, and the following three verses describe the result of God's protection. Verse 6 "elaborates on the statement, 'the Lord is your shade' and so, it would appear that verses 5 and 6 are connected to one another."[55] Verse 6 is written chiastically as seen in the following example:

    a. By day
      b. The sun
        c. No harm
      b. The moon
    a. By night

"The sun and the moon, which were often given divine powers in other religions, are demythologised and deprived of their power. Yahweh rules over these powers."[56]

The phrase "your going out and your coming in" extends the protection to all aspects of life. This all-inclusive protection will last forever, as stated by the last phrase of this psalm.

Affirmation that God is the Creator is key in resolving the absence of help. "The answer to the poet's question as to where help comes from begins with the confession that Yahweh is the Creator."[57] Help can come "only from the Lord, the Creator of heaven and earth."[58]

Conclusion

Creation represents a significant theme in the book of Psalms. This fact prompts several observations.

The first is that the use of Creation language widens the scope of the text. Suddenly, the text no longer speaks to only a specific group of people, but it speaks to *all* nations and often includes even animals or other parts of creation.

Second, Creation themes always carry the subtext of praise and are often interrupted by its spontaneous expressions. It is a direct response to creation. When the psalmists consider the works of God's hands, their first response is praise.

Third, the psalmists refer to Creation as a historical fact. These writers believed that creation took place at the beginning and was a result of God's hand or God's Word. Those who do not recognize creation as God's handiwork are called wicked.

Fourth, creation is never perceived as an accident. Even when the psalmist questions the reasons for creation, God assures him of a greater plan.

Fifth, creation is always looked at from the perspective of a sinful world. It is entwined with the life-death cycle and with imagery of a fallen planet and, thus, usually represents a post-Flood world.

Sixth, it is interesting to notice that when creation is linked with humanity, it often emphasizes the fleeting state of being; however, when creation is seen in connection with God or His law, it highlights the eternal quality of both. It is this mortal being that God placed in charge of all creation and, therefore, has a great responsibility for its protection.

Seventh, the Exodus story is often incorporated within the Creation story. They are both the result of God's power, and therefore, both invoke praise.

Finally, in comparison with other ancient Near-Eastern deities, Creation theology in the Psalms emphasizes monotheism. Objects, such as the sun, moon, stars, or seas, are turned into created servants of God that not only do as He says but also give Him praise.

Implications for the
Genesis Creation Account

The book of Psalms includes numerous allusions to and echoes of the Genesis Creation account. The numerous Creation themes discovered in the Psalms clearly underline the theological thrust of the Hebrew Bible. Creation and a Creator are assumed. However, one wonders what does the book of Psalms add to the biblical concept of creation? How did the psalmists understand the beginnings of our world?

First, from the reading the Psalms, it is clear that the authors believed in a literal creation that occurred through the word of God (especially Pss. 33; 104). Furthermore, God completed the entire creation; everything is part of His work. The psalmists leave no place for chance or an accident. God is the One who gave life and set the world in place.

Creation week, as such, is not clearly seen in the book of Psalms, aside from the implication of such a progression of Creation in Psalm 104 (which falls outside the focus of this study and has been dealt with in a separate chapter). On the other hand, there is also no indication of anything different from a literal seven-day Creation, as described in Genesis 1. In the Psalms, the God of creation is a God of blessing. These blessings are immediate. In this way, God's power to create is seen in events that are sudden and immediate. Therefore, it could be argued that, on the basis of present events, God created in the past in the same way. Therefore, the Psalms, in an indirect way, support the seven-day literal Creation.

The main addition to the Genesis account is God's sustaining power over His creation. This does not mean that creation was not finished in seven days; rather, it suggests that God did not excuse Himself after He finished His creation but continued to be a caring Father and Sustainer.

All the occurrences of the Creation theme in the Psalms are tied to present reality. The Genesis account ends with the seventh day. God saw that everything was very good—and rests. The narrative continues, describing the entrance of sin, followed by God's immediate commencement of the process of saving a fallen world. He is present in the narratives, but the narratives do not stress His creative power. On the other hand, God continues to maintain His creation in the book of Psalms. He continues to create and renew a chaotic world. Many psalms refer to this God as a Sustainer. This is not a God who created physical substance and then stepped out to see what would happen. The psalmists stress that God's ongoing creative power is evident in a newborn child, in a growing plant that is being watered by the rain, and even through anomalies in the natural world. In this way, the psalmists illustrate the fact that the world was created by God from the beginning to the end.

The Psalms never give any credence to a mythical creation. Creation is not based on metaphorical or symbolic ideas but on solid facts. These facts could be seen by the psalmists and can still be seen today. Literal creation in the Psalms is based on present reality. Therefore, the book of Psalms strengthens and builds on the historical force of creation, which was already established in Genesis.

Humans are the wonderful work of God's

hands. They exhibit God's wisdom. It is this understanding that causes the psalmists to praise and worship. They are set apart from other aspects of creation, but at the same time, they are created by the same Hand of the Creator.

Finally, the psalmists used Creation themes to express their wonder over God's greatness. They do not satisfy the reader with absolute answers. They themselves admit that there are mysteries, which cannot be understood easily. They cannot explain every detail of God's creation; they can only marvel at the way it works. Thus, the book of Psalms suggests that not every event, every act, or every matter can be explained by scientific observation. There are complexities that only God can understand. There are areas where His power is seen, but this power cannot be explained by study or observation. Ultimately, the psalmists leave the reader with a need to believe in God the Creator.

Notes

1. Samuel L. Terrien, *The Psalms: Strophic Structure and Theological Commentary* (Grand Rapids, MI: Eerdmans, 2003), 670.

2. John H. Eaton, *The Psalms: A Historical and Spiritual Commentary With an Introduction and New Translation* (London: T & T Clark, 2003), 481.

3. Gerald H. Wilson, *Psalms: From Biblical Text to Contemporary Life*, vol. 1 (Grand Rapids, MI: Zondervan, 2002), 557.

4. Konrad Schaefer, "Psalms," in *Berit Olam: Studies in Hebrew Narrative and Poetry*, ed. David W. Cotter (Collegeville, MN: Liturgical Press, 2001), 280.

5. George J. Zemek, "Grandeur and Grace: God's Transcendence and Immanence in Psalm 113," *Master's Seminary Journal* 1, no. 2 (1990): 133.

6. Martin S. Rozenberg and Bernard M. Zlotowitz, *The Book of Psalms: A New Translation and Commentary* (Northvale, NJ: Jason Aronson, 1999), 727.

7. James Luther Mays, *Interpretation: Psalms*, A Bible Commentary for Teaching and Preaching (Louisville, KY: John Knox Press, 1994), 136.

8. Michael D. Goulder, *The Psalms of the Return: Book V, Psalms 107–150* (Sheffield, England: Sheffield Academic Press, 1998), 160.

9. W. Graham Scroggie, *A Guide to the Psalms* (Grand Rapids, MI: Kregel, 1995), 3:108.

10. Zemek, "Grandeur and Grace," 129.

11. Cas J. A. Vos, *Theopoetry of the Psalms* (Pretoria: Protea Book House, 2005), 129.

12. Hans-Joachim Kraus, *Psalms 60–150: A Commentary* (Minneapolis, MN: Fortress, 1993), 215.

13. Rozenberg and Zlotowitz, *The Book of Psalms*, 570.

14. Kraus, *Psalms 60–150,* 215.

15. Rozenberg and Zlotowitz, *The Book of Psalms*, 568.

16. Schaefer, "Psalms," 181.

17. Kraus, *Psalms 60–150,* 99.

18. Ibid., 101.

19. Terrien, *The Psalms*, 541.

20. Rozenberg and Zlotowitz, *The Book of Psalms*, 454.

21. Zemek, "Grandeur and Grace," 129.

22. Scroggie, *A Guide to the Psalms*, 88.

23. Wilson, *Psalms*, 908.

24. Rozenberg and Zlotowitz, *The Book of Psalms*, 389.

25. Ibid.

26. James L. Crenshaw, *The Psalms: An Introduction* (Grand Rapids, MI: Eerdmans, 2001), 73.

27. James H. Waltner, "Psalms," in *Believers Church Bible Commentary*, eds. Elmer A. Martens and Willard M. Swartley (Scottdale, PA: Herald, 2006), 61.

28. Terrien, *The Psalms*, 127.

29. Wilson, *Psalms*, 204.

30. Mays, *Psalms*, 425.

31. Terrien, *The Psalms*, 874.

32. Mays, *Psalms*, 283.

33. Rozenberg and Zlotowitz, *The Book of Psalms*, 564.

34. James Limburg, "Psalms," in *Westminster Bible Companion*, eds. Patrick D. Miller and David L. Bartlett

(Louisville, KY: Westminster John Knox, 2000), 494.

35. Terrien, *The Psalms*, 909.

36. Mays, *Psalms*, 440.

37. Ibid., 441.

38. Scroggie, *A Guide to the Psalms*, 125.

39. Ibid.

40. Eaton, *The Psalms*, 476.

41. Limburg, "Psalms," 395.

42. Schaefer, "Psalms," 294.

43. Scroggie, *A Guide to the Psalms*, 182.

44. Terrien, *The Psalms*, 801.

45. Rozenberg and Zlotowitz, *The Book of Psalms*, 783.

46. Terrien, *The Psalms*, 802.

47. Crenshaw, *The Psalms*, 21.

48. Vos, *Theopoetry of the Psalms*, 256.

49. Goulder, *The Psalms of the Return*, 42.

50. Terrien, *The Psalms*, 11.

51. Norman C. Habel, " 'Yahweh, Maker of Heaven and Earth': A Study in Tradition Criticism," *Journal of Biblical Literature* 91, no. 3 (1972): 329.

52. Scroggie, *A Guide to the Psalms*, 205.

53. Vos, *Theopoetry of the Psalms*, 35.

54. Ibid., 254.

55. Ibid.

56. Ibid., 257.

57. Ibid.

58. Eaton, *The Psalms*, 425.

Genesis and Creation in the Wisdom Literature

Ángel M. Rodríguez

Old Testament scholars generally recognize that wisdom thinking and theology are directly related to the topic of creation and that creation provides a coherent perspective from which to study it by perhaps providing a way to integrate wisdom thinking into the theology of the Old Testament. This direct connection between wisdom thinking and creation justifies examining the possible role or influence of Genesis 1–3 on wisdom thinking.

Creation Motifs in the Book of Job

It is generally recognized that the author of Job was acquainted with the Creation account of Genesis and used it in the development of some of his arguments. The book contains a significant number of creation motifs and discussions.

Creation of Humans. Although we do not find a study of the origins of humanity in Job, the writer is acquainted with the creation of humans as recorded in Genesis. Elihu, when arguing that often humans do not ask for God's help, states that "no one says, 'Where is God my Maker' " (Job 35:10).[1] The participle translated as "the One who created me" pertains to the verb translated "to make, do, create," which is "the commonest verb for 'create' " in the Old Testament.[2] This is the same verb used in Genesis 1:26 when God said, "Let Us *make* man in Our image." Elihu is assuming that God is the Creator of humankind. Job also uses the same participial form to refer to God as "He who made me" (Job 31:15). He refers to himself as the "the work" of God's hands (14:15). The connection between the use of this verb in Job and in Genesis is strengthened by linking it to the "breath" of God and to "clay."

Job sees God as a Potter or Artisan: "Your hands fashioned ["to shape, form"] and made me altogether" (Job 10:8). He proceeds to clarify that concept by saying, "You have made me as clay" (v. 9). The verbs translated "to fashion" and "to make" are used as synonyms to refer "to God's act of creation."[3] "To fashion" stresses "the artistic skill of a craftsman in making an image"[4] or even an idol. Job conceives of God as an Artisan, who shaped and created humans from clay. Clay is the raw material used by the potter to produce what he intended to do. When used with reference to God, it points to God's sovereignty and care for humans (Jer. 18:4–8; Isa. 64:8). In the context of creation, clay is the raw material God used to create humans. This term is not used in Genesis 1; 2, but we find instead the phrase "of dust from the ground" (Gen. 2:7). In the book of

Job, "clay" and "dust" are practically used as synonyms (Job 10:9). Humans "dwell in houses of clay, whose foundation is in the dust" (4:19). When they die, they return to dust (34:15), an idea found in Genesis 3:19. The conceptual connection is quite clear.

In Genesis, the movement from clay to a living human being occurs when God breathes "into his nostrils the breath of life" (Gen. 2:7). This is also the case in Job: "As long as life is in me [literally, "the breath is in me"], and the breath of God is in my nostrils" (Job 27:3). The Hebrew term translated as "breath of life" designates the divine gift of life bestowed to humans at creation, which constitutes the dynamic nature of human life that is sustained by the "spirit of God."[5] They are both given "to human beings as life-giving powers."[6] When God withdraws both of them, the result is death (34:14, 15). The book of Job presupposes that the writer knew about the origin of humanity recorded in Genesis 2.

Some additional evidence strengthens this conclusion. In Job 31:33, Job is speaking: "Have I covered my transgressions like Adam, by hiding my iniquity in my bosom . . . ?" The only linguistic connection with Genesis is the term translated "Adam," which could be a proper name (Gen. 4:25) or a collective noun, "humankind" (1:27). This reference to Adam has been interpreted in different ways, but the most obvious one is to take it as referring to Adam. There is a clear allusion in the text to Adam's attempt to conceal his sin before the Lord by blaming Eve (3:12).

The second passage is found in one of the speeches of Eliphaz, in which he asks

Job, "Were you the first man to be born or were you brought forth before the hills?" (Job 15:7). Eliphaz is reacting to Job's attack against the wisdom of his friends. This passage deals with two different moments: existence and pre-existence. The first is about the moment when the first man was born or came into existence—the image of birth is used to speak about creation—and the second refers to the time before creation—before the hills were created. Was Job the first man created or was he created before anything else? Here, Psalm 90:2 could be useful: "Before the mountains were born or You gave birth to the earth and the world, even from everlasting to everlasting, You are God." This passage indicates that the verbs translated as "born" and "birth" can be used figuratively to refer to the divine work of creation. In this case, the birth of the "first man" designates the creation of the first human being and would at least contain an allusion to Adam. One wonders whether Eliphaz is satirically asking Job whether he thinks he is wiser than the first man or even than God Himself. The possibility of the allusion to Adam is quite strong.

The last passage to be considered here is Job 20:4, in which Zophar asks Job: "Do you know this from of old, from the establishment ["to place, to put"] of man ["Adam"] on earth?" The biblical background for this statement is Genesis 2:8: "The LORD God planted a garden toward the east, in Eden; and there He placed the man whom He had formed." The presence in verse 8 of the words translated "Adam" and "the man" make the connection between the two passages practically unquestionable. What

Zophar is bringing to the table "is traditional wisdom, which he pretends to be as old as Adam, and he marvels ironically that Job has not yet learned it."[7]

Alleged Existence of Other Accounts. Some have found in Job 33:6 evidence of a non-biblical study of the origin of humanity from Mesopotamia. In the text, Elihu is addressing Job: "I belong to God like you; I too have been formed out of the clay." It has been argued that in some myths dealing with the origin of humans the Akkadian word translated "to pinch off," takes as its object "clay." In one of the Akkadian myths, the goddess Mami "nipped off fourteen pieces of clay"[8] to create humans. In another one, two goddesses "nip off pieces of clay"[9] from the Abzu, give them human form, and place them in the womb of birth-goddesses, where the clay figures develop and are later born as humans. Based on this mythology, it has been suggested that in Job we find at least traces of a myth that is significantly different from what is narrated in the Genesis account.

One could perhaps give serious consideration to the previous interpretation if, first, it could be demonstrated that Elihu, coming from Uz and under the influence of Mesopotamian thinking, was not acquainted with the Creation account found in Genesis. But this is not the case. In Job 33:3, as already pointed out, he uses ideas now recorded in Genesis 2:7 to refer to the origin of his life: God gave him the breath of life. Second, Elihu is attempting to answer some of the arguments used by Job to support his views. In Job 13, Job argued that it appears to be impossible to enter into a dialogue with God. Now, Elihu says to

Job that since they are both humans, they can enter into a dialogue with each other. They both were created from clay (Job 10:9; 33:6), and God gave them the breath of life (27:3; 33:4). In other words, "their common humanity is traced to creation."[10] Elihu seems to be developing an argument based on the Creation narrative recorded in Genesis 1.

Concerning the meaning of the verb translated as "formed," the translation "to be nipped off" is only assigned to its usage in Job 33:6, and this is done under the influence of the Akkadian cognate. There are four other usages in this formation in the Old Testament. In three of which, the direct objects are the eyes. In such cases, the meaning seems to be "to blink or squint the eye" (e.g., Ps. 35:19; Prov. 6:13; 10:10). The phrase refers to a nonverbal communication consisting of a gesture that could express mockery, deception, or indifference. In one case, the direct object is lips: "He who compresses his lips brings evil to pass" (16:30), probably referring to a gesture of disdain or deception.

A Ugaritic cognate could also be useful in attempting to establish the meaning of the Hebrew verb translated as "formed." The Ugaritic word, like the Hebrew verb, has two slightly different meanings, namely "to nibble, to bite gently, to gnaw" and "to mold, to form."[11] The first usage is compatible with the passages in the Old Testament in which the verb translated "formed," when used in conjunction with "eyes" or "lips," means "to wink or squint" or "to compress." The Ugaritic verb is also used with "clay" to express the idea of shaping it into an effigy. This usage fits well into the meaning of the Hebrew verb in Job 33:6, thus, justifying the translation "formed out of the clay." Therefore, there is no need to postulate the presence of a Mesopotamian representation of the humankind's origin or traces of it in Job.

Creation and De-creation. Several scholars have noted the influence of the Creation account in the prologue and the third chapter of Job.

• *Prologue.* It has been suggested that if Job 1; 2 are read through the filter of Genesis 1–3, then there may be a correlation that is not accidental but is the result "of a conscious adaptation of Genesis to the fabric of the new narrative."[12] Only a few of the connections deserve consideration. Although the case is not as strong as one would like it to be, it could be argued that there seems to be an intertextual connection with Genesis. The description of the family and possessions of Job appear to be a fulfillment of God's command to Adam and Eve and to the animals to multiply and be fruitful (Job 1:2, 3; Gen. 1:22, 28). The blessing bestowed upon Adam and Eve has also been granted to Job (Job 1:10). The Creation narrative seems to "create the atmosphere"[13] for the story of Job, who is described as living in an idyllic state. This is reinforced by the reference to a seven-day cycle in Genesis, which is implied in Job (1:4, 5).

Job's idyllic state of being changes in a radical way, and he experiences de-creation. Having lost everything, he was left only with his wife. It is probable that the tragedy began during "the first day of the seven-day cycle, as his children celebrated 'in the eldest brother's house'

(Job 1:13). This is when creation should begin."[14] Job's first reaction to de-creation is summarized in the sentence: "Naked I came from my mother's womb, and naked I shall return there" (1:21). In Genesis 2, the human awareness of nakedness surfaces at the moment when, on account of sin, de-creation begins. Job is also realizing that he is heading toward death. The saying may be identifying the womb with the ground from which humans were taken and to which they will return (Gen. 3:19).

One more theological connection between the prologue of Job and Genesis 3 should be considered. In both cases, an adversary—the serpent, Satan—is in dialogue with another person: God in Job and Eve in Genesis. But the fundamental attitude of the adversary is the same. The theological concept of a cosmic conflict is present in both, and the adversary's primary object of attack is not Eve or Job; it is God Himself. In both cases, he attacks God's way of governing His creation. In the case of Eve and Adam, God is charged with restricting their self-expression and development by threatening them with death. In the case of Job, God is accused of having bought Job's service by protecting Job and his family; Satan insinuates that if God would only withdraw that protection and stop being Job's provider, Job would be able to express himself and would break his relationship with God, as Adam and Eve did.

The Creation account provides the background for the prologue of Job to emphasize the radical experience that Job went through. What he experienced was like the deconstruction of creation experienced by

Adam and Eve but with one difference: he was innocent. This made his experience more intriguing.

• *Job's First Speech.* Some have found intertextual connections between Job 3 and the Creation account in Genesis. It is argued that Job's first speech is "a counter-cosmic incantation designed to reverse the stages of the creation of the day of his birth, which were thought to be essentially the same as the stages of the seven-day creation of the world."[15] What Job is doing is expressing a "death wish for himself and the entire creation."[16] The following parallels have been identified:

	Job 3:3–13	Genesis 1:1–2:4
Day 1	let it be darkness (v. 4a)	let there be light (v. 3b)
Day 2	let not God above attend to it (v. 4b)	and [God] divided between the waters below the firmament and the waters above the firmament (v. 7b)
Day 4	that night . . . let it not be counted in the days of the year (v. 6b)	let there be light . . . to divide between the day and the night and let them be signs . . . for years (v. 14)
Day 5	those prepared to stir up Leviathan (v. 8b)	and God created the great sea monsters (v. 21a)
Day 6	Why did I not die from the womb? (v. 11a)	let us make man (v. 26a)
Day 7	for now I would be lying down and quiet, I would be asleep and at rest (v. 13)	and [God] rested on the seventh day from all His work . . . He sanctified it, because in it He rested (2:2, 3)

If the thematic connections are accepted, they would have to be interpreted in terms of reversal, or de-creation. But not all the parallels are persuasive. There is not a valid parallel for day two, and the third day is omitted. Overall, it could be argued that the Creation account of Genesis 1:1–2:4 seems to provide the theological background for Job's first discourse as he wishes for the impossible, the undoing of his creation. This is particularly the case with respect to the phrase "may that day be darkness" (Job 3:4), which is basically the opposite of that found in Genesis 1:3: "Let there be light." But probably the most radical contrast is the one of rest. After creation, God rested to celebrate the goodness of creation, but Job wants to rest in death, thus, denying the value of his life (Job 3:13).

There are other linguistic parallels: "days and years" (Gen. 1:14; Job 3:6) and light and night (Gen. 1:14; Job 3:3, 9). It may also be important to notice that there is a reference in Job 2:13 to a period of seven days and seven nights during which Job and his friends sat on the ground "with no one speaking a word." This is a period of inactivity and deep silence in contrast to Genesis 1, where God is active every day and His voice is constantly heard. It may also be useful to observe that Job's attempt to de-create his own existence takes place through the spoken word in the form of a curse, whereas God's creation takes place through the power of His spoken word that occasionally takes the form of a blessing (Gen. 1:22, 28). The idea that, in using Genesis as a background for the expression of his emotions and wishes, Job is aiming at the de-creation of the cosmos is foreign to the biblical text.

• *Creation and God's Speeches.* The divine speeches in Job 38:1–40:5 are developed around the topic of creation as God takes Job in a cosmic tour. De-creation is not present in the text, but the Genesis Creation account provides a background for the speeches. The first speech the Lord addresses to Job "consists of dozens of questions about the cosmos. They begin with creation and advance in a pattern that approximates the first chapter of Genesis"[17] (see Job 38:4–39:30). Of course, God is describing to Job creation as he experiences it, and consequently, we find in the speeches comments on the presence of death on earth (38:17). This is possible because the speeches are not primarily about the creation of the earth and all that is in it. They are not even about creation as it came out of the hands of the Creator. This is creation as Job and we encounter it today. But the speeches presuppose that God is the Creator, and this idea goes back to Genesis.

The first speech can be divided into two sections. The first one is mainly about the earth, the sea, the stars, and meteorological phenomena (Job 38:8–38). The second part is about the fauna (38:39–39:30). The speech begins with a reference to the moment when God is creating the earth (38:4–7). A building image is used for the divine act of creating the earth in which God is metaphorically described as "the architect (v. 5a), the surveyor (v. 5b), and the engineer (v. 6)."[18]

This is not another Creation narrative different from Genesis 1 but a metaphorical description of what we find in Genesis (vv. 9, 10). It is the theological background of Genesis that allows for the use of the metaphor. In the immediate context of the founding of the earth by the Lord, the separation of the waters or sea from the earth is mentioned. In Job 38:10, God separates the earth from the sea by setting limits to the sea in order for it not to encroach on earth. As in Genesis, this is creation by separation. Besides, in the rest of the speech, as will be seen, Genesis 1 plays an important role. The use of the building metaphor "emphasizes the wisdom and discernment required in its grand design"[19]—something that only God possesses.

A comparison of Job 38:4–38 with Genesis 1 suggests a significant number of linguistic connections between the two passages. The following list summarizes the evidence:

Job	Term	Genesis
38:4, 13, 18, 24, 26, 33	"earth"	1:1, 10–12, 15
38:8, 16	"sea"	1:10, 22, 26, 28
38:8, 29, 32	"come out"	1:12, 24
38:12	"morning"	1:5, 8, 13, 19
38:15, 19, 24	"light"	1:3–4, 5, 18
38:16, 30	"deep"	1:2
38:19	"darkness"	1:2, 4, 5, 18
38:21, 23	"day"	1:5, 8, 13, 14, 16
38:26	"human"	1:26, 27
38:27	"grass"	1:11, 12
38:29, 33, 37	"heavens"	1:1, 8, 9, 14, 15
38:30, 34	"waters"	1:2, 6, 7, 9, 10
38:38	"dust"	2:7

These linguistic connections are, to some extent, to be expected in a speech about the natural world. But the fact that, within the speech itself, there is a clear reference to God's creative activity (Job 38:4–7) indicates that the biblical writer was using the Creation account of Genesis as a theological background for the speech. As already indicated, God is depicted as an Architect and Builder who lays the foundation of the building, takes measurements, and then finishes the project by placing the cornerstone (vv. 4–6). From that moment on, the speech assumes that God is the Creator of everything there is in the cosmos. In this section, the speech is based on what God created during days two, three, and four of the Creation week.

a. Day 3	Creation of earth and sea	Job 38:4–11
b. Day 4	Creation of light to rule	Job 38:12–15
a. Day 3	Sea and earth	Job 38:16–18
b. Day 4	Dwelling of light and darkness	Job 38:19–21
c. Day 2	Meteorological phenomena	Job 38:22–30
b. Day 4	Stars	Job 38:31–33
c. Day 2	Meteorological phenomena	Job 38:34–38

The discussion is organized on the basis of the days of Creation using a couple of panels (ABA'B') and a chiasm (CBC'). The speech moves from the content of one day to the other to nurture curiosity and to introduce the unexpected. Therefore, Job could not anticipate what would come next in spite of his acquaintance with the Creation narrative.

The rest of the first speech and most of the second speech (Job 40:6–41:34) are based on days five and six of the Creation account and concentrates on the fauna or zoology. The material seems to be organized as follows:

a. Day 6	Wild animal: lion	Job 38:39, 40
b. Day 5	Bird: raven	Job 38:41
a. Day 6	Wild animals: mountain goat, deer, wild donkey, wild ox	Job 39:1–12
b. Day 5	Bird: ostrich	Job 39:13–18
a. Day 6	Domestic animal: horse	Job 39:19–25
b. Day 5	Birds: hawks and eagles	Job 39:26–30
a. Day 6	Wild animals: Behemoth and Leviathan	Job 40:15–41:34

The literary pattern found in this section is formed by three panels of the *a* plus *b* pattern and an incomplete one that creates a literary envelope for the content of the structure. The speeches presuppose the Creation narrative of birds and animals, as recorded in Genesis 1, but it provides much more information concerning the habitat of the animals and their behavior. The main purpose for using Genesis as a point of reference in the speeches is to provide for them an organizational pattern—a back and forth movement of the activities of days five and six. In other words, without Genesis 1 as a referent, the long list taken from the natural world will not show any particular order or pattern.

• *Summary.* This discussion has provided enough biblical evidence to suggest that what the book of Job says about creation is influenced by the Creation account of Genesis. This is particularly the case with respect to the origin of humans. The author and the speakers were well acquainted with the Creation narrative and used it whenever necessary to contribute to the development of the dialogue. In Job, the account of the creation of humans is used as a rhetorical tool to communicate several ideas. The first is the obvious one: it is employed to demonstrate the common origin of humankind (Job 33:6). Second, it highlights the fragility of human existence. Since life is fragile and brief—clay and breath—God should hasten to deliver Job from his pain or he will die (7:7, 21). Third, it is used to underline the value of human life. Since human existence was created by God and is, therefore, good, the Creator should not destroy it (10:8, 9; 27:3). Finally, Genesis's representation of the origin of humanity is used in Job to accentuate the superiority of God as Creator over humans as creatures (31:14, 15; 34:13–15).

In the prologue, the idea of the de-creation is influenced by the Creation account and is used as a background for the reversal of Job's fortunes. It is also employed to connect the adversary with the serpent of Genesis 3. De-creation theology is particularly present in the first full speech of Job in chapter 3. In the divine speeches, Genesis 1 not only contributes to the development of their ideology, but in some instances, it also contributes to the organization of some of their content. This presupposes that the author of Job was exceptionally well acquainted with the Creation narrative.

Creation Motifs in the Book of Proverbs

Proverbs adds a significant number of texts addressing aspects of Creation theology, clearly indicating that the writers knew about the Creation account of Genesis 1; 2. The new element, carefully developed in the book, is that God created through wisdom. This is stated very early in the book: "The LORD by wisdom founded the earth, by understanding He established the heavens" (Prov. 3:19).

Humanity and Marriage. God is "the Maker or Creator" of humans (Prov. 17:5), who, according to Proverbs 20:27, are also animated by the God-given "breath of life." In this passage, the term used for humans provides a useful linguistic match to Genesis 2:7. Humans are male and female, united by God in a marriage relationship: "He who finds a wife finds a good thing and obtains favor from the LORD" (Prov. 18:22). In this case, the word translated "good thing" is used in conjunction with the verb "to find," and it probably means "to find (one's) fortune,"[20] that is to say to find a person of great value. Its meaning is further clarified by the phrase "obtain favor from the LORD," which means that the husband has been blessed by the Lord. The implication of the text is that "the husband has little to do acquiring such a prize. She is a gift from God."[21] This idea goes back to Genesis 2:22–24, in which God brings Eve to Adam and blesses both of them. The concept of marriage found in Proverbs is the one established in Genesis. A man and a woman are united in the presence of God; He blesses them, and a partnership is instituted among the three of them. At that moment, the couple makes a covenant with and before the Lord, and the two of them establish a relationship of mutual, loving friendship.

Wisdom and Creation. The phrase translated "tree of life" is employed outside Genesis only in four passages in Proverbs. Even though it is used in three of these (Prov. 11:30; 13:12; 15:4) in a metaphorical sense, "the mere fact of the presence of this motif seems to provide a link to the important story of origins found in Genesis 1–3."[22] Concerning the use of the same phrase in Proverbs 3:18, it has been argued that this is a nonmetaphoric use of it, referring back to Genesis. The passage reads: "She [Wisdom] is a tree of life to those who take hold of her, and happy are all who hold her fast." The text gives the impression that, even here, the phrase is being used metaphorically to refer to the life-giving nature of wisdom. The allusion to the Garden of Eden is argued by indicating that, in the context, there is terminology that is common to both. For instance, in Proverbs 3:13 the noun "man" is used twice. This double use of the term is unique in the Hebrew Bible. The argument is that "the verse obviously applies to any individual in general, but designating him by [the word translated "man"] rather than one of its alternatives is dictated by desire to emphasize and allusion to [Adam] of the Garden of Eden story."[23] It is also argued that Proverbs 3:19, 20 resembles 8:22–31, where the role of wisdom in creation is discussed and where a connection is also found with Genesis 4:4, 10.

The most important argument, according to this interpretation, is based on the connection between Proverbs 3:17, 18. Verse 17 speaks of the ways and paths of wisdom that are pleasant and peaceful, and verse 18 begins with the tree of life. The suggestion is made that combining the words of the two verses yields the translation "her ways are the ways of/toward the Tree of Life."[24] It is then concluded that Proverbs 3:18 "signals us that the way (back) to the Tree of Life is through wisdom."[25] This reading of verses 17 and 18 is hardly defensible. But the close connection between way and tree of life found in both Proverbs and Genesis is significant and supports the argument that there is here, at least, an allusion to Genesis 2; 3. It is also likely that even if the phrase "tree of life" is

used metaphorically, the allusion to Genesis still stands. The text assumes that there was a tree of life and that literal access to it in the garden is no longer possible. It, then, proceeds to teach that we can again have access to it through divine wisdom.

Wisdom and the Study of the Origin of Humanity. Proverbs develops, in a unique way, the role of wisdom in the Creation of the world. This emphasis on wisdom is not present in Genesis, but it is not presented here as an alternative to the Genesis account. On the contrary, it enriches that account by considering the thoughts of the Creator. The key passage on the topic of Creation is Proverbs 8:22–31, which is part of a wisdom poem in the form of speech (vv. 4–36). In this passage, Wisdom is personified and invites humans to listen to her (vv. 4–11). The authority of her call to listen is based on her knowledge and her value for human existence (vv. 12–21) and on her close relationship with the Creator (vv. 22–31). She can be a reliable guide for humans (vv. 32–36).

The passage in verses 22–31 is not properly speaking about creation but about wisdom, but in the process, something very important is said about creation. With respect to creation itself, the passage could be divided in two sections. One of them is about the pre-creation condition, and the other is about creation itself. Although the main interest of the passage is not to describe creation along the lines of the Genesis Creation account, a connection with Genesis is undeniable. It is not a Creation account, but rather, a highly poetic description of creation.

• *Pre-creation State.* The pre-creation

state is depicted through negatives. This is done in Proverbs 8:24–26: "When there were no . . ." (v. 24), "before . . ." (v. 25), and "while He had not yet made" or "before he had made" (v. 26). A partial description of the pre-creation condition of some elements of the earth is also found in Genesis 2:5, 6, where similar terminology is employed ("No shrub of the field was yet; . . . no plant of the field had yet . . . ; there was no man"). In the case of Genesis 1, there is no description of the pre-creation state of the cosmos. Before cosmic creation, there was only God (v. 1), and this by itself indicates *creatio ex nihilo*.

According to Proverbs, before creation "there were no depths," no "springs abounding with water" (Prov. 8:24), and neither were there "mountains" or "hills" (v. 25). God had not yet made the earth, the fields, and "the first dust of the world" (v. 26). In other words, the earth as we know it, with water, mountains, hills, and dust, had not yet been created. According to Genesis, God created the earth (Gen. 1:2), the dust (2:7), and the "deep" (1:2), which is associated with "the springs" of water (or "the fountains of the deep," 7:11). The mountains and the hills are not mentioned in Genesis 1, but since they are part of the earth as we know it, they are included in the list of what was not there before creation.

• *Creation Itself.* The wisdom poem moves from pre-creation to Creation itself or to the moment when God was creating. Only a few examples are given of what He created, but they are framed by a reference to the heavens at the beginning of the list (Prov. 8:27) and to the earth at the end

(v. 29). This refers to Genesis 1:1: "In the beginning God created the heavens and the earth." In between these two, Proverbs emphasizes the skies and water. God is described in the passage as an Architect who is building the cosmos and the earth: "He established the heavens," "he inscribed ["to inscribe, decree"] a circle on the face of the deep" (Prov. 8:27b), "he made firm the skies above" (v. 28a), "fixed" ("to show oneself strong") the springs of the deep (v. 28b), set "boundaries" ("limit, regulation") to the sea (v. 29a), "He marked out ["to inscribe, decree"] the foundations of the earth" (v. 29c). The language describes the work of a being who is constructing nothing less than the cosmos.

• *Central Purpose of the Passage.* The main interest of the passage is not on the creation of the cosmos but on the significance of wisdom. The brief discussion of the pre-creation period has the purpose of establishing that divine Wisdom pre-existed, while the discussion about the divine act of Creation reveals that during Creation she was already with Him: "The LORD possessed me at the beginning of His way, before His works of old ["from of old"]" (Prov. 8:22); "From everlasting I was established" (v. 23); "When there were no depths I was brought forth ["to be in labor"]" (vv. 24, 25). The language used is highly figurative and is basically taken from the experience of human reproduction.

Scholars are divided with respect to the meaning of the verb translated "to acquire" in Proverbs 8:22. It is generally recognized that its basic meaning is "to acquire," from which other derived usages are possible ("to possess," "to buy," "to create," and "to beget").[26] What is strongly debated is whether the verb also means "to create." It has been suggested that this usage may be implied in only two passages, namely Genesis 14:19, 22. In the context of wisdom, the main possibilities are "to acquire," "to possess," "to beget." This means that the determining factor would have to be the immediate context.

The context clearly supports the idea of begetting. Wisdom herself unambiguously states that she came into being through birth: "I was brought forth," indicating that at some point she was born. The Hebrew verb used here is defined as "a comprehensive term for everything from the initial contractions to the birth itself."[27] It is, therefore, better to interpret the verb as referring to the moment of conception. The moment when the action of the verb took place is identified as "at the beginning," using the same Hebrew term employed in Genesis 1:1. "At the beginning of His way" is clarified as "before His works of old." When God began His work of creation, Wisdom was already with Him; He had already conceived her. In the next verse, the existence of Wisdom is apparently pushed back into eternity: "From everlasting I was established" (Prov. 8:23).

The new verb translated "established me" is also difficult. One translation indicates that it is "to pour out (a libation offering)," but this does not fit the context. In what sense was wisdom poured out? Where was it poured if nothing else had been created? There are two other possible readings of the verb. The first is to consider the verb to mean "to be woven, to be formed." This by-form is used in Isaiah 25:7b: "The veil [a woven "covering"] which is stretched ["to be woven, shaped"] over all nations." The second possibility is that the verb means "to weave, to shape," and "to be made into shape, manufactured." The meaning of the two verbs would be basically the same.

What would then be the meaning of the phrase "from everlasting I was being woven"? The best parallel would probably be Psalm 139:13b, in which the psalmist states: "You wove me in my mother's womb," denoting the process of gestation inside the mother. Interestingly, the parallel verb in that verse is "for you formed my inward parts." The two verbs express different ideas—one would designate the begetting, while the other would refer to the development of the embryo. In the case of Wisdom in Proverbs 8:22, 23, she is described as conceived or begotten by God (v. 22); in verse 23, her development is described as the process of weaving together the different parts of the embryo; and finally, in verses 24, 25, the moment of her birth is described.

Her birth seems to coincide with the act of Creation in the sense that, at that moment, what was not yet was created: "When He established the heavens, I was there, when He inscribed a circle on the face of the deep, when He made firm the skies" (vv. 27–29). Throughout the whole process of creation, Wisdom was with the Lord. She concludes saying, "Then I was beside Him, as a master workman; and I was daily His delight" (v. 30). As the Lord is creating, Wisdom is an object of His delight. It could very well be that the idea of delight is expressed in Genesis 1 through the use of the phrases "God saw that the light was good"

(Gen. 1:4, 10, 12, 18, 21, 25) and "it was very good" (v. 31). God rejoices as He contemplates the works of His hands. The Creation act is described in Proverbs 8:31, 32 as a cosmic playing activity ("to laugh, play"), indicating not only how joyful it was but also the effortlessness of the divine activity. Both God and Wisdom rejoice as the cosmos is coming into existence in a context free from conflict but filled with joy. This theology is also at the foundation of the theology of Creation in Genesis, where creation takes place free from conflict and as the result of the effortless power of God.

On the surface, it could appear that the Creation elements present in verses 22–31 seem to be quite different from what we find in Genesis, but that is not the case.

First, the image provided by these texts is that of a God who creates effortlessly, assigns roles to the different elements, and establishes limits for everything to function in proper harmony.

Second, the language of birth is exclusively associated with Wisdom. Under the influence of ancient Near-Eastern creation ideas, some have concluded that this passage depicts Wisdom as a goddess. But what the text seems to indicate is that wisdom is a personification of a divine attribute.

Third, as compared to Genesis, Proverbs 8 allows a look back before Creation into the origin of wisdom. Here, "wisdom originates from God's very self."[28] Genesis depicts a God who is fully active in creating, but here, He is portrayed as a God who had been conceiving and weaving wisdom—creating it— within Himself; this wisdom later became the objective reality of the cosmos humans know and of which they are a part. The brief

mention of the beginning of creation in Proverbs 8 has been more fully developed in Genesis 1; 2.

Fourth, the process of Creation that can be detected in this passage is totally compatible with that in Genesis 1; 2. In both cases, God is described as an Architect or Builder who separated things and assigned to them specific roles. It is true that Creation through the Divine Word is not fully visible in Proverbs, but it is not totally absent. In the poem, the order of Creation was established through the divine command, suggesting the presence of the spoken word. This is particularly the case in Proverbs 8:29: "When He set for the sea its boundary so that the water would not transgress His command." The word translated "boundary" could also be translated "law, regulation," and here, it would be designating the divine regulation governing the sea, which was not to be transgressed by it (notice the personification of the sea). The Hebrew word translated "command," means "mouth," but by extension, it expresses the idea of the "spoken command" or what comes out of the mouth as a command (Gen. 41:40; Josh. 15:13). The specific command given to the waters is explicitly mentioned in Job 38:11a: "Thus far you [the sea] shall come, but no farther." The phrase "would not transgress His command" means that the waters will not transgress what came out of the mouth of the Lord. This is a hint at Creation through the spoken word.

• *Summary.* The Creation theology found in Proverbs is related to the theology of Creation recorded in Genesis 1; 2. The creation of humans as male and female, united in marriage by the Lord, the references to the tree of life, and the overall theology of Creation in Proverbs 8:22–31 unquestionably demonstrate that the author of the book was acquainted with the Creation narrative in Genesis. The wisdom poem provides, through the use of highly figurative or metaphoric language, some insights not present in Genesis but compatible with it. It also expresses, in poetic form, ideas found in Genesis. The differences between the two enrich one another's depiction of divine Creation.

Creation Motifs in the Book of Ecclesiastes

It is generally accepted that the book of Genesis has exerted some influence on the book of Qohelet, the Hebrew name for Ecclesiastes. Of primary interest here is the topic of creation, and in this particular case, there are just a few passages where this influence is clearly present, indicating that the author was acquainted with Genesis 1–3. One could begin with one of the most frequently used words throughout the book, commonly translated "vanity." It seems to contain an echo of the name of the second son of Adam and Eve, Abel. The noun designates that which is transitory and ephemeral, like Abel who appeared for a brief period of time and then, like a vapor, was gone. Ecclesiastes universalizes the experience of Abel and describes all, except God, as vain, ephemeral, or empty of ultimate meaning.

There is only one reference in the book to God as Creator, which may or may not be a reference to Genesis 1: "Remember also your Creator" (Eccles. 12:1). The term translated "Creator" is a form of a verb used several times in Genesis 1, which is occasionally used to designate the Creator (Isa. 40:28; 42:5; 43:1, 15; 45:18; Amos 4:13).

The context of the passage suggests that Ecclesiastes had in mind Genesis. This is suggested by the allusion to the nature of humans in Ecclesiastes 12:7: "The dust will return to the earth as it was, and the spirit will return to God who gave it." This is within the conceptual world of the creation of Adam in Genesis 2:7, according to which God created him from the dust of the ground and gave him the "breath of life." Qohelet, the name given also to the narrator of Ecclesiastes, is now using this ideology to describe what takes place when humans die: what belongs to God returns to Him, and what was taken from the ground goes back to it (Gen. 3:19).

The idea that humans were created from the dust and that they will return to it is also mentioned in Ecclesiastes 3:19, 20. The context is a discussion of human mortality and the conclusion is that from that perspective humans are like the animals (v. 18). They were both created from the dust, they both have the same breath, and when they die, they return to the dust. Genesis establishes that animals and humans were created from the ground, albeit in significantly different ways (Gen. 1:24; 2:7), and they both are breathing creatures (1:30; 7:22). This is the biblical background for what Qohelet is, in its own peculiar way, arguing.

Qohelet establishes another connection with Genesis: "Behold, I have found only this, that God made man upright, but they have sought out many devices" (Eccles.

7:29). In his search, this is what Qohelet has found to be true, and it constitutes an important statement in the sense that humans are responsible for their own actions. This verse "is an obvious reflection on the first few chapters of Genesis,"[29] though the vocabulary is in some cases different. The verb translated "made" and the noun translated "man" are both used in Genesis 1:26 for the creation of humans—the use of man in both passages is generic. In agreement with the theology of Genesis, Qohelet indicates that originally humans were created upright (morally straight) but that they lost this uprightness through their own machinations. This theological reasoning is clearly based on Genesis 1–3.

The creation of the world is alluded to at the beginning of the book in a poem that introduces the question of meaning. The poem is about "the back and forth movements of all the basic elements of Creation.... And yet nothing really new happens: no advantage is gained. It all seems purposeless."[30] The elements of the cosmos mentioned in the passage seem to follow the order in which they are recorded in Genesis 1.

Ecclesiastes 1:3: The phrase "under the sun" is about light and sky and corresponds to the first and second days of the Creation account (Gen. 1:3–8).

Ecclesiastes 1:4: The reference to the earth corresponds to the third day (Gen. 1:9–13).

Ecclesiastes 1:5, 6: The statement "the sun rises and the sun sets" is an allusion to the fourth day (Gen. 1:14–19).

Ecclesiastes 1:7: The movement of rivers and sea could be correlated to the creation of life in the water during the fifth day (Gen. 1:20–23).

Ecclesiastes 1:8: That humans can speak, see, and hear corresponds to the creation of humans on the sixth day (Gen. 1:24–31).

The order of creation and its organized movement is read by Qohelet as indicating the absence of the new. "All," the totality of creation, has become, in itself, vain and purposeless. The term "all" is also used in Genesis 1 to designate the totality of creation, but it refers to a creation that, after coming from the hands of the Lord, was "very good" (Gen. 1:31). According to Qohelet creation is no longer what it was.

Qohelet is indeed aware of the Creation account, but he uses elements of that narrative to argue that creation by itself is vain and does not provide for humans' ultimate meaning. It is a dead end: "That which has been is that which will be ... there is nothing new under the sun" (Eccles. 1:9). Human existence itself is ephemeral and, like that of the animals, will finally dissolve. But in accordance with the Creation account, Qohelet recognizes that humans were originally created upright and that the condition in which they find themselves now is the result of their own choosing.

Conclusion

The three wisdom books discussed here contain a substantial number of references to the Creation account recorded in Genesis 1; 2. Arguments are developed that assume the reliability of the Creation account and its significance for the life of the writers and their audience. The references to the creation of humans, animals, the natural phenomena, and the earth found in these books are, at times, brief summaries, allusions, or even passing comments, but they are all compatible with those found in Genesis. The experience of pain and suffering and even death is contrasted with creation and understood as a de-creation experience. The original goodness is acknowledged, and the present condition of humans is credited to themselves.

The most penetrating contribution to the theology of Creation is found in the personification of wisdom and its connection to creation. God's creation includes wisdom, created in the mystery of the Divine Being before it found expression in the objective phenomena of creation as we know it. Within that theology, Creation through the Word is assumed and even indicated in the text of Proverbs. This theology enriches the content of the Creation narrative found in Genesis. The wise sages of the Old Testament were biblical creationists.

Notes

1. Unless otherwise noted, all scriptural references in this chapter are from the *New American Standard Bible.*

2. Helmer Ringgren, "עשׂה ʿāśâ," in *Theological Dictionary of the Old Testament,* 11:390.

3. M. Graupner, "עצב ʿāṣab," in *Theological Dictionary of the Old Testament,* 11:281.

4. John E. Hartley, *The Book of Job* (Grand Rapids, MI: Eerdmans, 1988), 186.

5. T. C. Mitchell, "The Old Testament Usage of Neshāmâ," *Vetus Testamentum* 11 (1961): 177–187.

6. H. Lamberty-Zielinski, "הַמְשָׁגְ neshāmâ," in *Theological Dictionary of the Old Testament,* 10:67.

7. David J. Clines, *Job 21–37* (Nashville, TN: Thomas Nelson, 2006), 484.

8. W. G. Lambert and A. R. Millard, *ATRA-HASĪS: The Babylonian Story of the Flood* (Oxford: University Press, 1969), 61.

9. "Enki and Ninmah," trans. Jacob Klein, *The Context of Scripture* 1, no. 159: 517.

10. Francis I. Andersen, *Job: An Introduction and Commentary* (Downers Grove, IL: InterVarsity, 1976), 267.

11. G. del Olmo Lete and J. Sanmartín, *Diccionario de la lengua ugarítica,* Aula Orientalis Supplementa 7, 8 (Barcelona: AUSA, 2000), 2:373.

12. Sam Meier, "Job I–II: A Reflection on Genesis I–III," *Vetus Testamentum* 39 (1989): 183.

13. Ibid., 187.

14. Ibid., 188.

15. Hartley, *The Book of Job,* 102, 103.

16. Ibid., 153.

17. Robert L. Alden, *Job* (Nashville, TN: Broadman & Holman, 1993), 369.

18. Norman C. Habel, *The Book of Job: A Commentary* (Philadelphia: Westminster Press, 1985), 537.

19. Habel, *The Book of Job,* 539.

20. *Hebrew and Aramaic Lexicon of the Old Testament,* 2:371.

21. Roland E. Murphy, *Proverbs* (Dallas, TX: Word, 2002), 138

22. Gerald A. Klingbeil, "Wisdom and History," in *Dictionary of the Old Testament: Wisdom, Poetry & Writings,* 872.

23. Victor Avigdor Hurowitz, "Paradise Regained: Proverbs 3:13–20 Reconsidered," in *Sefer Moshe: The Moshe Weinfeld Jubilee Volume: Studies in the Bible and the Ancient Near East, Qumran, and Post-Biblical Judaism,* eds. Chaim Cohen, Avi Hurvitz, and Shalom M. Paul (Winona Lake, IN: Eisenbrauns, 2004), 57.

24. Ibid., 60.

25. Ibid.

26. *Hebrew and Aramaic Lexicon of the Old Testament,* 3:1111–13.

27. A. Baumann, "ליח ḥyl," in *Theological Dictionary of the Old Testament,* 4:345.

28. G. Yee, "An Analysis of Prov 8:22–31 According to Style and Structure," *Zeitschrift für die alttestamentliche Wissenschaft* 94 (1982): 91.

29. Tremper Longman III, *The Book of Ecclesiastes* (Grand Rapids, MI: Eerdmans, 1998), 207.

30. Jacques B. Doukhan, *Ecclesiastes: All Is Vanity* (Nampa, ID: Pacific Press® Pub. Assn., 2006), 16.

Creation in the Prophetic Literature
of the Old Testament

Martin G. Klingbeil

Creation to this day," writes theologian Rolf Rendtorff, "has been one of the 'proverbial step-children' in the recent discipline of Old Testament theology."[1] While Rendtorff only diagnoses the problem, Brueggemann, in looking for a rationale, refers the responsibility for the peripheral position of Creation in theology to the dichotomy between Israelite faith and Canaanite religion, or history and myth, that found its way into biblical theology during the earlier part of the last century through scholars like Gerhard von Rad, who suggested that Creation was subservient to salvation, or Ernest Wright, who maintained that "Israel was little interested in nature."[2]

A number of scholars moved beyond the paradigm created by von Rad and recognized the prominence of Creation in the theological thinking of the Old Testament, both in terms of position and content.

In his work on Genesis 1–11, Claus Westermann places Creation in history through its expression in myth and ritual. Thus, it is the primeval event, and the stories told about and enacted upon it are part of the universal traditions of humankind. The biblical authors adapted these stories theologically for Israel and identified them as part of God's work of blessing, which, for Westermann, "really means the power of fertility."[3]

In direct and intentional contrast with von Rad, the doctrine has been described by Hans Heinrich Schmid as the horizon of biblical theology. Schmid relates Creation to world order, and by comparing it with creation beliefs in other ancient Near-Eastern cultures, he arrives at the conclusion that history is the realization of this order. "Only within this horizon could Israel understand its special experiences with God in history."[4]

Nevertheless, it appears that, in most cases, the dating of texts lies at the bottom of the question as to where to position Creation within the framework of Old Testament theology. Though the Bible begins with Creation, biblical theologies mostly do not, since traditional critical approaches to Old Testament texts do not allow for an early dating of Genesis 1–11. Most of these studies, von Rad's included, have rather taken Isaiah 40–55—the so-called Deutero-Isaiah—dated by critical scholars to postexilic times, as a chronologically secure paradigm for Creation in the Old Testament, against which other texts, including also Genesis 1–3, are then benchmarked. This leads inevitably to the conclusion that Creation is a late addition to the theological thinking of the Old Testament. Implicit in this approach is the danger of circular reasoning, since Creation texts are being dated on the basis of religious historical paradigms as late and are then used to date other Creation passages accordingly:

"It is obviously somewhat paralysing to realise that we form a picture of Israel's religious history in part on the basis of certain texts which, in turn, with the help of the picture obtained by historical research, we subsequently judge with respect to 'authenticity' and historical truth."[5]

Recognizing the unsatisfying results of such a dating scheme that is further informed by a particular school of thought with regard to Israelite religious history, a more adequate approach to the topic of Creation in the Old Testament should begin with a contextual reading of texts in the various bodies of Old Testament literature.

The prophetic literature of the Old Testament provides a rich tapestry for such a reading, since the implicit nature of prophecy in the Old Testament is reformative in nature—referring back to the historic deeds of YHWH in the past (Creation, Exodus, conquest, etc.) and, thus, motivating a return to Him in the respective present. While there are studies that have touched on the subject of Creation in individual prophetic books, there is need for a more synthetic treatment of the issue in question.

Methodological Questions

Two points need attention before evaluating the evidence of Creation in the Old Testament prophets. The first is the question of intertextuality, based on the observation that much of the prophets' messages evoke earlier texts, creating points of reference to events in the course of Israel's history but, at the same time, applying them to their present contexts. The second issue refers to the question of how one can identify references to Creation in the prophetic literature of the Old Testament.

Intertextuality. Intertextuality could be defined broadly as references between texts that can occur on multiple levels. However, its boundaries are often determined by the author's view of the composition of Scripture. Intertextuality networks texts in a way that creates new contexts and new meanings of old texts. Intertextuality also sometimes puts various texts on a complicated timeline and, thus, gives rise to chronological considerations that have been out of focus in biblical studies within the vogue of a critical approach to Scripture.

The following timeline will serve as the chronological framework in which the usage of Creation texts in the prophetic books has to be read:

Eighth Century B.C.	Seventh Century B.C.	Sixth and Fifth Century B.C.
Jonah	Nahum	Ezekiel
Amos	Habakkuk	Obadiah
Hosea	Zephaniah	Daniel
Micah	Joel	Haggai
Isaiah	Jeremiah	Zechariah
		Malachi

This rough timeline will help to demonstrate how the theological thinking during the period, reflected in the prophetic literature of the Old Testament, has been progressively shaped by a continuous hermeneutic of returning to Creation as the pivotal point of origin(s).

This also implies that the prophetic literature of the Old Testament is subsequent to Genesis 1–11, a point that can be argued both on a literary and historical level but that will hopefully become even more apparent when it can be demonstrated how the prophets were constantly "looking back" at Creation. Thus, Genesis 1–3 becomes the point of reference to which the prophets return when they employ Creation terminology and motifs.

Creation Markers. To recognize intertextual Creation markers, criteria must be sufficiently broad, thus moving beyond a purely semantic level, but also narrow enough to connect positively with the Creation account of Genesis. A broad range of devices that often belong to totally different discourses are employed by scholars to identify Creation in the prophets: allusion, tradition, motif, theme, imagery, metaphor, and so on. It is probably safe to divide these into three main groups: (1) lexical, (2) literary, and (3) conceptual.

• *Lexical Creation Markers:*

A. *Semantic Field.* Lexical markers in the prophets take the semantic field as point of departure centering on the theologically most specific term *bārā'*, or "to create" (Isa. 40:26; Amos 4:13). It further includes the term *yāṣar*, or "to form, shape" (Isa. 45:18); the rather generic *'āsāh*, or "to make, do," and its derivatives (Isa. 45:18; Jer. 10:12; Jon.

1:9); and the more solemn *pō'al* (Isa. 45:11, BHT), or "to do, produce" (45:9, 11). All these words, however, also describe activities beyond Creation as found in Genesis 1–3, which is an indicator of how the reflection on Creation served as a departure point for the creation of new meanings.

B. *Word Pairs.* Word pairs, like the term for "heaven or earth" (Isa. 37:16) or "darkness or light" (42:16; 45:7), represent strong reference markers to Creation.

C. *Quotes.* An author often interrupts the flow of argument with a quote to authenticate, substantiate, or expand the argument. Apart from direct quotes, which are usually introduced by a static formula (Dan. 9:13), there are also inverted quotes of the Creation account, such as Ezekiel 36:11, in which the order of verbs from the original Genesis 1:28 is reversed to call attention to the connection between the theology of Creation and re-creation (i.e., restoration after the Exile).

D. *Allusions.* Allusions create less intense lexical reference markers but are widely used in the prophetic literature of the Old Testament. An allusion is an incomplete or fragmented reference to another text and, thus, is less easily recognizable and more prone to misinterpretation. Nevertheless, when the prophet says in Zephaniah 1:3, "I will sweep away both man and beast; I will sweep away the birds in the sky and the fish in the sea,"[6] the allusion to Creation is made through reversing the order of creatures as they have been listed in Genesis 1, making a theologically significant statement of reversing Creation and separating from his Creator.

• *Literary Creation Markers:*

A. *Metaphors.* A number of metaphors

of God are employed by the prophets, and some of them function as Creation markers. The use of *yāṣar* (to form, shape) in reference to YHWH as a potter in Isaiah 45:9 serves as a good example for the Creation subtext of this metaphor.

B. *Poetry.* The authors of the Hebrew Bible used poetry to communicate important theological content. Interestingly, most of the contexts in which Creation texts are found in the prophets are poetic in nature. Though in itself not a sufficiently strong marker, the expression of poetry indicates the presence of a theologically important theme.

• *Conceptual Creation Markers:*

A. *Motifs.* Although YHWH as a King is another metaphor that could be mentioned in terms of Creation, in a broader sense, kingship can serve as a motif alluding to Creation. Kingship in Israel had to do with building and maintaining the divinely created world order. Though YHWH is the builder of Jerusalem after the Babylonian exile (Jer. 24:6), He is also the builder of Eve in Genesis 2:22. In both instances, the lexical Creation marker *bānāh* (to build) is used.

B. *Typologies.* Typologies preserve historicity of events or personalities from the past and project them theologically into the present. Creation as a historical event is used in the prophetic literature as a type for present and future restoration, and the concluding chapters of Isaiah use the reference to Creation as a type for the re-creation of a new heaven and earth (Isa. 65:17).

The prophets employed in their writings a wide range of Creation markers to refer to Genesis 1–3. Some of these markers are easily discernible, while others only establish loose links, in that way, creating a certain sliding scale on which intertextual relationships can be constructed. The frequency in which this hermeneutical procedure was invoked indicates that the prophets built their theology around pivotal themes, such as the Creation motif.

Creation in the Prophets

An exhaustive account of Creation in sixteen books of varied length, which account for almost one-third of the Old Testament, is not possible in the scope of this chapter. But a general overview of the prophetic books does offer the possibility of differentiating the intertextual Creation patterns.

• *Eighth-Century B.C. Prophets:*

Jonah, Amos, Hosea, Micah, and Isaiah represent an impressive mix of messengers and messages, with Jonah directing his prophecies toward the international arena, while Amos and Hosea address the northern kingdom. Micah and Isaiah prophesied in Judah before or until after the fall of Samaria. The geographic spread should give a good indication of the pervasiveness of Creation thought during this century.

A. *Jonah.* Jonah's message is replete with ecological content and, as such, is allusive of Creation. When introducing himself to the sailors, Jonah defines himself as a follower of the Creator-God in a language that is reminiscent of Creation and the Decalogue: "YHWH, God of heaven, I worship/fear who made the sea and the dry land" (Jon. 1:9, author's translation). Jonah sees himself surrounded by YHWH, the God of Creation, although ironically, he is not quite sure if he should worship or fear God.

Several creation elements appear in Jonah's poem in Jonah 2: he finds himself cast into the "heart of the sea" (v. 3; Gen. 1:10) and cast out of God's presence (Jon. 2:5) as Adam and Eve were cast out of Eden (Gen. 3:24); he passes through the chaotic waters (Jon. 2:5; Gen. 1:2) and finally descends to Sheol (Jon. 2:2) or the pit (v. 6). Jonah is sinking towards darkness and death, away from light and Creation, a process equivalent to de-creation.

In the whole book, obedient Creation is in juxtaposition to disobedient humanity, and the Creator is portrayed as continually being involved in His creation by throwing a storm at Jonah (Jon. 1:4), appointing a fish to his twofold rescue by letting it swallow the disobedient prophet (v. 17) as well as vomiting him onto solid ground (2:10). He furthermore prepares a plant (4:6), a worm (v. 7), and an east wind (v. 8) to bring His despondent servant to his senses. Creation is not just an event of the past but recurs through YHWH's permanent involvement in His creation and with His creatures. But foremost, all Creation is geared toward YHWH's salvation acts toward humanity, and the question that concludes the book of Jonah finds its answer in the book's presence in the canon, reiterating Jonah's belief in the supreme Creator-God, as initially ironically stated in his confession to the heathen sailors (1:9).

B. *Amos.* Creation in Amos is based on an analogy of history. YHWH is presented as a Creator who is continuously interacting with His creation. This occurs in a context of threatening judgment but also promising salvation. Creation terminology appears predominantly in the three hymns (Amos 4:13; 5:8, 9; 9:5, 6) that play a structuring role in the overall layout of the book.

Amos 4:13	Amos 5:8, 9	Amos 9:5, 6
He who forms the mountains, who creates the wind, and who reveals his thoughts to mankind, who turns dawn to darkness, and treads on the heights of the earth—the Lord God Almighty is his name.	He who made the Pleiades and Orion, who turns midnight into dawn and darkens day into night, who calls for the waters of the sea and pours them out over the face of the land— the Lord is his name. With a blinding flash he destroys the stronghold and brings the fortified city to ruin.	The Lord, the Lord Almighty— he touches the earth and it melts, and all who live in it mourn; the whole land rises like the Nile, then sinks like the river of Egypt; he builds his lofty palace in the heavens and sets its foundation on the earth; he calls for the waters of the sea and pours them out over the face of the land—the Lord is his name.

Creation language is predominant in these five verses, and a number of lexical Creation markers appear in the three passages: *bārā'*, or "to create"; *yāṣar*, or "to form"; and *'āsāh*, or "to make." Interestingly, all these markers are participles, a syntactic peculiarity throughout the book of Amos. God's creative activity in each instance is brought into relationship with the human sphere, indicating how Creation touches human life.

One can perceive a certain progression between the three hymns in terms of how God's intervention impacts humanity. In Amos 4:13, God reveals His judgment intentions to humankind, whereas Amos 5:8, 9 describes the destructive aspect of God's judgment. Amos 9:5, 6 finally describes the human reaction to the divine judgment. The startling aspect of Amos's presentation of Creation is that it is intrinsically linked to judgment, almost in such a way that Creation forms the explanation for destruction. What begins as a hymn of praise for YHWH the Creator becomes a threatening description of YHWH the Judge. This apparent contradiction has startled a number of scholars and most probably, and more deliberately, Amos's audience. The position of inherent security based on belief in the Creator-God is challenged by Amos, and what has provided a basis for a false religious autosufficiency becomes now the rationale for judgment, reversing the original function of the hymns. "By means of the hymns, Amos makes it clear that YHWH is not a God who could simply be controlled. He challenged certain positions of presupposed rights—by means of which the people presumed the right of existence—from the broader perspective of God's creation."[7]

Thus, Creation can be contextually oriented toward both comfort and judgment, whereas in Amos, it is mostly directed toward judgment. To accept YHWH as the Creator, also implies the acceptance of His power to de-create. On first sight, Creation used in this way is disassociated from salvation, but when judgment is understood as preliminary and partial to salvation, then de-creation becomes a necessary precursor for re-creation. Amos drives this point home by the formulaic usage of the expression "the LORD is his name" (Amos 4:13; 5:8; 9:6) indicating that this still is God; He "is not only the God who creates, but He also destroys."[8]

The book of Amos concludes with a glorious perspective on restoration after judgment (Amos 9:11–15), introduced by the eschatologically charged phrase "in that day." The passages allude to the Creation theme by employing building terminology (e.g., "to build," vv. 11, 14) and the metaphor of YHWH as King. Thus, within the theological thinking of Amos, the correct understanding of Creation becomes a prerequisite to the comprehension of re-creation.

C. *Hosea.* Creation in Hosea is closely linked to the theme of the Creation of Israel as a nation, again, as with Amos, in a context of pending judgment. Creation is not only analogous to history but is history itself.

Hosea begins to develop his Creation theology with an allusive description of de-creation in Hosea 4:1–3, in which an interesting reversal of the order of Creation as presented in Genesis 1 takes place. God is entering into a "controversy, a legal case" with or against Israel (Hosea 4:1). In the relationship-focused narrative context of Hosea, this could be better understood as a quarrel between husband and wife, which constitutes the underlying metaphor of the book. Based on Israel's sins (v. 2), Hosea

4:3 invokes judgment by introducing the anti-Creation theme: "Therefore the land will mourn, and all who live in it will waste away; the beasts of the field, the birds of the heavens, and the fish of the sea will be extinguished" (author's translation). The three groups of animals represent the three spheres in which life is found on earth. The reversal of the known Creation order in Genesis 1 invokes the idea of judgment as de-creation, in which Creation just shrivels up when confronted with and abused by sin.

The affinity between Hosea 6:2 and Deuteronomy 32:39 can hardly be overlooked in this context and constitutes another Creation motif in Hosea. The reference to YHWH as the One who puts to death but also resurrects is pointing to the God of Creation, a theme strongly developed in the Song of Moses. Hosea 8:14 picks up on the same motif, again establishing a relationship with the Pentateuch in using the divine Creation epithet "Maker," which also occurs repeatedly in the Song of Moses (Deut. 32:6, 15, 18). However, "the notion of Creation leads toward indictment and sentence, not toward praise."[9]

Possibly the strongest Creation text in Hosea is found in 11:1. It synthesizes the passages mentioned above into the metaphor of YHWH as the Creator and Procreator of Israel: "When Israel was a child, I loved him, and out of Egypt I called my son." This verse connects to Hosea 1:10 ("they will be called 'children of the living God' ") and to the Exodus, which is described in Creation terminology. Thus, the creation of Israel as a nation during the historic events connected with the exodus from Egypt becomes part of God's creation. Whom God elects, He also creates, and with that, an intimate and eternal bond is created like that between a father and his son. Beyond reiterating and enhancing Creation theology, the metaphor is pedagogic in its rhetoric: "By means of this theme of Israel's creation it is not so much the intention of Hosea to nuance the view that the people had of YHWH but, rather, to confront them with their own behaviour. They are faithless sons."[10]

D. *Micah.* Affinities and intertextual issues between the messages of Micah and Isaiah are numerous and have been noted by many scholars. The most often quoted passage in this context is the almost identical parallel found in Micah 4:1–3, 5; and Isaiah 2:2–5. Though the passage can be taken as an argument for a common prophetic message of the two prophets, for the purpose of this study, the focus rests on the Creation imagery transmitted in an eschatological setting via the metaphor of Mount Zion. According to Old Testament cosmology, Zion lies at the center of the created world, and Micah points to its establishment in terms of Creation terminology ("to establish" [Mic. 4:1]). Creation in Micah is focused on destruction and consequent re-creation in the context of the "day of the Lord" with its eschatological implications. The prophet builds a theological bridge between Creation in the beginning and in the end around the presence of God as symbolized by the Mount Zion metaphor.

E. *Isaiah.* As mentioned above, the so-called Deutero-Isaiah was the point of departure for Gerhard von Rad and others in establishing an Old Testament theology of Creation, based on the assumption that Isaiah 40–55 could be dated to the postexilic period. Nevertheless, recent studies that focus on the literary unity of Isaiah—though few scholars would take the argument to its logical conclusion, in other words, unity of authorship—show that Creation theology is present throughout the whole book.

Taking Isaiah's temple vision as a chronological departure point, Isaiah 6:1 describes YHWH along the lines of the heavenly king metaphor identified earlier as allusive to Creation. The song of the vineyard in Isaiah 5 presents an important aspect of Creation in demonstrating the interconnection of God's Creation and His intervention in history, placing it in the context of Israel's election. Verse 12 provides a further insight into Isaiah's Creation theology: sin is in reality not acknowledging God's deeds in Creation.

In Isaiah 17:7, the prophet takes up the theme developed by Hosea of YHWH as the "Maker" of humankind. The image of YHWH as the Potter of Isaiah 29:16 has already been identified above as Creation terminology and occurs in all three parts of the book (Isa. 45:9; 64:8). Creation in Isaiah focuses primarily on God's sovereignty over His Creation and humankind's failure to recognize His proper position within this world order.

Isaiah 40–55 has been called the center of Isaiah's theology; whereas, Isaiah 36–39 fulfills a bridging role carefully linking the previous chapters to the remainder of the book. It has been argued that the so-called Deutero-Isaiah introduces Creation as a new theological topic to the book, but the preceding observations show that the theme is "deeply continuous with the Isaian tradition."[11]

Though Creation terminology abounds in the whole book, Creation occurs in Isaiah 40–55 in connection with the Exodus and Conquest (Isa. 41:17–20; 42:13–17; 43:16–21; 49:8–12), placing Creation in history. Furthermore, Creation is positioned alongside redemption (44:24), pointing to the theological significance of the motif in introducing Cyrus as the agent of God's redemption. In this way, the Exodus serves as a typological guarantee for the future redemption from the Babylonian exile through Cyrus (v. 28). The theocentric manifestation that God forms light and creates darkness as much as peace and evil (45:7) serves as an introduction to the metaphor of God as a Potter (vv. 9–13), which illustrates the absolute sovereignty of God within the realms of human history.

The final part of the book of Isaiah (Isa. 56–66) focuses on the Creation of Zion with Isaiah 60–62 at the center of the section describing the glorious city. The book's grand finale in Isaiah 65; 66 adds an eschatological dimension to Creation theology in Isaiah, describing renewal and restoration in terms of Creation. But Creation in these last chapters refers not only to Zion as a place but foremost to its inhabitants who need re-creation and transformation: "Be glad and rejoice forever in what I will create, for I will create Jerusalem to be a delight and its people a joy" (65:18).

Summarizing Isaian Creation theology, the following becomes apparent. Creation in Isaiah 1–39 is focused on God's sovereignty over His creation and the establishment of a personal relationship with humanity, exemplified by the usage of the potter metaphor, which points back to Genesis 2. In Isaiah 40–55, the theme focuses on the creation of Israel as a nation in history by connecting Creation with the Exodus and theologically with salvation. In Isaiah 56–66, Creation is centered on the future re-creation of Zion and its people in response to the failure of a pre-exilic Israel. Thus, we have a sequential development of Creation theology in the book of Isaiah that follows a natural progression of thought.

• *Seventh-Century* B.C. *Prophets:*

A new century in the prophetic literature of the Old Testament is overshadowed by the sobering perspective of the fall of Samaria (722 B.C.) and an increasing urgency for the prophetic message to be heard as the Babylonian exile for Judah is approaching. As during the eighth-century, the prophetic word is often introduced by an international message, issued by Nahum against the Assyrians. Habakkuk enters with God into a dialogue about His people, while Zephaniah and Joel enlarge upon the eschatological meaning of the "day of the LORD" motif. Jeremiah, the weeping prophet, finally fails in averting with his message the Babylonian exile.

A. *Nahum.* Creation in Nahum is connected to the "day of the LORD," and the description of its characteristics is reminiscent of Creation terminology: "He rebukes the sea and dries it up; he makes all the rivers run dry. Bashan and Carmel wither and the blossoms of Lebanon fade. The mountains quake before him and the hills melt away. The earth trembles at his presence, the world and all who live in it" (Nah. 1:4, 5). Again, there is a context of de-creation that is driven by cosmological imagery.

B. *Habakkuk.* Habakkuk offers a similar perspective on Creation as Nahum in using Creation imagery in the context of de-creation during the theophany in the "day of the LORD": "He stood, and shook the earth; he looked, and made the nations tremble. The ancient mountains crumbled and the age-old hills collapsed but he marches on forever" (Hab. 3:6). In the following verses, Habakkuk describes the impact of YHWH's appearance on Creation (vv. 7–12). Through the destructive power of de-creation, however, salvation is accomplished: "You came out to deliver your people, to save your anointed one" (v. 13). Along the same lines, Creation imagery also serves as a point of reference for recognition of the Creator: "The earth will be filled with the knowledge of the glory of the LORD, as the waters cover the sea" (2:14).

C. *Zephaniah.* Zephaniah 1:3 introduces a reversal of Creation by listing the animals in a reversed order from that in which they were originally mentioned in the Creation account of Genesis 1. He furthermore uses the familiar word play between 'ādām, or "man," and 'ādāmâ, or "ground," known from Genesis 2:7. The reversal of Creation, however, transmits a strong theological message: "In Genesis ii, however, the pun is used to indicate man's dependence on that from whence he came, whereas Zephaniah uses it to show man's separation from his Creator, YHWH. A situation that involves a return to the age before Creation can result only in man's destruction."[12] Zephaniah is depicting the progressive loss of dominion over creation by humanity and its resulting de-creation.

D. *Joel.* Within the "day of the LORD" imagery, Joel employs Creation imagery to describe the impact of YHWH's theophany on Creation as part of that judgment day: "The sun and moon will be darkened, and the stars no longer shine. The LORD will roar from Zion and thunder from Jerusalem; the earth and the heavens will tremble. But the LORD will be a refuge for his people, a stronghold for the people of Israel" (Joel 3:15, 16). The term "heavens and earth" serves as a Creation indicator but, again, within a negative context of judgment. God's appearance to humanity is always connected to the experience of God in nature and the impact of His appearance on creation. The final verses of Joel return, however, to the topic of re-creation, describing the future of Zion in paradisiacal terms: "In that day the mountains will drip new wine, and the hills will flow with milk; all the ravines of Judah will run with water. A fountain will flow out of the LORD's house and will water the valley of acacias" (v. 18). The Garden of Eden mentioned earlier on (2:3) that has been destroyed by the locust plague is thus being re-created. Again, a linear motion from Creation to de-creation and finally re-creation can be observed with Creation being the overall paradigm that underlies history.

E. *Jeremiah.* Creation in Jeremiah is so omnipresent that only a representative number of key passages will be offered here. The book begins with reference to the creation of the prophet in his mother's womb (Jer. 1:5), using the lexical Creation marker for "to form, fashion," which can also be found in Genesis 2:7. The creation of humankind as part of the Creation week is repeated in every new creation of new human life.

A survey of Creation in Jeremiah has to include 4:23–26, which connects with strong linguistic markers to the Creation account, as found in Genesis 1. The oracle of doom presents possibly the most faithful account of de-creation, or the reversal of Creation, when compared to Genesis 1:2–2:4.

Though the Genesis account ends with the day of rest, or the Sabbath, Jeremiah's de-creation account ends with a day of fury. The deconstruction of Creation is taking place and one can be sure that the listeners (and subsequent readers) of the prophet's message recognized the Creation pattern. Creation becomes the paradigm for destruction and serves as the primeval point of departure for contemporary theology. "What acts and words could be more invested with power than those of Creation?"[13]

The antithesis to the doom oracle is provided in Jeremiah 31:35–37, in which two short sayings conclude the so-called book of comfort (vv. 30, 31), and in Creation language, point to the impossibility of YHWH destroying Israel. Yet, it is expressed along the lines of remnant theology with reference to the "seed of Israel" and its future hope. Both apparent opposite expressions, 4:23–26 and 31:35–37, show the range of possible applications of Creation theology within Jeremiah but, beyond that, show that Israel needs to acknowledge YHWH with regard to its present future: "Thus both extremes of expression bear witness to the theological claim that finally Israel must come to terms with Yahweh upon whom its future well-being solely depends."[14]

Jeremiah 10:12–16 is a hymn that celebrates YHWH's creative power, and it is replenished with Creation imagery: "But God made the earth by his power; he founded the world by his wisdom and stretched out the heavens by his understanding. When he thunders, the waters in the heavens roar; he makes clouds rise from the ends of the earth. He sends lightning with the rain and brings out the wind from his storehouses. Everyone is senseless and without knowledge; every goldsmith is shamed by his idols. The images he makes a fraud; they have no breath in them. They are worthless, the objects of mockery; when their judgment comes, they will perish. He who is the Portion of Jacob is not like these, for he is the Maker of all things, including Israel, the people of his inheritance—the LORD Almighty is his name" (vv. 12–16).

Although most commentators point to the contrast between the true God and the idols, the emphasis is rather on a contrast between YHWH as the Creator of life (Jer. 10:13) and humankind as (false) creator of life (v. 14). The focus is not on the idol but on its maker, who is "shamed" by his inanimate image, since he is not able to provide the creature with the necessary breath of life, which is the distinguishing characteristic of YHWH's Creation. "Idolatry is therefore a double sin. The worship of idols denies the reality of God's complete control over the cosmos because it involves the acknowledgement of other divine powers. . . . Worse still is the

pretense of creating life. In doing so, humankind lays claim to divine knowledge."[15]

• *Sixth- and Fifth-Century B.C. Prophets:*
The Babylonian exile and postexilic period caused a change in the prophetic messages, shifting its contents towards restoration or re-creation. While Ezekiel and Obadiah witness the downfall of Jerusalem and, as such, the ultimate fulfillment of the long-prophesied de-creation, Daniel brings an apocalyptic dimension to the topic. Re-creation becomes the prominent topic for postexilic Haggai and Zechariah, and Malachi finalizes the canonical prophetic chorus of the Old Testament with the restorative message around the second Elijah.

A. *Ezekiel.* David L. Petersen comes to the conclusion that "creation traditions are not important for Ezekiel's theological argument."[16] His argument, however, appears to be based on the assumption of an exclusive positive reading of the Creation account, which, as has been seen, forms only one part of the theological panorama for which Creation motifs were invoked. If understood in this way, Ezekiel "is not concerned with how the world itself came into existence, . . . but rather with re-forming a world gone awry."[17] Three passages will outline Ezekiel's theological use of Creation:

First, Ezekiel 28:11–19 is a prophetic oracle that centers on a description of the king of Tyre as a type for the anarchic Cherub, which has been interpreted since patristic times as pointing to the fall of Lucifer. A number of indicative Creation linguistic markers are present, yet the context of the passage is focused on the description of the hubris of a fallen angel who is staining a perfect world. As with Jeremiah, Creation language is employed as a powerful paradigm to describe the origin of sin.

Second, Ezekiel 31:1–18 transfers the same scenario into the realm of human history. The cosmic tree representing human kingship, a motif well known from ancient Near-Eastern iconography, is used as a metaphor for the downfall of the king of Assyria, which in turn, serves as a warning for Egypt's future judgment. The chapter describes the glory of the tree within Creation terminology and cosmology (Ezek. 31:4; Gen. 7:11) and connects it with paradise (Ezek. 31:8, 9, 16, 18). Creation terminology is employed to describe the downfall of two prominent nations, Assyria and Egypt. Thus, not only paradise but also human history has been spoilt.

Third, re-creation in Ezekiel and the reversal of de-creation as exemplified by the two previous passages can be found in Ezekiel 47:1–12 within the context of the vision of the future glory of the temple, which in itself serves as a Creation motif. This time the trees are growing again, not in rebellion against but under YHWH's power and provision of fertility (Ezek. 47:12). The sustaining agents of God's power are the rivers of paradise, which connect Ezekiel to the Creation account in Genesis 2:10–14. Ezekiel deliberately merges temple and Zion with paradise imagery, because the destruction of the earthly temple in Jerusalem and his own exile in Babylon has caused the place of God's presence to transcend to a heavenly realm, indicating that YHWH's presence is continuous and does not depend on human realities.

"As the connections between Ezek 47:1–12 and Gen 2:10–14 reveal, Ezekiel understood the symbol of Zion in a new way. Cut free from explicit reference to the temporal, political realities of kingship, priesthood, and the earthly temple, the temple-mountain and river of Ezekiel's last great vision stand as timeless symbols of divine presence. For Ezekiel, the earthly Zion, with its city and temple, was a bitter disappointment."[18]

Creation in Ezekiel is used to express divine (and the prophet's) disappointment over angelic rebellion and consequent human history, which replays that rebellion again and again. But the prophet moves beyond that in stating that God is able to re-create something new and eternal from the shreds of human history. One should be cautious, however, not to attribute an exclusive otherworldliness to Ezekiel's prophecies.

B. *Obadiah*. No explicit Creation terminology is employed in the book of Obadiah except for the usage of the Mount Zion motif (Obad. 1:17, 21), which stands in juxtaposition to the mountains of Edom (vv. 3, 4, 8, 9). The one who has made his "nest among the stars" (v. 4) will be brought low because of human wisdom and understanding (v. 8). Instead, the mountains of Esau will be governed from Mount Zion (v. 21).

C. *Daniel*. Few studies engage the book of Daniel with Creation theology, and those who take up the task usually focus on the mythological creation-struggle motif and its ancient Near-Eastern counterparts, as found in the description of the waters in Daniel 7:2, 3. According to Robert R. Wilson, in contrast to Genesis 1, the waters described in Daniel 7 are presented as returning to chaos, and the animals that surface from the waters are composite creatures that do not correspond to the order of Creation in Genesis 1. "The world has reverted to its pre-creation state and is clearly in need of re-creation."[19] This re-creation is achieved in the vision of the Ancient One who constitutes the second part of the vision (Dan. 7:9–14) with the word for "dominion" as the key word that appears eight times in this chapter. The failure of human dominion over the earth in history, as envisioned in Creation, is replaced by God's dominion over the universe through an everlasting kingdom.

But apart from Daniel 7, Jacques B. Doukhan has demonstrated more references to Creation in the prophetic book. Approaching the issue from a linguistic perspective, he arrives at the conclusion that "allusions to creation abound throughout the book and are attested one way or another in each of its chapters."[20] In the following, I have included the most significant allusions highlighted by Doukhan.

In Daniel 1:12, the four young men opt for a menu that echoes the pre-Fall diet found in Genesis 1:29, while the description of Nebuchadnezzar in Daniel 2:38 invokes Creation terminology when it employs the same attribute of dominion over the earth and all its creatures to the Babylonian king as Adam received in Genesis 1:28. Clay, which is part of the statue's feet, is used throughout the Bible in contexts alluding to Creation, indicating the religious aspect of spiritual Rome (Isa. 29:16; Jer. 18:2; Lam. 4:2). The word pair for "darkness and light" in Daniel's benediction (Dan. 2:22) echoes the Creation account of Genesis 1:4, 5. Another Creation word pair ("heaven

and earth") is found in Nebuchadnezzar's prayer after he returns to his senses in Daniel 4:35. Furthermore, the usage of the cosmic tree motif in Daniel 4 points to the Creation account (Gen. 2:9). The association of "evening-morning" in Daniel 8:14 is found in this sequence and meaning only in the Creation story (Gen. 1:5, 8, 13, 19, 23, 31). In the concluding chapter of the book, Daniel evokes Creation terminology by describing re-creation, which is taking place after the de-creation scenario of the previous chapter (Dan. 11). For the righteous ones, there is a passage from sleeping in the dust (12:2) to shining like the stars (v. 3) and, for Daniel in particular, from resting to standing up in the final day to receive his inheritance (v. 13).

The apocalyptic themes of transformation of history and final return to an Edenic state that are so recurrent in the book of Daniel are theologically grouped along a process from Creation to de-creation and finally re-creation—a topic encountered repeatedly in the prophetic literature of the Old Testament, whereas the timelines in Daniel are broader and informed by his apocalyptic perspective. Eschatology, which moves toward an end, imperatively necessitates a beginning, and the theme of Creation provides the theological rationale against which eschatology can take place.

D. *Haggai.* In Haggai 1:10, the prophet invokes the heaven and earth figure of speech, demonstrating how the postexilic community's lack of faithfulness is causing nature's or Creation's blessings to be interrupted. Further on, Haggai employs the same word pair in order to describe how the created order is affected by the "day of the Lord" but this time from a Messianic perspective: "This is what the Lord Almighty says: 'In a little while I will once more shake the heavens and the earth, the sea and the dry land. I will shake all nations, and what is desired by all nations will come, and I will fill this house with glory,' says the Lord Almighty" (Hag. 2:6, 7).

E. *Zechariah.* Zechariah describes God as the continuous Sustainer of creation: "Ask the Lord for rain in the springtime; it is the Lord who sends the thunderstorms. He gives showers of rain to all people, and plants of the field to everyone" (Zech. 10:1). The "plants of the field" connects with the "plant[s] of the field" of Genesis 2:5. Springtime and fertility are caused by the ongoing process of "creating" the storm clouds. Zechariah's second oracle is introduced by using a distinct Creation terminology, however, with a significant rearranging of the various elements: "The word of the Lord concerning Israel. The Lord who stretches out the heavens, who lays the foundation of the earth, and who forms the human spirit within a person, declares ..." (Zech. 12:1). While the stretching out of the heavens is not a direct linguistic Creation marker, it nevertheless recaptures the action of Genesis 1:6, 7 and is found throughout the Old Testament (Ps. 104:2; Job 9:8; Isa. 44:24) in connection to Creation. It is also interesting to note that the object of "forms" in Zechariah 12:1 is not humankind itself, as in Genesis 2:7 but "the spirit of man."

"One has the sense that there is a traditional set of Creation vocabulary, but that it could be arranged in various acceptable patterns. Heavens, earth, humanity, and spirit provide the crucial building blocks. Zechariah 12:1 combines them into an innovative and adroit manner."[21]

Interestingly, Zechariah 12:1 serves within the given literary genre as a validation for the following oracle, which is a description of Israel's new and victorious role among the nations, a new creation of the nation on the day of the Lord.

F. *Malachi.* Malachi concludes the cycle of Old Testament prophets with a rhetorical question that links the God-as-Creator metaphor to the God-as-Father metaphor: "Do we not all have one Father? Did not one God create us? Why do we profane the covenant of our ancestors by being unfaithful to one another?" (Mal. 2:10). Creation here is being transformed to the intimate level of a father-son or husband-wife (vv. 14, 15) relationship, which echoes the intimate Creation account of Genesis 2. Creation in the last book of the Old Testament and, in its final analysis, is not centered on cosmogony but on a personal relationship between God and humanity as already hinted at in the order of Creation.

Summary and Conclusion

In trying to establish the broader lines of Creation in the prophetic literature of the eighth century b.c., it becomes apparent that Creation is progressively anchored in history, theologically made relevant in salvation and paradigmatically centered in the introduction of the triad of Creation, de-creation, and re-creation.

Creation in the prophetic literature of the seventh century b.c. is historically contextualized by the impending Babylonian exile, whereas the triad of creation, de-creation, and re-creation becomes more and more prominent with the prophets beginning to look beyond the inevitable judgment toward restoration.

The usage of Creation during the final two centuries of Old Testament prophetic literature is clearly future oriented, whereas a theological abstraction has taken place that can be related to the disappearance of the physical temple and monarchy. Though Creation is still the overarching paradigm that spans human history, the focus has moved toward the end of that arch, which, as in the case of the book of Daniel, takes on apocalyptic and also Messianic concepts.

Creation in the prophetic literature of the Old Testament is employed as a constant literary and theological reference that connects to a historical past, motivates the interpretation of the present, and moves toward a perspective for the future by means of a continuous contextualization of the topic via the triad: creation, de-creation, and re-creation. This reference point is anchored in the Creation account as found in Genesis 1–3.

"The final authors of the Hebrew Bible understood creation not as *one* topic among others or even one of lower significance. For them creation was the starting point, because everything human beings can think and say about God and his relation to the world and to humankind depends on the fact that he created all this."[22]

The intertextual markers that refer to Creation in the prophets indicate that they saw Creation as a literal and historical given; reference is made indiscriminately to the Creation account as presented in both Genesis 1 and Genesis 2. The intertextual movement indicates clearly that as much as Creation forms the starting point of much of the prophetic theological discourse, all markers of Creation, as discussed in this study, point back to the Creation model presented in Genesis 1–3. Creation was the point of departure for their worldview. They clearly explained and interpreted the world from this perspective. Any discussion of whether the prophets considered Creation anything other than a historical event or used it only for literary or theological purposes cannot be sustained from the textual data and would be projecting a nineteenth-century A.D. rationalist debate into a first-millennium B.C. context in which it would have otherwise not existed.

Notes

1. Rolf Rendtorff, "Some Reflections on Creation as a Topic of Old Testament Theology," in *Priests, Prophets and Scribes: Essays on the Formation and Heritage of Second Temple Judaism in Honour of Joseph Blenkinsopp*, eds. Eugene Ulrich et al., *Journal for the Study of the Old Testament*, supplemental series 149 (Sheffield, England: Sheffield Academic Press, 1992), 204–212.

2. G. Ernest Wright, *The Old Testament Against Its Environment* (London: SCM, 1950), 71.

3. Claus Westermann, "Creation and History in the Old Testament," in *The Gospel and Human Destiny*, ed. Vilmos Vatja (Minneapolis, MN: Augsburg, 1971), 30.

4. Stefan Paas, *Creation and Judgement: Creation Texts in Some Eighth Century Prophets*, Oudtestamentische Studiën 47 (Leiden, Netherlands: Brill, 2003), 12.

5. Ibid., 29

6. Unless otherwise noted, all scriptural references in this chapter are from the New International Version.

7. Paas, *Creation and Judgement*, 324.

8. Ibid., 429.

9. David L. Petersen, "Creation in Ezekiel: Methodological Perspectives and Theological Prospects," in *Society of Biblical Literature Seminar Papers, 1999* (Atlanta, GA: Scholars Press, 1999), 207.

10. Paas, *Creation and Judgement*, 431.

11. Richard J. Clifford, "The Unity of the Book of Isaiah and Its Cosmogonic Language," *Catholic Biblical Quarterly* 55 (1993): 16.

12. Michael DeRoche, "Zephaniah I 2–3: The 'Sweeping' of Creation," *Vetus Testamentum* 30, no. 1 (1980): 106.

13. Ibid., 152.

14. Ibid., 159.

15. Dominic Rudman, "Creation and Fall in Jeremiah X 12–16," *Vetus Testamentum* 48, no. 1 (1998): 68.

16. Petersen, "Creation in Ezekiel," 499.

17. Julie Galambush, "Castles in the Air: Creation as Property in Ezekiel," in *Society of Biblical Literature Seminar Papers* 38 (Atlanta, GA: Scholars Press, 1999), 147.

18. Steven Tuell, "The Rivers of Paradise: Ezekiel 47:1–12 and Genesis 2:10–14," in *God Who Creates: Essays in Honor of W. Sibley Towner,* eds. William P. Brown and S. Dean McBride Jr. (Grand Rapids, MI: Eerdmans, 2000), 189.

19. Robert R. Wilson, "Creation and New Creation: The Role of Creation Imagery in the Book of Daniel," in *God Who Creates: Essays in Honor of W. Sibley Towner,* eds. William P. Brown and S. Dean McBride Jr. (Grand Rapids, MI: Eerdmans, 2000), 201, 202.

20. Translated from Jacques B. Doukhan, "Allusions à la création dans le livre de Daniel," in *The Book of Daniel in the Light of New Findings*, ed. Adam S. van der Woude (Leuven, Belgium: University Press and Peeters, 1993), 289.

21. Petersen, "Creation in Ezekiel," 210.

22. Rendtorff, "Some Reflections on Creation," 207.

Biblical Creationism and Ancient Near-Eastern Evolutionary Ideas

Ángel M. Rodríguez

Archaeologists have found a significant amount of written and iconographic materials in the ancient Near East that have helped scholars gain a better understanding of the Sumerian and Akkadian cultures and religions. More recently, there has been an emphasis on the influence of those cultures on Western thinking.

Egypt, however, has always intrigued the Western world to the point of fascination. Egyptian ideas are quite widespread in the West and are commonly found in popular media. Interestingly, some elements of the cosmogonies—theories of the origins of the cosmos or of conscious beings—of the ancient Near East, including Egypt, phrased in mythological language, have found a more sophisticated expression in modern cosmogony and some theories on the origin of life.

Origin of the Gods and Cosmogony in the Ancient Near East

Before Creation. Egyptians raised the question of origins by asking, first, what was there before creation or beyond the actual cosmos. They recognized that there was no final answer to that question. When addressing that specific concern, they used statements of denial. Thus, for instance, Egyptian texts would say that before creation there was no space, no matter, no names, and there was neither birth nor death. Nothing had yet come into being. This formula was used to indicate a radical difference between what is and what was not. Here are some more typical examples:

- "When the heaven had not yet come into being, when the earth had not yet come into being, when the two river banks had not yet come into being, when there had not yet come into being that fear which arose because of the eye of Horus. . . .
- "When the heaven had not yet come into being, when the earth had not yet come into being, when men had not yet come into being, when the gods had not yet been born, when death had not yet come into being. . . .
- "When two things in this land had not yet come into being."[1]

But Egyptians also speculated that beyond the cosmos could be found what was always there, namely darkness and a limitless ocean or primeval waters called Nun. This was a lifeless, motionless state of absolute inertness and nonexistence.

Origin of Life. Since before creation there were no gods, then, properly speaking, creation does not begin with cosmogony but with a theogony, an explanation for the origins of deity, that leads to a cosmogony.

In fact, one of the common and fundamental characteristics of ancient Near-Eastern cosmogonies is that they all begin with a theogony. For Egyptians in particular, the next logical question would have been, how did "what is" come into being? How did the gods come into existence? The answer they provided was more developed than that of anywhere else in the ancient Near East.

An Egyptian text states that Amun is the god "who was in the very beginning, when no god had yet come into being, when no name of anything had yet been named."[2] According to the Creation theology that originated in Hermopolis, Amun was the creator-god. The statement just quoted implies that he was already existent at the beginning or that he was eternal, but that is not the case. It is at this point in Egyptian thought that elements of evolutionary thinking surface. But before examining these ideas, it is helpful to know more about the main Egyptian theological centers.

There were four main theological centers in Egypt, each with different approaches to and emphases on creation. Some of the basic elements of the creation myths were common to all. In the theology of Heliopolis, the creator-god was Atum. In that of Hermopolis, creation was the result of eight primeval gods' actions, though Thoth was also considered a creator-god. In Thebes, the creator-god was Amun, and the theological emphasis was on divine transcendence. And finally, in Memphis the theology of creation believed that Ptah was the creator-god. Its main emphasis was on creation through the word.

These different systems were notably similar in many ways and were not necessarily in competition with each other. The Heliopolitan theology of origins is best known and the most significant of the early Egyptian cosmogonies. It has provided the basis for all later speculations about origins in Egypt. In this theology, the creator-god is Atum, and the origin of this god goes into the realm of evolutionary ideas:

> "*The background of creation*
> I am the Waters, unique, without second.
>
> "*The evolution of creation*
> That is where I evolved,
> On the great occasion of my floating
>   that happened to me.
> I am the one who once evolved—
> Circlet, who is in his egg.
> I am the one who began therein, (in) the
>   Waters.
> See, the Flood is subtracted from me:
> See, I am the remainder.
> I made my body evolve through my own
>   effectiveness.
> I am the one who made me.
> I built myself as I wished, according to
>   my heart."[3]

The first sentence is spoken by Nun, the personified waters before creation. The speaker in the rest of the text is Atum, the creator-god. The event took place a long time ago, when all that was there were the primeval waters. Atum describes and explains how he came into being in the absence of life. Therefore, the myth portrays an important Egyptian understanding of the origin of matter and life.

Atum's existence begins within the waters

through a process of self-development or evolution. The evolutionary process begins with the sudden appearance and development of an egg within the waters of nonexistence. After a long, undetermined era, the egg or Atum rises and floats on the surface of the waters, where it will evolve into the primeval mound or hill where Atum will stand. At this stage, Atum and the mound are a unity of undifferentiated matter—a cosmic stem cell. The egg and the mound are Atum at different stages of development: "I made my body evolve through my own effectiveness. I am the one who made me."[4]

Such a description speaks of self-causality and total independence from anything else. The Egyptians are describing what would be called today a "cosmic singularity," totally independent of any external force of divine origin. This is the moment when life springs into existence by itself.

The Egyptian verb translated "to evolve" means "to change, develop, evolve."[5] It is used quite often to refer to Atum as self-evolving. With the creation of space, air, and sky, Atum will evolve even more to become the sun-god, Re or Atum-Re. This creation myth is a mythological expression of the spontaneous generation of a unique life from which all life will develop. This could be called an "act of original spontaneous genesis."[6] This has led an Egyptologist to suggest that some Egyptian texts deserve "to be considered a contribution to the philosophical or scientific literature on evolution."[7]

Some Egyptian ideas discussed above are also found in Sumerian and Akkadian texts. According to some, creation occurs by means of spontaneous generation and sexual reproduction. As in Egypt and in modern science, in the Mesopotamian civilization it was "assumed that everything now in existence went back to a simple element."[8] According to *Enuma Elish,* the simple element was two bodies of water. It is in the mixing of the two that they acquire spontaneously divine procreative powers, personified as the god Apsu (sweet water) and the goddess Tiamat (seawater). It is within these two that the gods are formed.

The idea of spontaneous generation, implicit in the previous text, is explicitly expressed in a bilingual Sumero-Babylonian incantation:

"Heaven was created of its own accord. Earth was created of its own accord. Heaven was abyss, earth was abyss."[9]

This is a case in which the "spontaneous generation of heaven and earth (namely, the universe) is proclaimed, but then we are told that there was in fact no heaven or earth but only a body of water, which is the implication of the third line quoted."[10] Within this body of water, the gods apparently generated themselves. Another Babylonian text contains a prayer to the moon god Nanna-Suen, a creator-god, expressing the idea of spontaneous generation: "O lord, hero of the gods, who is exalted in heaven and on earth, father Nanna, lord Anshar, hero of the gods. . . . Fruit which is self-created, of lofty form."[11]

The concept of the self-generation of the moon was quite common and was associated with the fact that during the month it grew in size, then disappeared and died, after which it returned to life through its own power. In any case, it was from these self-created deities that the rest of the cosmos came into being. In other words, the simple diversified itself. This idea is explored more carefully by the Egyptians.

Diversification of Life. Atum is not simply Atum but the totality of the cosmos. Like the cosmic egg in modern cosmogony, everything in the cosmos was compressed in Atum. In a sense, it could be said that he " 'turned himself into' the cosmos. Atum was not the creator, but rather the origin: everything 'came into being' from him."[12] It is through a process of differentiation that undifferentiated matter will shape the cosmos. This process begins with the origination of Shu (male) and Tefnut (female). They constitute, in Egyptian cosmology, the air or void that separates the sky from the earth.

Probably more important in this belief is the creation of sexually differentiated deities. Their creation is described in different ways—through masturbation or sneezing—but there is a text in which a more analytical approach is taken when relating the origin of Shu. It is recited in the first person singular by the deceased, who is identifying himself or herself with the personality or soul of Shu:

> "I am the *ba* of Shu, the god mysterious (?) of form:
> It is in the body of the self-evolving god that I have become tied together.
> I am the utmost extent of the self-evolving god:
> It is in him that I have evolved. . . .

> I am one who is millions, who hears the affairs of millions. . . .

> "It is in the body of the great self-evolving god that I have evolved,
> For he created me in his heart,
> Made me in his effectiveness,
> And exhaled me from his nose. . . .

> "I am one exhale-like of form.
> He did not give me birth with his mouth,
> He did not conceive me with his fist.
> He exhaled me from his nose."[13]

The creation of Shu and his twin sister Tefnut is not through procreation but through development and differentiation. Another text says, "I was not built in the womb, I was not tied together in the egg, I was not conceived by conception."[14] He is part of the process of self-evolution or development of Atum. From the mythological perspective, one could perhaps conceive of Atum as an androgynous monad who is now evolving into a plurality or, at first, into a duality of gender differentiation. The process of the transformation or the actualization of the potentiality of the original undifferentiated matter begins with Shu and Tefnut.

From this point on, the Heliopolitan theology of creation is mainly based on procreation among the gods, but even there, the idea of the self-development of Atum is maintained. It is through procreation that the potential compressed in Atum—the millions in him—will actualize itself. In the Heliopolitan cosmogonic model, "the central concept is the 'coming into being' of the cosmos, as opposed to its creation."[15] It may not be too farfetched to suggest that Heliopolis, in a sense, deals "with the rules of the big bang."[16]

Time and Creation. In the Sumero-Babylonian literature, time was one of the basic elements from which everything that now exists originated. The idea is found in a text dealing with the ancestry of Anu. There is a pair of gods called Duri (male) and Dari (female). The combination of the two names means "ever and ever,"[17] indicating that time was considered to be fundamental in the emergence of everything else.

This is intriguing, because "conceiving something immaterial like time as a prime element represents sophisticated thinking."[18] It is clear that the idea of time as a personified creator is ancient and is also found in Phoenician, Iranian, and Indian speculations and among some Greek thinkers. In the case of Phoenicia, the god Oulomos is mentioned in its cosmology. The name is etymologically related to the Hebrew term for "eternity, world." Among the Greeks, the god Chronos played an important role in creation. In the semi-philosophical cosmology of Pherecydes of Syros, Chronos or Time is personified and described as the one without beginning, who created without a consort—from his semen—fire, wind, and water. And from these three elements, the world came into existence.

The matter of the time, the moment when creation took place, is not addressed in the Egyptian literature. It is clear that the Egyptian understanding of time was primarily linear. It has been suggested

that there was an Egyptian god of time and that his presence may be reflected in the Egyptian god Thoth, who "is the god of the moon and of the lunar calendar and, thus, of time."[19] He reckoned time and distinguished months and years. Thoth had a wide range of responsibilities (e.g., nature, cosmology, writing, science), including that of creator-god in Hermopolis. If this suggestion is valid, there was an Egyptian god of time who participated in the creation of the cosmos.

In Egypt belief, creation occurred at "the first time," which "does not just mean the beginning. It only means the beginning of an event.... 'Time' does not exclude the period after the event; on the contrary, it implies that other 'times' followed, in principle times without number."[20] There is no expression "millions of years" to refer to the time from the origin of the creator-god to the end of all things. The use of "millions of many millions (of years)"[21] should not be only understood as a way of expressing the idea of eternity but as a statement of a deep-time chronology that would lead to the end of the cosmos.

The well-ordered cosmos is not eternal and neither are the gods and humans who inhabit it. An Egyptian text announces the return of everything to their state before creation. It is found in the Book of the Dead and in manuscripts dating back to about the eighteenth- and nineteenth-century B.C. dynasties (1450–1200 B.C.). The text narrates a conversation between Atum and Osiris:

"O, Atum, what does it mean that I go to the desert, the Land of Silence, which has no water, has no air, and which is greatly deep, dark, and lacking?"

"Live in it in contentment."

"But there is no sexual pleasure in it."

"It is in exchange for water and air and sexual pleasure that I have given spiritual blessedness, contentment in exchange for bread and beer"—so says Atum.

"It is too much for me, my lord, not to see your face."

"Indeed, I shall not suffer that you lack. . . ."

"What is the span of my life"—so says Osiris.

"You shall be for millions of millions (of years), a lifetime of millions. Then I shall destroy all that I have made. This land will return into the Abyss, into the flood as in its former state. It is I who shall remain together with Osiris, having made my transformations into other snakes which mankind will not know, nor gods see."[22]

This is indeed a very dark view of the future of the cosmos, quite similar to what some contemporary cosmologists anticipate happening millions of years from now. The expanding universe, they say, may experience a big crunch that will bring everything, including life itself, to an end. The Egyptians also believed that the whole cosmos will be pulled back into itself, thus returning to the darkness and inertia of the pre-creation watery condition. A Ptolemaic text states that, at that

moment, "there is no god, there is no goddess, who will make himself/herself into another snake."[23] It would appear that, at the end, only Atum and Osiris remain in that they "change back into the enduring, original form of a snake, that is, into the same form—or rather formlessness—which the eternal enemy of the gods, Apopis, possesses as a power of chaos."[24] But the phrase "having made my transformations into other snakes which mankind will not know, nor gods see" could indicate that they do not exist. What cannot be known by humans and cannot be seen by the gods is what does not exist. But perhaps there was also the possibility of rebirth and, therefore, the chance for a new beginning.

Origin of Theogonic and Cosmogonic Speculations. The speculations of the Egyptians concerning the origin of life and matter are, to some extent, based on their observation of nature and the conclusions drawn from it. The idea of the primeval mound was probably based on their experience during the flooding of the Nile. During the summer, the river began to swell until it covered the flat lands beyond its banks. The waters brought with it an excellent deposit of fertilizing silt. As the waters began to decrease, the first things that appeared were mounds of fertile mud ready to be seeded. When the mounds of slime were bathed by the rays of the sun, there was an explosion of new life on them. This led the Egyptians to conclude "that there is special life-giving power in this slime."[25]

The Egyptians had also observed the dung beetle—the scarab—specifically the so-called rollers, which the Egyptians associated with the fertile mounds. The female makes a spherical ball of dung inside of which she deposited her eggs. At the proper moment, the young emerge from the dung ball as through a spontaneous generation of life. The scarab became a symbol of life. The Egyptian word for "scarab" is related to the word for "to develop, evolve" and to the solar deity Khepri. It seems obvious that the observations of a natural phenomenon and the interpretation given to it were used by the Egyptians to develop the basic elements of their cosmogony. Their initial point of departure was from below.

A similar situation occurs in Mesopotamian myths. Ancient Mesopotamians began from what they observed in nature and through speculations projected it back to primeval times. Their speculations were apparently based "on observations of how new land came into being. Mesopotamia is alluvial, formed by silt brought down by the rivers. It is the situation at the mouth of the rivers where the sweet waters, Apsû, flow into the salt waters of the sea, Ti'āmat, and deposit their load of silt . . . to form new land that has been projected backward to the beginnings."[26] They, like the Egyptians, moved from what took place in nature as they knew it to cosmogonic speculations.

Influence of Ancient Near-Eastern Theogonies

Creation myths in Egypt and Mesopotamia begin with a theogony and are based on the spontaneous generation of life, divine life, out of which a process of diversification was initiated that brought into existence everything else. These ideas were well known throughout the ancient Near East and influenced Greek mythology.

Scholars in Greek classic literature have realized that the ancient Near East was not only the geographic context of Greece but also its cultural context and that Greek religion was influenced by the ancient Near East. It is now well accepted that Hesiod's *Theogony*, written around 700 B.C., was influenced by ancient Near-Eastern theogonic myths. Scholars are still debating how these ideas reached Greece. Current consensus considers the Phoenicians as the mediators of elements of ancient Near-Eastern theogonies and cosmologies throughout the Aegean area.

Hesiod's *Theogony* is a masterful piece of literature that influenced Greek cosmogony in significant ways. In it, Hesiod narrates the origin of the gods and the cosmos from the very beginnings to the final triumph of Zeus. In describing the origin of the gods, Hesiod wants the Muses to inform him about the origin of everything. Here is the beginning of the theogony:

"In truth, first of all Chasm came to be, and then broad-breasted Earth, the ever immovable seat of all the immortals who possess snowy Olympus' peak and murky Tartarus in the depths of the broad-pathed earth, and Eros, who is the most beautiful among the immortal gods, the limb-melter—he who overpowers the mind and the thoughtful counsel of all the gods and of all human beings in their breasts. . . .

"From Chasm, Erebos and black Night came to be; and then Aether and Day came forth from Night, who conceived and bore them after mingling love with Erebos. . . .

"Earth first of all bore starry Sky, equal to herself, to cover her on every side, so that she would be the ever immovable seat for the blessed gods; and she bore the high mountains, the graceful haunts of the goddesses, Nymphs who dwell on the wooded mountains. And she also bore the barren sea seething with its swell, Pontus, without delightful love; and then having bedded with Sky, she bore deep-eddying Ocean and Coeus and Crius and Hyperion and Iapetus and Theia and Rhea and Themis and Mnemosyne and golden-crowned Phoebe and lovely Tethys. After these, Cronus was born, the youngest of all, crooked-counseled, the most terrible of her children; and he hated his vigorous father."[27]

The text suggests that at the beginning, when there was nothing, Chasm (Chaos), Earth, Tartarus, and Eros originated by themselves. The process of diversification was ready to begin. Out of Chasm, in what appears to have been an emanation or a self-development, came Erebos and Night. Earth self-generated Sky (Ouranos) and Pontus (Sea). The other gods came into existence through procreation. The text becomes a succession myth, describing the supremacy of Sky and how Cronus (corn harvest god) castrated him and assumed supremacy. Zeus rebelled against his father Cronos, became the supreme god, and fought against the Titans and the monster Typhon. The basic thrust of the narrative is similar to the *Enuma Elish* with its emphasis on succession and overcoming the enemy in order for Marduk to become the supreme god. Creation through self-generation and procreation, fundamental in Mesopotamia and Egypt, is also present in Hesiod's book.

Ancient Near-Eastern Anthropogonies

Some of the ancient Near-Eastern myths dealing with anthropogony—the origin of humans—also include ideas that are today associated with evolutionary thinking. This does not seem to be the case in Egypt, where there is no myth dealing with the creation of humans. Instead, a simple statement became the common Egyptian view on the topic. The creator-god says,

"I made the gods evolve from my sweat,
While people are from the tears of my
Eye."[28]

Somehow, the sun-god had temporary blindness and from the tears of his weeping eye humans came into existence. Therefore, to be human "means that he is destined never to partake in the clear sight of god; affliction blights everything he sees, thinks and does."[29] In other words, the understanding of humans portrayed in this mythological fragment is negative.

In Sumerian literature, some texts address the original condition of humans that contain concepts associated today with natural evolution. In the Babylonian cosmogonic introduction to the "Disputation Between Ewe and Wheat," the text describes the primitive condition of humans as follows:

"The people of those distant days
Knew not bread to eat,
They knew not cloth to wear;
They went about in the Land with naked
limbs
Eating grass with their mouths like
sheep,
And drinking water from the ditches."[30]

Nothing is said in this text about how these humans were created. What the text describes happened in a very distant time, suggesting that, since then, the condition of humans has changed. They behaved like animals and did not know anything about agriculture and animal husbandry. Notice that at this early stage of human development humans ate only grass. The idea is not that they were vegetarians but that they were like animals, feeding themselves from the grass and drinking water like animals. They looked and behaved like animals. This comes very close to what are called today "hominids." The text goes on to indicate that the gods "discover the advantages of agriculture and animal husbandry for themselves but their human servants, without those means, could not satisfy them. Enki, wishing to increase human efficiency for the ultimate benefit of the gods, persuades Enlil to communicate to the human race the secrets of farming and animal husbandry."[31] In this case, the "evolution" from a prefully human condition to humans as social beings occurred through divine intervention. What is important is that, according to this text, "the human race was originally created animallike."[32]

This same two-stage development is applied to the experience of an individual in the

Akkadian epic of Gilgamesh, probably written around 1900 B.C. The story line is about Gilgamesh, the ruler of the city of Uruk. He was a semidivine being who, because of his powerful personality, "drove on his poor subjects; neither men nor women ever had respite from him. The people of Uruk complained to the gods, who realized that Gilgameš needed somebody equal to himself to measure himself against. And so they created Enkidu, the savage, who grew up in the steppe, far away from human settlements."[33] Here is the portion of the text describing him:

"[On the step]pe she created valiant
Enkidu, Offspring of, . . . essence of
Ninurta.
[Sha]ggy with hair is his whole body,
He is endowed with head hair like a
woman.
The locks of his hair sprout like Nisaba
He knows neither people nor land;
Garbed is he like Sumuqan.
With the gazelles he feeds on grass,
With the wild beasts he jostles at the
watering-place,
With the teeming creatures his heart
delights in water."[34]

The full text refers to Enkidu several times using an Akkadian term meaning "primal or primeval man." It is used in some texts in contrast to another term that designates the king as a "thinking-deciding man." The terminology as well as his behavior and physical appearance suggest that this text refers to a being who is neither an animal nor a fully developed human being. He seems to be very close to what we would call today a "hominid."

Enkidu transitions from his wild life and behavior to the life of culture with the help of a harlot and becomes a close friend of Gilgamesh.

Texts like these are not common in the Sumerian and Akkadian literature, making it difficult to understand their full import. But in Sumerian and Babylonian thinking, "the beginning of human existence was neither a golden age nor a period of pristine simplicity. On the contrary, life was savage, and man differed little, if at all, from other animals. Primal man was a beast, and the Babylonian Enkidu was primal man [reborn]."[35] These texts represent a view of humans that links them quite closely to the animal world. The connection is so close that humans are, in fact, depicted closer to the animal world than to that of humans, properly speaking.

Biblical Creation Narrative

It would be difficult to deny that the ancient Near-Eastern cosmogonic ideas discussed above were totally unknown in Israel. The Old Testament speaks about a significant amount of political and cultural contacts between Israel, Egypt, and Mesopotamia. We would suggest that the biblical Creation account, in describing the divine actions through which God actually brought the cosmos into existence, was deconstructing the alternative theories or speculations of origins available in the ancient Near East. Consequently, the biblical narrative can be used as well to deconstruct contemporary cosmogonies and natural evolution.

Creation and God. It would probably be correct to say that the most striking difference between ancient Near-Eastern creation narratives and the biblical one is the total absence of a theogony in the biblical Creation narrative. In fact, it does not appear anywhere in the Scripture. This is so unique that it places the biblical Creation account within a different conceptual paradigm, as compared to any other Creation narrative. In the context of ancient Near-Eastern theogonies and cosmogonies, the biblical Creation narrative is an exquisite anomaly. The biblical text assumes the pre-existence of and a radical distinction between Elohim or YHWH and the cosmos. To the question asking what there was before Creation, the biblical answer is: "In the beginning God created." He is not the Self-Created One but the One who was and is. This carries with it some important theological and cosmogonic implications.

First, the similarities between the biblical Creation account and those from the ancient Near East are mainly superficial. The new biblical paradigm excludes any derivation of the biblical view of Creation from ancient Near-Eastern sources and would consider such a derivation to be an attempt to force upon the biblical text what is foreign to it. Scholars are now more careful when seeking to identify ancient Near-Eastern influences on the biblical writer. The truth is that "given our present knowledge ... it is difficult to prove that any single work is the source of Genesis 1."[36]

Second, in contraposition to the idea that the cosmos is the result of the coming into being of God and everything else—surprisingly similar to process theology—the biblical text does not know anything about a cosmos that is the result of the self-evolving of God or that is emerging from within God. The phrase "in the beginning" is pronounced as a corrective and rejection of the common belief that Creation began with a theogony. There is a beginning, but it is a beginning of creation—not of God. Creation is about a divine function and not about divine ontology. It is probably this biblical conviction that has contributed to the development of science in the Christian world. In biblical theology, Creation is desacralized, and it is, therefore, open for human study and analysis.

Third, since Creation is not the result of a god who is evolving, the cosmos does not come into existence through inner struggles. In ancient Near-Eastern cosmogonies, evil is part of the creation process itself and is directly related to the development of a diversity of gods and goddesses from the creator-god—be it through procreation or direct self-development. Creation out of chaos, according to which God had to struggle with primeval forces of disorder to establish order and harmony, is not present in the biblical Creation narrative. In contraposition to such ideas, Creation is the result of God's effortless work. The singularity of the Creator-God does not allow for any other cosmogony.

1. *Creation and the Emergence of Life.* The biblical text makes another exclusive claim: the life we experience, enjoy, and see on earth is not an extension of the divine life but a mode of life created by God and, therefore, essentially different from His. To communicate this idea, the biblical text describes Creation as taking place through the Divine Word. Creation as the self-development of God or as divine procreation is replaced by creation through the Word of God and the breath of life. Even the inanimate world is created through God's command. Through His speech, God brings into existence light (Gen. 1:3) and the expansion (v. 6), and He separates light from darkness (v. 4), water from water (v. 7), and land from water (v. 9). All this happens through the divine command. The raw materials do not have the power to realize themselves. This power comes from outside the sphere of the raw materials and reaches them through the Divine Word. Life is created in the same way.

The flora comes into existence from within Creation itself but not through the power of natural forces. The statement "let the land produce vegetation" (v. 11)[37] may suggest the natural emergence of life from the inanimate, but that is not the case. The idea is that the barren land is unable to produce grass and trees by itself; it needs to hear the voice of the Lord commanding grass and trees to come into existence all over the ground. The Word of God mediates the creation of such life and, at the same time, establishes the way things will continue to be. The perpetuation of grass and trees is possible, because the Creator established it that way. He created a natural law.

God created fish to teem in the waters and birds to fly in the sky (v. 20). Fish do not sprout out of the water by themselves but, like the birds, are created to live within a particular habitat. It is through the divine command that this takes place and not as the result of the intrinsic power of nature. This is life created through the Divine Word. Concerning animals, we read, "Let the land produce living creatures" (v. 24). This does not mean that the earth participated in the creation of animals or that it had the potential to produce animals. It is only the divine command that creates the animals out of the earth. The rest of the text indicates that the earth is their natural environment—"all the creatures that move along the ground" (v. 25). In other words, the command is "addressed to the earth as the place where these creatures are to live."[38] Life is created exclusively through the Divine Word.

In the case of humans, their life is created in a unique way: God "breathed into his nostrils the breath of life" (Gen. 2:7). The text does not say that God gave them His breath of life but that He breathed into them the breath of life. To have the breath of life means to be alive, and the divine breathing of it into humans simply means the "giving of life to humans, nothing more."[39] This is not life emanating from the divine life to take a new form or to go through further self-developments. This is God creating human life.

In the biblical narrative, life does not create itself at any stage in the process of coming into being. Its origin remains hidden in the mystery of the divine act of Creation. Once created, life is empowered by the Creator to perpetuate itself through procreation. This is based on the creation of gender differentiation, and therefore, it is a potential that is part of life itself and that humans can explore and understand. The origin of life is inaccessible for scientific analysis, but its nature and perpetuation through procreation are not.

The biblical text implicitly rejects the idea that the diversification of life is the result of a self-created life evolving or developing into a multiplicity of forms. The biblical paradigm depicts a God who effortlessly creates life in its different forms, thus excluding the development of one form of life into a different one. Each creation of life is described in the text as an event in itself, and that particular life does not evolve or develop in any way into the creation of other forms of life. This is an amazing thought in the context of ancient Near-Eastern creation stories. The only thing that provides coherence and unity to the different expressions of life in the biblical Creation narrative is the fact that there is only One Creator.

2. *Creation and Time.* Ancient Near-Eastern creation accounts do not date the moment of creation. They, like the Bible, speak about a beginning that includes the creation of time. There is no awareness of what is called today "deep time"—geologic time in billions of years. As noted earlier, Egyptian cosmogonies make reference to millions of years, running from creation to de-creation, and perhaps in that sense, it would be possible to introduce some notion of deep time. In natural evolution, deep time is the creator that brings into being the cosmos and all forms of life found on this planet.

Such ideas contrast in significant ways with the information provided by the biblical text in which a chronology of millions of years and the existence of a god of time are unknown. This does not mean that the biblical Creation narrative is not interested in time. As a matter of fact, there is throughout the narrative a significant amount of emphasis on time and its direct connection to the origin of life on the planet, but time is not raised to the status of creator. Time is created by God to frame His creative acts; it is under His rule. When it comes to the creation of life on the planet, deep time is totally absent from the text. Everything takes place in a week (Exod. 20:11). This particular biblical emphasis on time excludes the ancient Near-Eastern idea of the self-development of undifferentiated divine essence into millions by means of time.

• *Origin of Humans.* The biblical Creation narrative distances itself from ancient Near-Eastern representation of human origins by emphasizing the uniqueness of the creation of humans and the essential differences between humans and animals. Although some similarities can be detected, they are placed at the service of different ideologies. It is obvious that the primeval human, who in ancient Near-Eastern texts looked and behaved like an animal, is totally absent from the biblical text.

1. *Creation and Role of Humans.* The uniqueness of humans is emphasized in the biblical text by describing their true nature and role within the created world. The general tendency in ancient Near-Eastern texts is to undermine the value and uniqueness of human life and existence. The most common reason for the creation of humans in the Sumerian and Babylonian narratives lacks any interest in the self-value of humans. They were created as a result of the selfish concerns of a group of small deities who rebelled against working for the major deities. According to *Enuma Elish*, Ea, the father of Marduk, created humans

from the blood of the rebellious god Kingu: "They bound him (Kingu), brought him to Ea, imposed punishment on him (and) severed his arteries. From his blood he formed mankind. He imposed on him service for the gods and (thus) freed them."[40] Humans were created from an inferior, evil god to relieve the gods from their burdensome and exhausting responsibilities. Humans were the servants of the gods.

In the biblical text, humans are created in God's image to enjoy fellowship with Him (Gen. 1:26, 27). The image was not something that, through time, they were able to develop, but something granted to them as a gift when they were created on the sixth day of the Creation week. As God's image, they were rational, free beings, able to communicate with God through language (2:17, 20; 1:28; 3:10). As made in His image, humans were to represent Him to the rest of the created world (1:26). In contrast to the biblical depiction of humans, ancient Near-Eastern incipient evolutionary ideas devalued humankind.

2. *Animals and Humans.* In contrast to the ancient Near-Eastern tendency to blur any distinction between humans and animals during primeval times, the biblical text emphasizes the differences between them. This is affected in different ways.

First, both animals and humans are created by God, but only humans were created in God's image. This explains the fact that humans had dominion over the animals and that Adam did not find a suitable helper for him among them (Gen. 2:20). Second, in the biblical account animals and humans come into existence in different ways. At the command of God, animals and birds are created or formed from the earth (v. 19), but in the case of humans, God formed them from the dust of the ground and breathed the breath of life into them (v. 7). The situation is different in ancient Near-Eastern texts. In the Sumerian text called the "Eridu Genesis," dated to around 1600 B.C., the creation of animals is described as follows:

"When An, Enlil, Enki, and Ninḫursaga
Fashioned the dark-headed (people),
They had made the small animals (that
    come up) from (out of) the earth
Come from the earth in abundance
And had let there be, as befits (it), ga-
    zelles,
(Wild) donkeys, and four–footed beasts
    in the desert."[41]

This is a case in which the origin of animals is somewhat similar to the biblical narrative. In both cases, all types of animals are created by bringing them out of the earth. In the case of the Sumerian text, this happens through the cosmic marriage—an idea totally absent from biblical cosmogony. The creation of humans is alluded to in the text (the gods fashioned humans), but no details are given. This text should be compared with another Sumerian one known as "Hymn to E'engura." In it, the creation of humans occurs when the gods are fixing the destinies, creating the year of abundance, and building the temple. In this text, the creation of humans is also related to the cosmic marriage and could be described as the emergence of humans:

"When the destinies had been fixed for

all that had been engendered (by An),
When An had engendered the year of
    abundance,
When humans broke through earth's
    surface like plants,
Then built the Lord of Abzu, King Enki,
Enki, the Lord who decides the desti-
    nies,
His house of silver and lapis lazuli."[42]

When the two texts are compared, it is clear that no distinction is made between the way humans and animals were created. They both broke through the earth's surface, emerging from it as a result of the cosmic marriage. The singularity of humankind at the moment of its origin is not emphasized at all.

A third important distinction between humans and animals is found in the diet assigned to them (Gen. 1:29, 30). This will become a major point of dispute between the woman and the serpent, one of the beasts of the field. According to Genesis 3:1, the serpent says to the woman, "Did God really say, 'You must not eat from any tree in the garden?' " The Hebrew text could be translated as a statement of fact: "God indeed said to you that you should not eat of any tree in the garden." It could also be a statement of surprise: "So, God has said to you that you should not eat from any tree in the garden!" Whether it is a question or not is not of decisive importance. It is the implication of the statement that is important.

It is clear that "the tempter begins with suggestion rather than argument."[43] He is suggesting that God said something about human diet different from what Eve knew.

What the tempter is attempting to instill in Eve's mind is that humans have been forbidden by God to eat from the trees of the garden. It has been suggested that the phrase "not from any tree" should be translated "not of every tree,"[44] but the fact is that the proper translation of the Hebrew phrase is "not at all," and in this particular passage, it should be translated "from no tree at all." Besides, the answer given by Eve to the serpent clearly indicates that she understood the phrase to mean "from no tree at all." Though the serpent insinuated that humans had been forbidden by God to eat from the trees of the garden, Eve, using the language of Genesis 1:29, clarifies that they can eat from the "fruit-bearing trees" of the garden.

Therefore, the topic of discussion presented by the serpent is about food. It is about what God assigned humans to eat. It is a little strange that the enemy would use this line of argumentation to initiate the conversation. But the topic of food is an important one in the Creation narrative. In Genesis, God is the One who determines what His creatures should eat (Gen. 1:29, 30; 2:17; 3:18). Diet set humanity apart from the animal world and constituted part of the order of Creation. They, like the rest of the animal world, were vegetarians. The animals were to feed themselves with "green plant[s]" (1:30), but humans were only to consume "seed bearing plant[s]" and "every tree that has fruit with seed in it" (v. 29).

This is an important marker of differentiation. In Genesis 2:16, 17, the Lord indicated that Adam and Eve were "free to eat from any tree in the garden" with one exception. The emphasis in Genesis 2 is on the fruit of the trees as part of human diet. By suggesting that humans should not eat from the trees of the garden, the enemy may have been trying to alter or weaken the dietary boundary that contributed to the differentiation of humans from animals.

One wonders whether the insinuation was that humans and animals basically belong to the same category of creatures—they were both to eat green plants. If that were the case then, the serpent was attempting to bring Eve to its own level of existence. What was at stake was the conception of humans as the image of God. Already quoted is an ancient Near-Eastern text, according to which primeval humans behaved like animals, "eating grass with their mouths like sheep and drinking water from the ditches."[45] In that text, there is no dietary differentiation between humans and animals. This appears to be what the serpent is attempting to introduce in the biblical narrative. By devaluing humans, the serpent forces Eve to react, to defend herself, and consequently, she becomes more vulnerable. Humans, she says, are to be differentiated from animals: "We may eat fruit from the trees in the garden, but God did say, 'You must not eat fruit from the tree that is in the middle of the garden' " (Gen. 3:2, 3a). The rejection of this apparent attempt to group humans and animals together, indispensable in evolutionary thinking, deconstructed some ancient Near-Eastern anthropogonies.

3. *Self-Evolving of Humans.* The idea that it is possible for humans to evolve from one level of existence to a higher one is

found in Genesis, but it is not endorsed by the biblical writer. It is placed in the lips of the serpent after Creation week. It is introduced in the narrative as an alternative to the divine plan for humans, and unfortunately, it captured their imagination. This represented a new worldview that was offered to humans by the serpent. According to it, humans have the potential within themselves to evolve into something unimaginable; they could be by themselves immortal and totally independent from God (Gen. 3:4, 5). They could leave behind their previous mode of existence and evolve or self-develop into a divine mode of existence. The biblical text rejects this worldview by describing the negative results of embracing it.

Instead of progress, humans were significantly dehumanized and unable to properly relate to each other and to God. One wonders whether hiding among the trees and putting on leaves as a kind of garment was not pointing to the fact that humans were identifying themselves with the trees (Gen. 3:8, 10). If that is a valid reading of the text, then, in seeking to be like God, they had fallen almost to the level of the flora. The fact that an animal was instrumental in their fall suggests that they lost their dominion over the fauna, thus damaging the image of God. This permanent loss of dominion over the fauna appears also to be expressed through the new garments that the Lord provided for them made from the skin of animals (v. 21).

Though in Genesis 1; 2 the distinction between humans and animals is clearly maintained, in Genesis 3, the distinction begins to deteriorate. An animal entered into a dialogue with Eve and deceived her, God explicitly states that humans will exist in conflict with this animal (v. 15), and finally, God clothes them with the skin of animals. All of these imply the human loss of their dominion over the fauna that God had entrusted to them. Dressing them with the skin of animals indicates that they are no longer in the condition in which they were before—they are now closer to the animals. But there is more. As a result of the Fall of Adam and Eve, the human diet is altered, and humans will also eat green vegetables or legumes (v. 18, "green plants of the field"), bringing them closer to elements of the animal diet.

The human quest for self-development or evolving into the divine and the acquisition of self-preservation—immortality—proved to be a failure. Yet, both ideas found fertile ground in the religions of the ancient Near East. Egyptian, Mesopotamian, and Hittite religions developed well-established rituals to facilitate the transition of the individual from this life to the other life. The movement from the human level to the divine took place particularly in the sphere of the king who, in some cultures, was considered to be divine or who was transformed into a god after dying. In this last case, the evolutionary goal was reached in the sphere of the spiritual world and connected evolutionary ideas with spiritualistic concerns. What is particularly important in the biblical narrative is that at the moment when evolutionary ideas are insinuated the biblical text rejects them by emphasizing their negative impact on human existence.

Conclusion

In the study of the history of evolutionary ideas, the literature of the ancient Near East should be taken into consideration. Behind the myths are some interesting reflections and speculations about the origin of life and its development from simple elements like water, matter, and time. These self-created elements are personified in the myths as divine beings who evolve or self-develop into the multiplicity of phenomena that can now be observed and experienced. None of this is, properly speaking, natural evolution as it is understood today, but it does contain elements of the evolutionary ideology promoted today in some scientific circles. In that sense, the ancient Near-Eastern views should be considered part of the history of the idea of natural evolution.

Once it is recognized that such ideas were part of the cultural and religious environment of the people of God in the Old Testament, the reading of the biblical Creation account reveals the uniqueness of its cosmogony and anthropogony. In revealing how YHWH created the cosmos, life in general, and human life in particular, the biblical text was indeed deconstructing the elemental evolutionary views present in the Egyptian and ancient Near-Eastern cosmogonies and anthropogonies. It can then be suggested that the biblical text is to be used as a hermeneutical tool to evaluate and deconstruct contemporary scientific evolutionary theories and speculations related to cosmogony and anthropogony. It is surprising to realize that an ancient text, the biblical Creation account, could have had such a unique role in the ancient world and that it can continue to address the same concerns in a technological and scientific global culture. Qohelet, who was very much interested in creation, said it well: "There is nothing new under the sun" (Eccles. 1:9).

Notes

1. Hellmut Brunner, "Egyptian Texts: Myths," in *Near-Eastern Religious Texts Relating to the Old Testament*, ed. Walter Beyerlin (Philadelphia, PA: Westminster, 1978), 6.

2. Ibid., 7.

3. "Cosmologies: From Pyramid Texts Spell 714," trans. James P. Allen, *The Context of Scripture* 1, no. 2: 6, 7.

4. Ibid., 7.

5. James P. Allen, *Genesis in Egypt: The Philosophy of Ancient Egyptian Creation Accounts* (New Haven, CT: Department of Near-Eastern Languages and Civilizations, 1988), 29.

6. Jan Assmann, *The Search for God in Ancient Egypt*, trans. David Lorton (Ithaca, NY: Cornell University Press, 2001), 122.

7. Siegfried Morenz, *Egyptian Religion*, trans. Ann E. Keep (Ithaca, NY: Cornell University Press, 1973), 169.

8. Wilfried G. Lambert, "Myth and Mythmaking in Sumer and Akkad," in *Civilizations of the Ancient Near East*, ed. J. Sasson (New York: Scribner, 1995), 3:1829.

9. Ibid.

10. Ibid.

11. Hartmut Schmökel, "Mesopotamian Texts: Sumerian 'Raising of the Hand' Prayer to the Moon God Nanna-Suen (Sin)," in *Near-Eastern Religious Texts Relating to the Old Testament*, ed. Walter Beyerlin (Philadelphia, PA: Westminster, 1978), 104.

12. Assmann, *Search for God in Ancient Egypt*.

13. "From Coffin Texts Spell 75," trans. James P. Allen, *The Context of Scripture* 1, no. 5:8, 9.

14. "Cosmologies: From Coffin Texts Spell 76," trans. James P. Allen, *The Context of Scripture* 1, no. 6:10.

15. Assmann, *Search for God in Ancient Egypt*, 120.

16. Gertie Englund, ed., "Gods as a Frame of Reference," in *The Religion of the Ancient Egyptians: Cognitive Structures and Popular Expressions* (Uppsala: S. Academiae Ubsaliensis., 1989), 15.

17. Lambert, "Myth and Mythmaking," 1829.

18. Ibid.

19. Carolina López-Ruiz, *When the Gods Were Born: Greek Cosmogonies and the Near East* (Cambridge, MA: Harvard University Press, 2010), 158.

20. Morenz, *Egyptian Religion*, 166.

21. Allen, "From Coffin Texts Spell 76," 30.

22. "Cosmologies: Book of the Dead 175: Rebellion, Death and Apocalypse," trans. Robert K. Ritner, *The Context of Scripture* 1, no. 18:28.

23. Quoted in Erik Hornung, *Conceptions of God in Ancient Egypt: The One and the Many* (Ithaca, NY: Cornell University Press, 1982),163.

24. Ibid., 164.

25. John A. Wilson, "Egypt: The Nature of the Universe," in Henri Frankfort et al., *The Intellectual Adventure of Ancient Man: An Essay on Speculative Thought in the Ancient Near East* (Chicago: University of Chicago Press, 1946), 50.

26. Thorkild Jacobsen, *The Treasures of Darkness: A History of Mesopotamian Religion* (New Haven, CT: Yale University Press, 1976), 169.

27. Glenn W. Most, *Hesiod, Theogony, Works and Days, Testimonia* (Cambridge, MA: Harvard University Press, 2006), 13–15.

28. "Cosmologies: From Coffin Texts 1130," trans. James P. Allen, *The Context of Scripture* 1, no. 17:26.

29. Quoted by Hornung, *Conceptions of Gods*, 150.

30. "Disputations: The Disputation Between Ewe and Wheat," trans. H. L. J. Vanstiphout, *The Context of Scripture* 1, no. 180:575.

31. Richard J. Clifford, *Creation Accounts in the Ancient*

Near East and in the Bible, Catholic Biblical Quarterly Monograph Series 26 (Washington, DC: Catholic Biblical Association of America, 1994), 46.

32. Ibid., 44.

33. Aage Westenholz and Ulla Koch-Westenholz, "Enkidu—the Noble Savage?" in *Wisdom, Gods and Literature: Studies in Assyriology in Honour of W. G. Lambert*, eds. A. R. George and I. L. Finkel (Winona Lake, IN: Eisenbrauns, 2000), 439.

34. E. A. Speiser, trans., "The Epic of Gilgamesh," in *The Ancient Near East,* ed. James Pritchard (Princeton, NJ: Princeton University Press, 1958), 1:74.

35. William Moran, "The Gilgamesh Epic: A Masterpiece From Ancient Mesopotamia," in *Ancient Near East*, 4:2328.

36. Clifford, *Creation Accounts in the Ancient Near East,* 141.

37. Unless otherwise noted, all scriptural references in this chapter are from the NEW INTERNATIONAL VERSION.

38. W. D. Reyburn and E. M. Fry, *Handbook on Genesis,* United Bible Society Handbooks (New York: United Bible Societies, 1997), 48.

39. Claus Westermann, *Genesis 1-11* (Minneapolis, MN: Fortress, 1994), 207.

40. Schmökel, "Mesopotamian Texts," 84.

41. Thorkild Jacobsen, *The Harps That Once ...: Sumerian Poetry in Translation* (New Haven, CT: Yale University Press, 1987), 146.

42. Clifford, *Creation Accounts in the Ancient Near East,* 29, 30.

43. Derek Kidner, *Genesis: An Introduction and Commentary* (Downers Grove, IL: InterVarsity, 1967), 72.

44. G. Ch. Aalders, *Genesis: Volume 1* (Grand Rapids, MI: Zondervan, 1981), 99.

45. "Disputations," 575.

"When Death Was Not Yet"

Jacques B. Doukhan

The question of the origin of death is interpreted differently, depending on whether one holds to the theory of evolution or to the biblical story of Creation. Evolution teaches on the basis of observation that death is a natural and necessary process in the hard struggle for life—death is a part of life. The Bible, on the contrary, asserts that death was not a part of the original plan.

From the testimony of biblical Creation, four arguments can be used to support this assertion: (1) the world was originally created good, (2) the created world was therefore not yet affected by death, (3) death was not planned, and (4) death will no longer be in the new re-created world of the eschatological hope. Literary clues in the biblical text suggest that not only was death not a part of God's Creation but that the biblical text attests to even a specific intentionality about this assumption.

The "Good" of Creation

The use of the Hebrew word *bārā'*, translated as "create," to describe God's operation of Creation and the regular refrain "it was good," to qualify His work testify to the goodness of Creation.

The divine work of Creation is rendered through the use of the term for "it was good," which is often used in parallelism with "to do, to make" (Isa. 41:20; 43:1, 7; 45:7, 12, 18; Amos 4:13). It implies a positive connotation that is on the opposite range of meanings to the negative ideas of destruction and death. In addition, "to do, to make" denotes the concept of producing something new, which has nothing to do with the former condition (Isa. 41:20; 48:6, 7; 65:17), and marvels, which have never been seen before (Exod. 34:10).

This usage of the "to do, to make" does not therefore allow the sense of separating, which has sometimes been advocated. This interpretation does not take the following arguments into consideration:

• *Semantic Argument.* Although the Genesis Creation story contains a series of separations, this does not mean that the Hebrew word means "separate." If it were the case, why did the biblical author choose to use it seven times in the Creation narrative (Gen. 1:1, 21, 27 [three times]; 2:3; 2:4a), instead of another specific word for "separate," which is used in the same context when the idea of separation is really intended (1:4, 6, 7, 14, 18)?

• *Logical Argument.* Other biblical occurrences of "to do, to make" would not make sense if the verb were translated "separate" instead of "create" (see especially Gen. 1:21; Exod. 30:10; Deut. 4:32; Isa. 45:12). Also, the fact that "to do, to make" has only God as a subject, whereas the word for "separate" has generally humans as subject, testifies to the fundamental difference of meaning between the two verbs.

• *Syntactical Argument.* The use of the same emphatic particle of the accusative *et*, after the verb *bārā'*, introducing one or several objects (Gen. 1:1; 21, 27), implies the same syntactical relation between them and, thus, supports the interpretation of "create" rather than "separate." This implies different syntactical relations, with the use of a different set of prepositions.

• *Ancient Near-Eastern Argument.* In ancient Egypt, as well as in Mesopotamia, the divine operation of Creation is similarly rendered by the verbs "create," "make," "build," and "form" but never by the verb "separate" or "divide."

• *Translation Argument.* The Septuagint translates the word generally by "create" (seventeen times) and "make" (fifteen times) but never by "separate" or "divide."

The divine work of Creation is at each stage of its progress unambiguously characterized as "good" (Gen. 1:4, 10, 18, 21, 25) and, at the end of the last step, as "very good" (v. 31). The meaning of the Hebrew word for "good" needs to be clarified here. Indeed, the Hebrew idea of "good" is more total and comprehensive than what is implied in the English translation. It should not be limited to the idea of function, meaning that only the efficiency of the operation is intended here. Rather, the word *good* may also refer to aesthetic beauty (24:16; Dan. 1:4; 1 Kings 1:6; 1 Sam. 16:36), especially when it is associated with the word for "see," as is the case in the Creation story (Gen. 1:1, 4, 10, 12, 18, 21, 25, 31).

The word *good* may also have an ethical connotation (1 Sam. 18:5; 29:6, 9; 2 Sam.

3:36)—a sense that is also attested in our context of the Creation story, especially in God's recognition that "it is not good that man should be alone." This divine statement clearly implies a relational dimension, including ethics, aesthetics, and even love and emotional happiness, as the immediate context suggests (Gen. 2:23; Ps. 133:1). This divine evaluation is particularly significant as it appears to be in direct connection to the first Creation story, which was deemed as good.

In the second Creation story (Gen. 2:4b–25), the word for "good" occurs five times, thus playing the role of a key word in response to the seven occurrences of good in the first Creation story (Gen. 1:1–2:4a). This echo between the two Creation stories on the word *good* sheds light on its meaning. While the term for "not good" alludes negatively to the perfect and complete Creation of the first Creation story, the phrase translated as "good and bad," the word and its contrary, suggests that the word *good* should be understood as expressing a distinct and different notion than "bad, evil." The fact that Creation was "good" means, then, that it contained no evil.

The reappearance of the same phrase in Genesis 3:22 will confirm this argument from another perspective. The knowledge of good and evil, suggesting discernment or knowing the difference between right and wrong, was possible only when "Adam was like one of us [God] in regard to the distinguishing between good and evil."[1] The verb "was" refers to a past situation. It is only when Adam was like God—not having sinned yet, that is, from the perspective of pure good—that Adam was still able to distinguish between good and evil.

The same line of reasoning may be perceived, somewhat in a parallel way, in regard to the issue of death, which is in this context immediately related to the issue of the knowledge of good and evil. Indeed, the tree of life is associated with the tree of the knowledge of good and evil (Gen. 2:9) as they are located at the same place "in the midst of the garden" (v. 9; 3:3). And Adam is threatened to lose life as soon as she or he fails to distinguish between good and evil (2:17). For just as good (without evil) is the only way to be saved from evil, life (without death) is the only antidote to death.

It is also noteworthy that this divine appreciation of good does not concern God. Unlike the Egyptian stories of creation that emphasize that a god created only for his own good, for his own pleasure, and that his progeny was only accidental, the Bible insists that the work of Creation was deliberately intended for the benefit of God's Creation and essentially designed for the good of humans (Ps. 8). Indeed, the two parallel texts of Creation in Genesis 1; 2 teach that perfect peace reigned initially. In both texts, humankind's relationship to nature is described in the positive terms of ruling and responsibility. In Genesis 1:26, 28, the word for "to have dominion," which is used to express humankind's relationship to animals, belongs to the language of the suzerain-vassal covenant and of royal dominion without any connotation of abuse or cruelty.

In the parallel text of Genesis 2, humankind's relationship to nature is also described in the positive terms of covenant.

Humankind gives names to the animals and, thereby, not only indicates the establishment of a covenant between humankind and them but also declares lordship over them. That death and suffering are not part of this relationship is clearly suggested in Genesis 1 by the fact that this dominion is immediately associated with the food designated to both humans and animals; it is just the product of plants (vv. 28–30). In Genesis 2, the same harmony is pictured in the fact that animals are designed to provide companionship for humans (v. 18).

At this point in the story, humankind's relationship to God has not suffered from any disturbance. The perfection of this relationship is suggested through a description of that relationship given in only positive terms: Genesis 1 mentions that humankind has been created "in the image of God" (vv. 26, 27), and Genesis 2 reports that God was personally involved in creating humans and breathed into them the breath of life (v. 7).

Likewise, the relationship between man and woman is blameless. The perfection of the conjugal unity is indicated by mentioning that humankind has been created in Genesis 1 as male and female (v. 27) and, in Genesis 2, through Adam's statement about his wife being "bone of my bones and flesh of my flesh" (v. 23). The whole Creation is described as perfect. Unlike the ancient Egyptian tradition of origins, which implies the presence of evil already at the stage of Creation, the Bible makes no room for evil in the original Creation. Significantly at the end of the work, the very idea of perfection is expressed through the word *wayĕkal* (vv. 1, 2), qualifying the whole Creation. This Hebrew word, generally translated "finished" (NKJV) or "completed" (NIV), conveys more than the mere chronological idea of end; it also implies the quantitative idea that nothing is missing, and there is nothing to add, again confirming that death and all the evil were totally absent from the picture.

Furthermore, the biblical text does not allow for the speculation of a pre-Creation in which death and destruction would have been involved. The echoes between introduction and conclusion indicate that the Creation referred to in the conclusion is the same as the one that is mentioned in the introduction.

The "heavens and earth" that are mentioned in Genesis 2:4a, at the conclusion of the Creation story, are the same as in Genesis 1:1, the introduction of the Creation story. The echoes between the two framing phrases are significant.

"In the beginning God created the heavens and the earth" (v. 1).

"This is the history of the heavens and earth when they were created" (2:4).

The fact that the same verb "created" is used to designate the act of Creation and with the same object ("heavens and earth") suggests that the conclusion points to the same act of Creation as that in the introduction. In fact, this phenomenon of echoes goes even beyond these two lines. Genesis 2:1–3 echoes Genesis 1:1 by using the same phrase but in reverse order: the words *created, God, heavens and earth* of Genesis 1:1 reappear in Genesis 2:1–3 as "heavens and earth" (Gen. 2:1), "God" (v. 2), "created" (v. 3). This chiastic structure

and the inclusion "God created," linking Genesis 1:1 and Genesis 2:3, reinforce the close connection between the two sections in the beginning and the end of the text, again confirming that the Creation referred to at the end of the story is the same as the Creation referred to in the beginning of the story. The event of Creation found in Genesis 1:1–2:4a is then told as a complete event that does not complement a prework in a far past (gap theory) nor is to be complemented in a postwork of the future (evolution).

The "Not Yet" of Creation

It seems, in fact, that the whole Eden story has been written from the perspective of a writer who already knows the effect of death and suffering and, therefore, describes these events of Genesis 2 as a "not yet" situation. Significantly, the word translated as "not yet" is stated twice in the introduction of the text (Gen. 2:5) to set the tone for the whole passage. And further in the text, the idea of "not yet" is implicit. The "dust" from which humankind has been formed (v. 7) anticipates the sentence of chapter 3: "To dust you shall return" (v. 19). The tree of knowledge of good and evil (2:17) anticipates the dilemma of humankind later confronted with the choice between good and evil (3:2–6).

The assignment given to humankind was to "keep" the garden in its original state, which implies the risk of losing it, therefore anticipating God's decision in Genesis 3 to chase them out of the garden (Gen. 3:23) and entrust the keeping of the garden to the cherubim (v. 24). This same word is used in both passages, showing the bridge between them—the former pointing to the latter, suggesting the "not yet" situation. Likewise, the motif of shame in Genesis 2:25 points to the shame they will experience later (3:7). The same idea is intended through the play on words between "naked" and the "cunning" of the serpent; the former (2:25) is also an anticipation of and points forward to the latter (3:1) to indicate that the tragedy that will later be initiated through the association between the serpent and human beings has not yet occurred. Indeed, as Walsh noticed, "There is a frequent occurrence of prolepsis in the Eden account."[2]

Death Was Not Planned

The biblical text goes on in Genesis 3 and describes an unplanned event and reversal of the original picture of peace into a picture of conflict: conflict between animals and humans (Gen. 3:1, 13, 15), between man and woman (vv. 12, 16, 17), between nature and humans (vv. 18, 19), and finally, between humans and God (vv. 8–10, 22–24). Death makes its first appearance since an animal is killed in order to cover humankind's nakedness (v. 21) and is now clearly profiled on the horizon of humankind (vv. 19, 24). The blessing of Genesis 1 and 2 has been replaced with a curse (Gen. 3:14, 17). Indeed, the original ecological balance has been upset and only the new incident of the sin of humankind is to be blamed for this. This theological observation is also reflected in the literary connection between the biblical texts. It is indeed significant that Genesis 3 is not only telling the events that reversed Creation; the story of Genesis 3 is written in a reversed order to the story of Genesis 2, following the movement of the chiastic structure:[3]

A Settlement (2:5–8)	C' Separation (3:1–3)
B Life (2:9–17)	B' Death (3:14–21)
C Union (2:18–23)	A' Expulsion (3:22–24)

The correspondence between the sections is also supported by the use of common Hebrew words and expressions. This literary reversal of motifs (settlement-expulsion, life-death, union-separation) confirms the intention of the biblical author, namely that sin provoked the reversal of the original Creation.

Later, this is the same principle behind the eruption of the Flood, since the cosmic disruption is directly related to the iniquity of humankind (Gen. 6:13). As Clines notes, "The flood is only the final stage in a process of cosmic disintegration which began in Eden."[4] More particularly, the picture of the harmonious relationship between humankind and animals depicted in Genesis 1 is again disrupted after the Flood (9:1–7). The literary bridge between the two passages indicates that the relationship was upset after the Creation and is not a natural part of it. Among a number of common motifs, the same concern with the relationship between humankind and animals is found. The parallelism is striking:

Genesis 1:28–30	Genesis 9:1–4
A God blessed man	A' God blessed man
B Be fruitful and multiply; fill the earth	B' Be fruitful and multiply; fill the earth
C Have dominion over all animals	C' Have dominion over all animals
D Food for humankind: plants	D' Food for humankind: animals

The parallelism works not only in the fact that both passages use the same words and motifs but also that these occur in the same sequence. No doubt the connection between the two passages is intended. One important difference, however, concerns the relationship between humankind and animals. Although it is packed with the same ingredients—humankind, animals (beast, birds, and fish), and food given by God—the nature of this relationship has changed. While in Genesis 1, humankind's relationship to animals is made of peace and respect (see above on vv. 29, 30), in Genesis 9 it is made of fear and dread on the part of every beast, which is "given into your hand" (9:2). The reason for this change is suggested in the texts. Since the peaceful relationship in Genesis 1 is associated with the herbal food for humankind and the conflict relationship in Genesis 9 is associated with the animal food, the conclusion may be drawn that it is the dietary change, implying the killing of animals, that has affected the humankind-beast relationship.

In other words, the picture of conflict is not understood to be original and natural but must have come as a result of an ecological imbalance, which is due essentially to death—the fact that humans (as well as animals) started hunting. In that connection, it is noteworthy that the consumption of herbal food was a part of Creation, as death was not yet implied at that stage; this is confirmed by the second Genesis Creation story, which specifies that the eating of fruit preceded and, therefore, excluded the appearance of death (2:16, 17).

It is significant that the overwhelming majority of occurrences of the technical word for death refer to human beings, rarely applies to animals (Gen. 33:13; Exod. 7:18, 21; 8:9 [13]; 9:6ff.; Lev. 11:39; Eccles. 3:19; Isa. 66:24), and is never used for plants per se. The same perspective is reflected in the use of the word for "life," whose departure is the equivalent of death, which also applies generally to humans, sometimes to animals, but never to plants.

The reason for this accent on human death (versus animals and plants) lies in the biblical concern for human salvation and the place of human consciousness and human responsibility in the cosmic destiny. For death is related to human sin, as noted in Romans 6:23. Sin belongs essentially to the human sphere (Gen. 2:17; Num. 27:3; Deut. 24:16; Ezek. 3:18; Jer. 31:30). It is significant that the first and the last appearances of death in the history of humankind, in the Bible, are associated with human sin and human destiny (Gen. 2:17; Isa. 25:8; Rev. 21:3, 4).

The old lesson that "no man is an island" is invariably registered in the pages of the Bible with all the responsibility and the tragic destiny this organic connection implies for humankind. Thus, the biblical view of death is essentially different from the one proposed by evolution. While the belief in evolution implies that death is inextricably intertwined with life and, therefore, has to be accepted and eventually managed, the biblical teaching of Creation implies that death is an absurdity to be feared and rejected. Evolution teaches an intellectual submission to death.

The Hebrew view of death also stood apart in the ancient Near East. Though the Canaanites and the ancient Egyptians normalized or denied death through the myths of the gods of death, the Bible confronts death and utters an existential shout of revolt and a sigh of yearning (Job 10:18–22; 31:35, 36; Rom. 8:22).

For the biblical authors, death is a contradiction to the Creator-God, who is pure life. The expression "God [or the LORD] is alive" is one of the most frequently used phrases about God. Holiness, which is the fullness of life, is incompatible with death. In the Mosaic law, the blood was forbidden to be consumed, precisely because the "life of the flesh is in the blood" (Lev. 17:11; see also Gen. 9:4); corpses were considered unclean, and any person who had been in contact with death would become unclean for seven days and, for that period of time, would be cut off from the sanctuary and the people of Israel (Num. 19:11–13). Priests who were consecrated to God were even forbidden to come near a dead person; they were prohibited from entering a graveyard or attending a funeral, except for a close relative (Lev. 21:1, 2; Ezek. 44:25). All these commandments and rituals were meant to affirm life and to signify the Hebrew attitude toward death as the result of sin.

When Death Shall Be No More: An Argument From the Future

It should not come as a surprise, then, that the biblical prophets understood hope and salvation only as a total re-creation of a new order in which humankind and nature will enjoy God's last reversal, where Creation will be totally good again, will no longer affected by sin, and where death will be no more (Isa. 65:17; 66:22; Rev. 21:1–4). In this new order, good will no longer be mixed with evil, as death will no longer be mixed with life. It will be an order in which the glory of God occupies the whole space (v. 23; 22:5). As Irving Greenberg points out, "In the end, therefore, death must be overcome, 'God will destroy death forever. My Lord God will wipe the tears away from every face.' (Isaiah 25:8). . . . In fact, since God is all good and all life, ideally there should have been no death in God's Creation in the first place."[5] The hope for the new Creation of heavens and earth, where death shall be no more, provides us with an additional confirmation that death was not a part of God's original Creation.

Summary and Conclusion

The biblical story of origins teaches that death was not a part of the original Creation for four fundamental reasons, provided by the biblical testimony of Creation:

1. *Death was not a part of Creation, because the story qualifies Creation as good, that is, without any evil.*

2. *Death was not yet, because the story is characterized as a not-yet situation, from the perspective of someone whose condition is already affected by death and evil.*

3. *Death was due to human sin, which resulted in reversing God's original intention for Creation.*

4. *That death was not intended to be a part of God's original Creation is evidenced in the future re-creation of the heavens and earth, where death will be absent.*

Close literary reading of the Genesis texts suggests that there is even a deliberate intention to emphasize these reasons to justify the absence of death at Creation:

1. *In the first Creation story (Gen. 1:1–2:4a),* the sevenfold repetition of the word for "good" reaches its seventh sequence in the term for "very good."

2. *In the second Creation story (Gen. 2:4b–25),* the twofold repetition of the word for "not yet" and the prolepsis anticipates the "not yet" of Genesis 3.

3. *In the story of the Fall (Genesis 3), the literary reversal expresses the cosmic reversal of Creation.*

The scientific difficulty to assume that death was not part of the original Creation is an honest struggle. For us, it is indeed impossible to conceive life without death, just as it would be philosophically impossible to conceive good without evil. Only the imagination of faith that takes us supernaturally beyond this reality would allow us to transcend and even negate our condition. Only the visceral intuition of eternity, the life granted by God to all of us ("He has put eternity in their hearts" [Eccles. 3:11]), and the imagination of faith could help us to see beyond the reality of our present condition that death has indeed nothing to do with life.

Notes

1. Author's literal translation, cf. Young's Literal Translation: "And Jehovah God said 'Lo, the man was as one of us as to the knowledge of good and evil.'"

2. Jerome T. Walsh, "Genesis 2:4b–3:24: A Synchronic Approach," *Journal of Biblical Literature* 92 (1977): 164.

3. I am indebted here (with slight modifications) to Zdravko Stefanovic, "The Great Reversal: Thematic Links between Genesis 2 and 3," *Andrews University Seminary Studies* 32 (1994): 47–56.

4. David J. A. Clines, *The Theme of the Pentateuch* (Sheffield: JSOT Press, 1978), 75.

5. Irving Greenberg, *The Jewish Way: Living for the Holidays* (New York: Simon & Schuster, 1988), 183.